A Blessed Shore

(left) King Richard II (1367–1400) kneeling in front of King (Saint) Edmund, King (Saint) Edward the Confessor, and Saint John the Baptist. The Wilton Diptych. Erich Lessing/Art Resource, New York.

(right) Saint Mary and the choir of angels, from the Wilton Diptych. Erich Lessing/Art Resource, New York.

A Blessed Shore

England and Bohemia from Chaucer to Shakespeare

Alfred Thomas

CORNELL UNIVERSITY PRESS
ITHACA AND LONDON

DA
47.9
.C94
T48
2007

Copyright © 2007 by Cornell University

All rights reserved. Except for brief quotations in a review, this book, or parts thereof, must not be reproduced in any form without permission in writing from the publisher. For information, address Cornell University Press, Sage House, 512 East State Street, Ithaca, New York 14850.

First published 2007 by Cornell University Press

Printed in the United States of America

Library of Congress Cataloging-in-Publication Data

Thomas, Alfred.
 A blessed shore : England and Bohemia from Chaucer to Shakespeare / Afred Thomas.
   p. cm.
 Includes bibliographical references and index.
 ISBN 978-0-8014-4568-2 (cloth : alk. paper)
 1. Travelers—England—History. 2. Travelers—Czech Republic—Bohemia—History. 3. England—Relations—Czech Republic—Bohemia. 4. Bohemia (Czech Republic)—Relations—England. 5. England—Civilization—Czech influences. 6. Bohemia (Czech republic)—Civilization—English influences. 7. Bohemia (Czech Republic)—In literature. I. Title.

 DA47.9C94T48 2007
 914.37104'224—dc22

2007005921

Cornell University Press strives to use environmentally responsible suppliers and materials to the fullest extent possible in the publishing of its books. Such materials include vegetable-based, low-VOC inks and acid-free papers that are recycled, totally chlorine-free, or partly composed of nonwood fibers. For further information, visit our website at www.cornellpress.cornell.edu.

Cloth printing   10 9 8 7 6 5 4 3 2 1

For Kathryn Tanner

Contents

Acknowledgments	ix
Note on Quotations, Translations, and Czech Names	xi
Introduction	1
1. *Imitatio Mariae:* Anne of Bohemia as Cultural and Religious Mediatrix	18
2. Imperial Designs: Art and Ideology at the Ricardian and Luxembourg Courts	65
3. "Master Adversary": Wyclif's Influence in Bohemia	98
4. "The Wycliffite Woman": Reading Women in Fifteenth-Century Bohemia	119
5. *Peregrinus et alter Ulysses:* Leo of Rožmitál's Mission to England (1466)	149
6. Shakespeare's Bohemia: English Men and Women in Renaissance Prague	167
7. Three Men in a Boat: Waldstein, Hollar, and Comenius in Seventeenth-Century England	196

Conclusion	209
Appendix. "The Wycliffite Woman": A Rhymed Translation	213
Bibliography	217
Index	229

Acknowledgments

I would like to acknowledge the encouragement and help of many scholars and friends in the course of writing this book: Rita Copeland, Dyan Elliott, Kati Evans, Tricia George, Paul Griffith, Anne Hudson, Michael Flier, Kathryn Kerby-Fulton, Mary Beth Rose, Miri Rubin, Beryl Satter, Pamela Selwyn, František Šmahel, William Stoneman, David Wallace, Joan and (the deeply missed) Stuart Williams, and Karen Winstead.

Vera Shack helped me with the final preparation of the manuscript while Mike Slager was a resourceful and conscientious research assistant. I would also like to thank the staff of the following libraries where I was privileged to conduct research: the Bodleian Library, Oxford University; the British Library, London; Cambridge University Library; the Newberry Library, Chicago, and the Houghton Library, Harvard University. I also acknowledge the gracious generosity of the Dean and Chapter of Westminster Abbey in allowing me access to the Chapel of Saint Edward the Confessor, where I was able to examine the beautiful and moving double tomb of Richard II and Anne of Bohemia. Last but not least, I would like to express my gratitude to John Ackerman, director of Cornell University Press, for supporting this project; Karen Laun for her patience and professionalism as manuscript editor, and Gavin Lewis for his excellent copyediting.

Note on Quotations, Translations, and Czech Names

All translations of Czech, French, German, and Latin sources are my own, unless otherwise stated. To facilitate those readers not familiar with foreign languages, I quote in English in the body of the text and provide the original in the footnotes only when necessary. Quotations from *Pearl* are provided in Middle English and in modern English translation. Quotations from Chaucer are in the original Middle English throughout. All quotations from Chaucer and Shakespeare are taken from *The Riverside Chaucer* and *The Riverside Shakespeare*.

Czech proper names and place names are provided in their original form except when they occur regularly or when common practice demands their English usage, for example, John Hus, Peter Chelčický, Agnes of Bohemia, King Wenceslas, and Queen Sophie.

A Blessed Shore

Introduction

When most people today think of Bohemia, it is not the ancient kingdom in east-central Europe which usually comes to mind. Rather, it is that cosmopolitan refuge for self-exiled modern writers and artists whose location varies according to political circumstance. In the words of César Graña and Marigay Graña: "Bohemia has been variously defined as a mythical country, a state of mind, a 'place of youth and disenchantment,' a 'tavern by the wayside on the road of life.' Thomas Mann defined it as 'nothing but social irregularity, a guilty conscience to be resolved in levity': Shakespeare called it a desert near the sea."[1]

The setting of Bohemia in *The Winter's Tale* (1609–11) is perhaps the first literary instance of what has come to be known as "bohemia" in the modern sense: a place of refuge for those who do not—or cannot—feel at home in their place of origin. In this study I shall argue that this notion of "bohemia" has its roots in the premodern kingdom of Bohemia or—to be more precise—in the kingdom of Bohemia as an imagined place. The desert endowed by Shakespeare with a sea coast

---

[1] *On Bohemia. The Code of the Self-Exiled*, ed. César Graña and Marigay Graña (New Brunswick, 1990), xv.

is not simply a feature of Greek romance but mediates between reality and imagination.

Since Ben Jonson's famous jibe it has been a persistent literary commonplace that Shakespeare was ignorant of the landlocked status of the ancient kingdom in east-central Europe. For many scholars Bohemia was a convenient dramatic prop rather than a reflection of an actual place. But if the kingdom of Bohemia was a matter of indifference to Shakespeare, why did he bother to make it the setting of his play at all? One obvious explanation is that the playwright inherited the setting of Bohemia from his immediate source, Robert Greene's prose romance *Pandosto. The Triumph of Time* (1588). Shakespeare did not simply reproduce Greene's romance in a mechanical fashion but switched the settings of *Pandosto,* to make Bohemia, rather than Sicilia, a land of exile for Perdita, the abandoned baby daughter of jealous King Leontes. Thus for Shakespeare Bohemia has quite a different function than for Greene: a refuge for an innocent persecuted by an unjust and tyrannical ruler.

The idea of fleeing to Bohemia may seem the stuff of romance to us today but in the early seventeenth century many English men and women did just that. During the reigns of Elizabeth I and James I there was a steady traffic of English exiles to Habsburg central Europe. Most of these exiles were Catholics unable to practice their faith freely in England. Although the English Reformation dates to the reign of Henry VIII, the real problem for English Catholics began in 1570 when Pope Pius V issued his bull *Regnans in excelsis* which excommunicated Elizabeth I and freed her subjects from allegiance to her rule. Up to that point the queen had more or less tolerated her Catholic subjects; but when she was excommunicated, fear for her life and crown led Elizabeth to intensify the persecution of the recusant population.

This, of course, begs the question why Shakespeare switched the setting of his play. Is the exiled Perdita a personification of the Catholic emigration? Is Shakespeare secretly expressing sympathy for the plight of those who left England for Bohemia? And if this was the case, did Shakespeare know where Bohemia was? These questions will be addressed in chapter 6. The point I wish to make here is that premodern Englishmen were not always ignorant of Bohemia and were in fact more inclined to go there than Bohemians were likely to go to England. When people visited England, they found it odd, exotic, and anomalous. In the words of Paul Murray Kendall, "England lay on the perimeter of the world, edged by the ocean that stretched westward no man knew whither."[2]

The point of origin for premodern Englishmen (and Europeans in general) lay in the east rather than in the west. If the west was the biblical locus of paradise lost, the east was the site of paradise regained. In the words of Iain Higgins:

> For Adam and Eve on their journey from Paradise into History, east was the direction of exile, loss, and new beginnings. Behind them lay the unpeopled enclosure of a naturally blissful life, barred now by cherubim and a flaming sword, while ahead lay a cursed existence on "the subjected Plain," soon to be the boundless scene of manual and maternal labor, fraternal murder, and further exile for some of their progeny. For their medieval Christian descendants in Europe, though, east was the direction of return, restoration and old beginnings: in short, of origins. By traveling east they could make their way to the very "navel of the earth," the divinely privileged theatre where the new Eve and the second Adam had made possible the return journey from History to Paradise.[3]

For medieval man the Orient was not simply an exotic space, as it would become in the Romantic era; it was synonymous with paradise itself. The anonymous author of the Middle English poem *Pearl* identifies the precious pearl both with the Orient and with the Celestial Jerusalem, which in the Book of Revelation is described as a city made of translucent stones and precious gems. The author of *Pearl* was indebted to the popular *Travels of Sir John Mandeville*. In a precious illuminated manuscript of the *Travels* made for the Bohemian court of Wenceslas IV ca. 1400 (now in the British Library), we see the eponymous knight and his companions set off in their ship from the English coast. Sir John looks back reassuringly to his companions but his hand gestures in the opposite direction toward the mysterious east where paradise is located. Similarly, in the Wilton Diptych, a moveable altarpiece commissioned by Richard II ca. 1395, the young king and his

[2] Paul Murray Kendall, *The Yorkist Age* (New York, 1965), 1.
[3] Iain Macleod Higgins, *Writing East. The "Travels" of Sir John Mandeville* (Philadelphia, 1997), 1.

three patron saints, Edmund the Martyr, Edward the Confessor, and John the Baptist, face the right-hand panel where the Virgin and Child, surrounded by eleven angels, are seen in a flowery meadow sprinkled with cut flowers. Richard kneels in a rocky waste land with a sinister forest in the background, but his rapt gaze and his hands raised in prayer are directed eastward toward the celestial vision of the Virgin and Child (frontispiece).

Only in the Renaissance, as the exploration of the Americas got underway, did the western hemisphere begin to supplant the east in the European imaginary. Coterminous with the growing reputation of the New World as the repository of untold wealth was the political and cultural decline of east-central Europe. Following the disastrous Battle of the White Mountain near Prague (1620), which ended the power of the Bohemian Estates and the independence of the kingdom of Bohemia for the next three centuries, the flow of English men and women to Bohemia dwindled to a trickle. Prior to that fateful event Bohemia had enjoyed a reputation as a haven of religious tolerance for two hundred years. The Austrian branch of the Habsburgs had presided over an empire which was more tolerant toward its non-Catholic subjects (Jews and Protestants) than it had previously been or would be again in the premodern period. This positive view of Bohemia as synonymous with ecumenical tolerance coincided with Protestant England itself. But prior to the Reformation the English authorities regarded Bohemia as the kingdom of heresy, whose beautiful city of Prague with its great university had been destroyed by fanatics and schismatics. This negative view of Bohemia was revived when Emperor Rudolf II's eventual successor, the bigoted Ferdinand II, reneged on his predecessors' commitment to religious tolerance, paving the way for the disastrous Thirty Years' War (1618–48).

Philip Massinger's tragedy *The Picture* (1629) follows Greene's *Pandosto* in identifying Bohemia not with a bucolic idyll but with deranged jealousy. The story of the unstable nobleman Matthias who is convinced of his faithful wife's infidelity inevitably recalls Shakespeare's Leontes; but whereas Shakespeare had switched the setting of Greene's *Pandosto* to make Bohemia a positive place, Massinger makes it a bad place—or at least, the background against which bad things are done—thereby reflecting the prevailing Protestant hostility to the triumph of the Counter-Reformation in that country. Thus literary representations of Bohemia throughout the early modern period were not frozen by the prescriptions of the romance genre but were continuously inflected and shaped by the fluctuating and changing political fortunes of the region itself.

Given the political and cultural importance of east-central Europe in the premodern period, it is surprising that scholarship dealing with the contacts between England and Bohemia has been such a one-sided affair, with the Germans and Czechs shouldering the burden of research. Josef Loserth's study *Hus und Wiklif* (1884) is now largely outdated, but it was pioneering in its day as was Constantin Höfler's monograph on Anne of Bohemia (1871). Höfler overlooked Queen Anne's influence on English culture, seeing her significance mainly in terms of her dynastic and diplomatic importance as the consort of an English king. But his book was groundbreaking in exploring the relationship between England and the Holy Roman Empire at a time when the British were more concerned with their far-flung colonies than their historical connection to Europe.

Part of the reason for Chaucer's attachment to European culture was the fact that nationalism had yet to fragment the cultural and political map of the continent into ethnic groups, each regarding itself as superior to and more culturally "central" than its neighbor. Rather, the premodern cultural map of Europe was a constantly shifting kaleidoscope in which the center/margin binary was unstable and protean. If Paris was a fixed center of the international court culture in the later Middle Ages, it had many competitors in the form of the Angevin kingdom of Naples, the Italian city-states of Florence and Milan, and Luxembourg Bohemia. It was precisely because Chaucer saw England as marginal to these cultural centers that he aspired to emulate and rival his continental masters, Guillaume de Machaut, Boccaccio, Petrarch, and Dante.

It was only in the nineteenth century that this center/margin binary became solidified with Austria, Britain, France, and Germany forming the "great powers" and colonized countries like Bohemia, Ireland, and Greece constituting the "small nations." Following the foundation of an independent Czechoslovak Republic in 1918, Czech scholars emphasized the importance of the premodern Anglo-Bohemian relationship (mainly the influence of the English reformer John Wyclif in Bohemia) for reasons which were not wholly separate from their political dependency on the great powers which had brought their republic into being. Loserth's dismissal of Hus as an unoriginal thinker completely dependent on Wyclif had in some sense been motivated by the Austrian desire to undermine the intellectual pedigree of burgeoning Czech nationalism. František Bartoš's study *Husitství a cizina* (*Hussitism and Abroad*) (1931), on the other hand, placed an emphasis on Hus' nationalism which said as much—if not more—about the Czechs' defensive reaction to the threat of German militarism in the early 1930s than it did about early fifteenth-century religious politics. In other words, the Czech scholarly interest in the Anglo-Bohemian connection in the premodern period was to some extent determined by the modern political relationship between Britain and Czechoslovakia. It is no coincidence, therefore, that Josef Polišenský's little book *England and Czechoslovakia* was originally delivered as a lecture to the Students' British Society at the Charles University at Prague on November 8, 1945, following the end of the Nazi occupation of Czechoslovakia. It was published in 1947, just one year before the Communists came to power, during a brief period of democracy in which the Czechs were able to express their positive sentiments toward the Western democracies. A second, expanded edition of the book—retitled *Britain and Czechoslovakia. A Study in Contacts*—appeared in 1968, the year of the Prague Spring, which saw the brief and ill-fated experiment with Western liberalism and "socialism with a human face."

Polišenský's main contribution to the history of Anglo-Bohemian relations was his important monograph *Anglie a Bílá Hora* (*England and the White Mountain*) (1949), a study of England's role in the uprising of the Bohemian Estates. The publication of Polišenský's study one year after the Communist takeover of Czechoslovakia reveals the immense relevance of the past in the Czech mind and how even remote historical events often mirror the contemporary situation: the loss of Bohemian independence following the crushing defeat of the Protestant army at the Battle of the White Mountain in November 1620 could be seen as a historical watershed analogous to the end of Czechoslovak democracy.

But the Czechs have not been alone in subordinating interpretations of the past to the very different realities of the present. In failing to look beyond England—and English as a modern academic subject—Anglo-

Introduction   7

American historians and literary historians often reproduce the insular perspectives of their own time and place, projecting back onto medieval and early-modern England the monocultural and monolinguistic conditions of contemporary Britain and the United States. As recently as 2005 the distinguished biographer of Richard II echoed the infamous words of British Prime Minister Neville Chamberlain at the Munich Agreement of 1938 in asserting that "to most Englishmen at the time, no less than to their successors later, Bohemia was a faraway land of which they knew little."[4] But medieval Bohemia was not the same as twentieth-century Czechoslovakia. In the second half of the fourteenth century Bohemia was the richest and most prosperous part of the Holy Roman Empire; the king of Bohemia was also the Holy Roman Emperor, and Prague was his residential seat and his administrative capital. Bohemia was not the plaything of empire, as in the nineteenth and twentieth centuries, but the heart of empire, the origin of major geopolitical policies and diplomatic initiatives. It is significant that it was the king of Bohemia rather than the king of England who first broached the subject of a dynastic alliance between the House of Luxembourg and the House of Plantagenet in the form of a marriage between Richard II and Anne of Bohemia.

By contrast, England was geographically and politically marginal for most of the premodern period while English was by no means the international language it is today. Even in Britain itself, Latin was the language of the Church prior to the Reformation and French the spoken and literary language of the upper classes until the fifteenth century.[5] In the medieval and early modern periods English remained an insular language, spoken exclusively on the British mainland. In the western part of Britain, Gaelic, Welsh, and Cornish were still vibrant and spoken languages. On the Continent English diplomats were required to speak with their European counterparts in Latin, French, or Spanish. In 1575 Sir Philip Sidney was sent on a diplomatic mission to Prague to offer the queen's condolences to Emperor Rudolf II on the recent death of his father, Maximilian II. One reason why Elizabeth I chose the young and inexperienced Sidney as her special ambassador

---

[4] Nigel Saul, *The Three Richards. Richard I, Richard II and Richard II* (London, 2005), 141.

[5] William Calin, *The French Tradition and the Literature of Medieval England* (Toronto, 1994), 3–16.

to the Habsburg court was because of his knowledge of foreign languages. During his trip Sidney consulted with the Protestant German princes in French and spoke to the emperor himself in Latin. In England itself foreigners were not expected to be familiar with the national language. Before Katherine of Aragon came to England as the bride of Prince Arthur, his mother and grandmother, Elizabeth of York and Lady Margaret Beaufort, wrote to the Spanish court requesting that the princess learn French so that they could converse with her on her arrival.[6] When Philip of Spain, son of the Habsburg Emperor Charles V, came to England in 1554 to marry Queen Mary Tudor, the couple conversed in Spanish or possibly French, since the prince consort could not speak English.[7]

By contrast with England, Bohemia was not only at the geographic heart of Europe but also at certain periods its political and cultural center. Twice in this period Prague became the residence and capital of the Holy Roman Emperor, the first time in the reign of Charles IV of Luxembourg (1316–78) and again in the reign of the Habsburg Rudolf II (1552–1612). Not surprisingly, the late fourteenth and late sixteenth centuries represented two periods when Englishmen gravitated towards Prague in far greater numbers than Bohemians traveled to London. Some were sent on diplomatic missions to represent the English monarchy: Sir Simon Burley, the king's tutor, to negotiate the marriage of Richard II to Anne of Bohemia in 1381, and Sir Philip Sidney in 1575 to establish stronger links with the Austrian Habsburgs.

As a consequence of the dynastic links forged by the marriage of Richard II and Anne of Bohemia in 1382, Bohemian visits to England became a regular feature of the late fourteenth and early fifteenth centuries. The first Bohemians to arrive in large numbers were the members of Queen Anne's entourage. Like all foreign queen consorts in the medieval period, Anne was accompanied by large numbers of servants and ladies-in-waiting. One of these was Agnes of Lancencrona, who became a figure of scandal in 1387 when it was revealed that the king's favorite, Robert de Vere, earl of Oxford, had abandoned his wife, a granddaughter of Edward III, in her favor. In the early fifteenth century Bohemian disciples of John Wyclif visited Oxford, eager to find

---

[6] J. L. Laynesmith, *The Last Medieval Queens. English Queenship 1445–1503* (Oxford, 2004), 211.

[7] David Loades, *Mary Tudor. A Life* (Cambridge, Mass., 1989), 225.

the master's books and take home copies for further dissemination. The first travel account of late medieval England was by Bohemian visitors in the second half of the fifteenth century. Bohemian and Moravian visitors to England continued in the Tudor and Stuart era, culminating in the arrival of the illustrious scholar and pedagogue John Amos Comenius in 1641.

It is the principal aim of this book to demonstrate the significance of these political, diplomatic, and cultural links in the premodern period with a special focus on the long fifteenth century when the kings of England and Bohemia were confronted with major outbreaks of heresy. The influential religious ideas of Wyclif spread to Bohemia at the beginning of the fifteenth century, facilitated by the Anglo-Bohemian dynastic alliance and the marriage of Anne of Bohemia to Richard II in 1382. Although Richard and Anne were scrupulously orthodox in their religious beliefs, Queen Anne's ability to read the New Testament in Latin, German, and Czech inspired the English Lollards to demand the translation of the Vulgate into the English tongue. Conversely, the Czechs saw the Wycliffite Bible as the validation of their own claim to read the Gospels in the vernacular. The question of which came first—the English or the Czech Bible—is less important than the perception of which came first: the Lollards looked to Bohemia as the place where their reformist aspirations could be implemented, while the Hussites regarded Wyclif's England as the homeland of their reform agenda. The well-known contacts between Lollardy and Hussitism, however, have obscured the fact that such links were in some sense the outgrowth of a preceding tradition of orthodox rapprochement between England and Bohemia. Anne of Bohemia is a crucial figure in this overlooked history of orthodoxy. Chapter 1 highlights her important role as a religious as well as a cultural mediatrix between her native land and her adopted home.

By the beginning of the fifteenth century Bohemia and England were in the grip of reformist fever. Henry IV, the Lancastrian usurper of Richard II's throne, attempted to curtail Lollard dissent with the antiheretical statute *De heretico comburendo* (1401). Meanwhile, Czech students, resident at Oxford and sympathetic to the ideas of Wyclif, brought back copies of his books to Prague where they were not only saved from orthodox bonfires but were disseminated and translated into Czech. Allied with a native Bohemian tradition of reformist thought originating in the fourteenth century, the welcome importation of Wyclif's teachings to Bohemia transformed the erstwhile orthodox heart of the empire into a volatile center of militant heresy. At the Council of Constance (1414–18) Henry V of England and the Emperor Sigismund, king of Hungary and future king of Bohemia, collaborated in an attempt to root out heresy. Sigismund actually visited England in 1414 to consult with his English ally.

But this book hopes to explore a more subtle connection between England and Bohemia that is not limited to "relations" in the empirical or positivist sense. In mediating between romance and reality, poetry and politics, Shakespeare's Bohemia says something profound about how all cross-cultural encounters blur the boundary between fictional and historical truth. For Shakespeare Bohemia functions as a utopia, a site, in the words of Michel Foucault, "with no real place" and "yet with a general relation of direct or inverted analogy with the real space of society."[8] As Foucault points out, placeless places of this kind are like a mirror, wherein the subject finds an idealized vision of himself. Bohemia functions as an inverted mirror image of England, a space of both difference and affinity.

Although it is my partial concern to rescue premodern Bohemian culture and history from the relative neglect in which it has languished through scholarly oversight and political amnesia, it is not my aim to assume the Czech point of view as such. This would undermine the objective assumptions upon which this study rests and would perpetuate the habit of subordinating scholarship to the expedient needs of political and cultural rapprochement. To take the Czech side, as it were, by placing Bohemia obstinately at the center of European affairs would subscribe to such a subjectivist and partisan position. The Czech Republic—along with Slovakia, Poland, and Hungary—has recently become part of the European Union. This, I believe, is the historical and cultural fate of east-central Europe. The role of the literary historian, in my view, is not to hasten this unifying process in a prescriptive fashion but to describe the complex political, historical, and cultural circumstances which enabled it to happen. The twenty-first-century unification of Europe brings full circle the geopolitical vision of a medieval Holy Roman Empire—inherited from Classical

---

[8] Michel Foucault, "Of Other Spaces," *diacritics* 16 (1986): 22–27 at 24.

and Carolingian antecedents—that arose at the dawn of the second millennium.

Bohemia played an especially prominent and important role within the medieval Holy Roman Empire. The king of Bohemia was the imperial cupbearer and one of the seven electors of the Empire. In the twelfth and thirteenth centuries, the Přemyslid rulers of Bohemia increasingly identified with German language and culture and encouraged first German peasants to cultivate the fertile border lands of the kingdom and later German knights and *ministeriales* to settle in its heartland, partly to offset the influence of the Slav nobility.[9] Charles IV's double title of Holy Roman Emperor and king of Bohemia was the realization of King Přemysl Otakar II's dream of making Bohemia the political and cultural center of the Empire. It was the latter's success in extending his territories as far as the Adriatic that provided the historical pretext for Robert Greene's—and Shakespeare's—romantic vision of Bohemia on the sea.

If the dream of reaching the sea was characteristic of certain central European rulers, the island rulers of England were conversely susceptible to the fantasy of a continental empire. King Arthur is, of course, the ultimate fictional embodiment of this fantasy. In Geoffrey of Monmouth's twelfth-century *Historia Regum Britanniae* the legend of Arthur makes its first significant literary appearance in England. Geoffrey's Arthur takes on the full might of Rome and conquers all of Europe in a counter-conquest fantasy of the earlier Roman invasion of the British Isles. Geraldine Heng sees a parallel between the transformation of this local British warrior into a crusading warrior on an imperial scale and the Christian colonization of the Holy Land initiated by the First Crusade in 1095: "the story of King Arthur ... begins in the East."[10] The apotheosis of a shadowy, minor figure of western provenance into the embodiment of an eastern empire was not limited to the world of literary fantasy. Insofar as Geoffrey's *Historia* purported to represent historical truth, its influence was far-reaching and pervasive. It is not surprising that the Plantagenet kings of England identified so closely with King Arthur, for he at once presaged and described their own imperial ambitions. The cult of Arthur became particularly important

---

[9] Geoffrey Barraclough, *The Origins of Modern Germany* (Oxford, 1962), 254.
[10] Geraldine Heng, *Empire of Magic. Medieval Romance and the Politics of Cultural Fantasy* (New York, 2003), 21.

during the reign of Edward I, reflecting that king's determination to dominate Wales and Scotland. The Arthurian romance *Escanor* by Girart of Amiens was dedicated to Edward's queen Eleanor of Castile and advanced the Plantagenets' dynastic ambitions in Scotland. By contrast, the Francophile Luxembourg rulers of Bohemia shied away from identifying with a ruler so closely associated with English imperialism. If Arthur features at all in Bohemian sources such as chronicles and courtly romances, it is as a minor—even comic—figure.[11]

Although Edward I's empire was limited to Wales and Scotland, it bore the imprint of a more ambitious imperial fantasy. The polygonal towers of Caernarfon Castle in North Wales were "deliberately reminiscent of the walls of Constantinople and its principal tower was to be crowned by a triplet of turrets each bearing an imperial eagle."[12] In emulating and identifying with the Byzantine Empire, Edward revealed a lust for territorial expansion that exceeded his immediate domains in England and France. Edward I's brother, Richard, earl of Cornwall (d. 1271), played out these more ambitious continental fantasies. Richard put forward his candidacy for the title of Holy Roman Emperor in the disputed election of 1257, along with Alfonso X of Castile and Přemysl Otakar of Bohemia (1253–78). This period of interregnum had been marked by strife since the death of Frederick II in 1250. The election of Rudolf of Habsburg in 1273 ended the interregnum but also the imperial dreams of the Bohemian king and the English earl.

Richard of Cornwall's self-styled title of king of the Romans was the first instance of direct English ambitions in central Europe, but it was not unique. The grandson of Edward III and son of the Black Prince, Richard II (1367–1400) aspired to become Holy Roman Emperor in respect of his wife Anne of Bohemia's status as the daughter of an em-

---

[11] For Edward's deployment of Arthurian romance to legitimize his expansionist policies, see Beate Schmolke-Hasselmann, *The Evolution of Arthurian Romance. The Verse Tradition from Chrétien to Froissart*, translated by Margaret and Roger Middleton (Cambridge, 1998), 267–72. For antipathy to Arthur in Bohemia, see Alfred Thomas, "King Arthur and His Round Table in the Culture of Medieval Bohemia," in *The Arthur of the Germans*, ed. W. H. Jackson and S. A. Ranawacke (Cardiff, 2000), 249–56.

[12] R. R. Davies, *The First English Empire. Power and Identities in the British Isles 1093–1343* (Oxford, 2000), 32. Caernarfon had associations with the Roman Empire since the Emperor Constantine's father was allegedly buried there. See Michael Prestwich, *Edward I* (New Haven, 1997), 214.

peror and sister of an emperor-elect. Richard may have lacked his grandfather's and father's military prowess, but he was no less ambitious than they were; indeed, his very lack of martial experience may have fueled his imperial fantasies which he displaced onto and sublimated in his grandiose building projects at Westminster. The Wilton Diptych is saturated with references to his wife's dignity as the daughter of an emperor and Richard's desire to become one. The diptych was probably intended as a moveable altarpiece to accompany the king as he moved around his kingdom, including two voyages undertaken to Ireland. Michael Bennett has pointed out that in the 1390s "Richard's peripatetic style was reminiscent of German imperial practice."[13] In gyrating around his kingdom as if it were an empire, Richard was consciously emulating the imperial progresses of his father-in-law Charles IV, who was constantly moving from one residence to another. Even Richard's mode of governance was reminiscent of Luxembourg practice. Richard's use of his own household (Chamber) officials in central and local government not only anticipates Tudor strategies for undermining the power of the magnates; it finds a contemporary parallel in the controversial kingship of Anne of Bohemia's half-brother Wenceslas IV.[14]

Like Richard, Wenceslas was to meet the stiff, armed resistance of the nobility in the pursuit of such policies. Wenceslas' failure to control his magnates was one of the reasons why he was eventually deposed as emperor-elect. In Richard's case, the dream of an imperial crown would remain just that, but one with a strong geopolitical logic behind it. At the end of the fourteenth century, Richard II appeared to be the only hope of Christendom, which was being undermined from within by a divided church and threatened from without by Turkish invasion.[15] Charles VI of France suffered from frequent bouts of insanity while Wenceslas was deposed as emperor-elect by the German princes in 1399. As the power and influence of Luxembourg Bohemia declined, Plantagenet England seemed poised to become the dominant player in European politics.

Chapter 1 discusses English artistic and poetic reactions to Anne

---

[13] Michael J. Bennett, "Richard II and the Wider Realm," in *Richard II. The Art of Kingship,* ed. Anthony Goodman and James L. Gillespie (Oxford, 1999), 187–204 at 200.
[14] Nigel Saul, *Richard II* (New Haven, 1997), 37.
[15] Michael Bennett, *Richard II and Revolution of 1399* (Stroud, 1999), 3.

of Bohemia, daughter of Emperor Charles IV and queen of England (1366–94). As John Gower's reference to the "guise of Beawme" (the fashion of Bohemia) in the epilogue of his *Confessio Amantis* suggests, Bohemian culture in the last two decades of the fourteenth century represented the height of European culture and something to be emulated at the English court of Richard II. Hence, in the prologue of Chaucer's *The Legend of Good Women,* Alceste's admonition to the poet-narrator to write a positive, pro-feminine palinode to the misogynist deficiencies of *Troilus and Criseyde* was a subjective projection of Chaucer imagining what Anne might have thought about his earlier work, a judgment based on his objective awareness of her cosmopolitan family and education.

Chapter 2 explores the political and ideological implications of Anne's English apotheosis. For her beloved spouse, Richard II, Anne was more than a mere consort and devoted partner; as the daughter of an emperor she was also the validation of his own claim to the imperial throne, which he zealously pursued following Anne's untimely death of the plague in 1394. If Anne was the source and embodiment of Richard's fantasies of imperial greatness, she equally inspired John Wyclif's justification for the translation of the Latin Bible into the vernacular. In 1381 Anne brought to England copies of the New Testament in Czech, German, and Latin, a fact that Wyclif cites in his *De Triplici Vinculo Amoris* to justify the translation of the Vulgate into the English tongue. This pro-vernacular cause was taken up by the Lollards after Wyclif's death.

In some ways the Lollards' appropriation of the example of Anne's devotion to the vernacular Bible to assert their reformist claims was based on perception as much as reality, since they were relying on the second-hand anecdote of Thomas Arundel, archbishop of Canterbury, at Anne's funeral in Westminster Abbey that the Queen desired to have the Bible in English "with the doctors' glosses upon them." This kind of mediated perception also characterized the Bohemian reformers' response to John Wyclif in the early fifteenth century. As discussed in chapters 3 and 4, the reception of Wyclif's theological and political ideas in Bohemia sheds light upon local preoccupations and preconceptions, and reveals the profound differences as well as affinities between the English and Bohemian heresies. If Wyclif's arguments against ecclesiastical corruption pointed ahead to the total subordination of the English church to the state in the reign of Henry VIII, Peter Chelčický's reaction to Wyclif anticipated the absolute separation of church and state in the United States. Similarly, the anonymous fifteenth-century Catholic satire "The Wycliffite Woman" reveals the extent to which Wyclif's reformist ideas were tied up with notions of gender roles in fifteenth-century Bohemia as well as the general medieval tendency to equate heresy with abnormal sexual and gender relations. The reformers were seen to have assumed the dominant, "masculine" position in the social hierarchy.

As a consequence of the Bohemian heresy and its various offshoots, the Czechs became synonymous in the European imagination with deviance and dissent. It was to mitigate such criticism that Baron Leo of Rožmitál and Blatná (ca. 1425–82) traveled to the courts of Europe—including the English court of Edward IV in 1466—on behalf of the excommunicated Hussite King George of Poděbrady and with the blessing of Emperor Frederick III. King George was keen to strengthen his ties to the Catholic rulers of Europe after more than twenty years of religious civil strife. The king had been excommunicated by the pope in 1465 and hoped that his brother-in-law's diplomacy would help to restore diplomatic relations with the rest of Europe and end the fifty-year isolation of his kingdom. As chapter 5 explores, Rožmitál's mission received a lavish welcome from Edward IV, who had come to the English throne five years before by force of arms.

The Bohemian visitors were fascinated by England and captivated by its fertile beauty. Their description of it as a "little sea-girt garden" anticipates Shakespeare's famous evocation of his native land in *Richard II*:

> This royal throne of kings, this sceptred isle,
> This earth of majesty, this seat of Mars,
> This other Eden—demi-paradise—
> This fortress built by nature for herself
> Against infection and the hand of war,
> This happy breed of men, this little world,
> This precious stone set in the silver sea,
> Which serves it in the office of a wall,

> Or as a moat defensive to a house
> Against the envy of less happier lands;
> This blessed plot, this earth, this realm, this England.
> (2.1.40–50)[16]

Lord Rožmitál's embassy was neither the first nor the last imperial contact with England. In 1414 Anne of Bohemia's brother, Sigismund, king of Hungary and Holy Roman Emperor, paid a personal visit to Henry V to negotiate an Anglo-Imperial alliance. Almost a century later the Habsburg Emperor Charles V twice visited England (in 1520 for three days and in 1522 for six weeks) with the same diplomatic intention and to discuss the prospect of his marriage to his cousin Mary Tudor, the infant daughter of Henry VIII. Within a few years of the emperor's visit, Tudor England had repudiated the Catholic faith and had become a stronghold of belligerent Protestantism. Bohemia, however, preserved a tradition of religious tolerance right up to the fateful Battle of the White Mountain in 1620. Chapter 6 discusses how several English recusants emigrated to Bohemia, among them the Jesuit priest Edmund Campion who was sent from Rome to Bohemia in 1574 to take up the professorship of rhetoric at the University of Prague. In 1584 the recusant Elizabeth Jane Weston emigrated with her family to Rudolfine Bohemia and became one of the most outstanding neo-Latin poets of her day, fluent in Czech, German, French, English, and Italian. To be sure, not all visitors to Bohemia at this time were disaffected Catholics. In his *Taylor his Travels: From the City of London in England, to the City of Prague in Bohemia* (1621), the Englishman John Taylor promoted the cause of the Protestant Estates in their resistance to Habsburg hegemony. But even Taylor had to admit that Catholics, Protestants, and Jews were permitted to worship alongside each other in the streets of Prague. Taylor's account is interesting for these objective insights; but, on the whole, it is far from disinterested, mediating between a personal travelogue and a colonizing call to arms in which the brave English and Scots are urged to fight on behalf of their sovereign's daughter, Elizabeth Stuart, Queen of Bohemia. Moreover, his rhapsodic descriptions of the fertile Bohemian countryside have more

---

[16] William Shakespeare, *The Riverside Shakespeare*, ed. G. Blakemore Evans (Boston, 1974), 813.

in common with the mythic Land of Cockaigne than with the observations of a dispassionate traveler.

Chapter 7 deals with the experience of Bohemians and Moravians in England before and after the fateful battle of the White Mountain in 1620: the Protestant nobleman Zdeněk Brtnický of Waldstein paid a visit to Elizabethan England in 1600 and was received by the queen at Hampton Court; the engraver Wenceslas Hollar left Bohemia in 1627 and ended up settling in England where he achieved fame as the greatest portrayer of seventeenth-century London; and the famous pedagogue and thinker John Amos Comenius visited England during his exile in Sweden in 1641.

Straddling the late medieval and early modern periods, this book aims not only to dismantle the fallacious synchronic distinction between England and continental Europe; it also highlights the artificial diachronic taxonomies of "medieval" and "Renaissance." As David Wallace has pointed out in critiquing the traditional view of Chaucer's "medieval" stupefaction at witnessing the glories of "Renaissance" Italy for the first time, there is "no magical divide (or Alpine peak) . . . between Chaucer and Shakespeare; perhaps the terms 'medieval' and 'Renaissance' might be assigned to the trash can of historiography (and hence of literary history)."[17] The lines of demarcation that traditionally divide "medieval" England from "Renaissance" Italy are equally illusory in the case of England and Bohemia. Wallace is right to affirm that "the Prague connection may have served as a conduit bringing Italian culture to England."[18] But in exploring the relations between premodern England and Bohemia, this book constantly confronts the difficulty in distinguishing between life and art, self and other, in the representation of these relations. In invoking as my title the conceit of Bohemia on the sea, my intention is not to exploit an old and tired literary cliché, but to give renewed vigor to its latent significance: that Chaucer's and Shakespeare's Bohemia is neither simply a geographic place nor an English misrepresentation of it, but a fascinating intermingling of the real and the imaginary, fact and fiction.

---

[17] David Wallace, *Chaucerian Polity. Absolutist Lineages and Associational Forms in England and Italy* (Stanford, 1997), 11.
[18] Ibid. 6.

Chapter 1

Imitatio Mariae

Anne of Bohemia as Cultural and Religious Mediatrix

Unlike Isabelle of France or Margaret of Anjou, foreign consorts to politically ineffectual kings (Edward II and Henry VI respectively), Anne of Bohemia, queen of England from 1382 to 1394, did not wish to exercise political power. Rather, she was content to play the traditional role of intercessor between her querulous husband, Richard II, and his disaffected subjects. Like Philippa of Hainault, who famously appealed to her husband—the bellicose Edward III—to spare the lives of the six burghers of Calais, Anne kneeled before her irate husband to request his clemency toward the disobedient citizens of London in 1392. She also interceded, unsuccessfully, with the rebellious Lords Appellant to spare the life of the king's tutor, Sir Simon Burley, following the Merciless Parliament of 1388.

The fact that Anne was content to play such a politically prescripted role has sometimes led scholars to regard her as culturally insignificant as well. The principal aim of this chapter is to show that medieval notions of femininity were sufficiently complex and fluid to transcend the active/passive model assigned to women in modern constructions of gender identity. Recent scholarship on Anne of Bohemia has begun to show that she was far from the passive and minor figure sometimes assumed.¹ Previously her reputation, such as it existed at all, rested largely upon metonymic details (for example, the fashionable clothes she brought to England) or incidental anecdotes which reveal little or nothing about her as a person in her own right, such as the secret marriage of her Bohemian lady-in-waiting, Agnes Lancencrona, to the king's favorite, Robert de Vere, earl of Oxford, in 1387.²

It is true that there is little empirical evidence that Queen Anne was especially interested in the literary arts. Apart from the Bodleian Library book of hours which bears her name, nothing from Anne's library has survived; and even that attribution is highly questionable.³ But the lack of an extant library or inventory of books does not necessarily mean that the individual in question did not have intellectual pursuits. No trace survives of a personal book collection in the case of Anne's father, Charles IV, who was one of the most educated rulers in the Middle Ages and a passionate patron of the arts.⁴

Most of the references to Anne in the contemporary chronicles dismiss her as inconsequential. Shortly after her arrival in England in December 1381, the Westminster writer complained that too much dowry money had been paid "for this tiny piece of flesh" ("pro tantillo carnis porcione").⁵ Disparaging comments such as these have encouraged some historians to take a similarly dim view of Anne's cultural significance. Citing the chroniclers' objection to her excessively large Bohemian retinue, Nigel Saul claims that the queen was unpopular in England from the moment she arrived in the country.⁶ But such com-

---

[1] See Paul Strohm, "Queens as Intercessors," in *Hochon's Arrow. The Social Imagination of Fourteenth-Century Texts* (Princeton, 1992), 95–119; David J. Wallace, "Anne of Bohemia, Queen of England and Chaucer's Emperice," *Litteraria Pragensia* 5/9 (1995): 1–16; Andrew Taylor, "Anne of Bohemia and the Making of Chaucer," *Studies in the Age of Chaucer* 19 (1997): 95–119; John M. Bowers, *The Politics of Pearl. Courtly Poetry in the Age of Richard II* (Woodbridge, 2001).

[2] Nigel Saul, *Richard II* (New Haven, 1997), 121.

[3] Bodleian Library, Oxford, M.S. Lat. Liturg. F. 3. Only two letters from Anne's chancery have survived and these are routine business documents. See *Letters of the Queens of England 1100–1547*, ed. Anne Crawford (Stroud, 1994), 102–6.

[4] Barbara Drake Boehm, "Charles IV. The Realm of Faith," in *Prague, The Crown of Bohemia 1347–1437*, ed. Barbara Drake Boehm and Jiří Fajt (New York, 2005), 23–33 at 24.

[5] Strohm, *Hochon's Arrow*, 106.

[6] Saul, *Richard II*, 85.

plaints about foreign consorts were commonplace in the Middle Ages and need to be treated with skeptical caution. The anonymous author of the Czech *Dalimil Chronicle* (ca. 1314) laments the Bohemian rulers' practice of marrying foreign—and especially German—princesses. Speaking through the voice of duke Oldřich, who took a Czech peasant girl named Božena as his wife in preference to a German consort, the chronicler warns that a German princess would bring her German entourage to Bohemia and would teach her children German rather than Czech.[7] It is true that unlike the author of the *Dalimil Chronicle,* the English chroniclers of Richard II's reign did not have a specific political agenda. But the xenophobic distrust they display toward Anne and her entourage is typical of medieval chroniclers in general.

A purely positivist approach to Anne of Bohemia, then, yields little, if any, contribution to our knowledge of her personality and cultural preferences. The problem, however, may lie less in the paucity of sources than in the inadequacy of historical methodology. Traditional historiography tends to perpetuate a rather crude model of medieval femininity: women were active and ambitious like Margaret of Anjou or passive and inconsequential like Anne of Bohemia. Yet medieval models of gender construction were altogether more pliant and protean than this restrictive binary allows. In his perceptive study of medieval queens as intercessors, Paul Strohm highlights the co-existence of active and passive attributes in the intercessory figures of Esther and the Blessed Virgin Mary as role models of medieval queenship:

> Even the most venerable precedents for intercessory queenship contain high—even flagrant—degrees of internal contradiction. Consider, for example, the cases of Mary and Esther, the two most influential exemplars of all. The crucial texts bearing on each case emphasize a range of virtues regarded as "feminine" in their emphasis on queenly access to mercy or compassion, personal experience of abjection or sorrow, and deference to established authority. Yet Mary and Esther also possess undeniable trappings of regality, not only symbolic power as epitomized through ceremony and splendid array, but access to practical wisdom and the worldly authority to enforce its dictates.[8]

---

[7] *Staročeská kronika tak řečeného Dalimila,* ed. Jiří Daňhelka (Prague, 1988), 2 vols., vol. 1, lines 12–32 (chapter 42).

[8] Strohm, *Hochon's Arrow,* 96–97.

In this chapter I shall not be primarily concerned with Anne's political persona, since it has already been dealt with so expertly by Professor Strohm. Rather, the ideological implications of Anne's marriage to Richard II will be addressed in the next chapter, while the present chapter is concerned with Anne's role as a cultural and religious—rather than as a political—intercessor or "mediatrix." By this term I mean that the binary active/passive which Strohm so deftly dismantles in his analysis of Anne's political role can also be fruitfully applied to her less well documented role as a transmitter of culture from her native Bohemia to her adopted England. The problem of assessing Anne's cultural influence on English life is particularly fraught when we turn to the case of Geoffrey Chaucer, who alludes several times to Anne in his work. Yet it is not immediately apparent how a woman who spoke French to her husband and her courtiers would have been interested in commissioning works of literature written in English such as *Troilus and Criseyde* or *The Legend of Good Women*. Clearly the either/or alternatives offered by the active/passive binary of femininity—did Anne commission Chaucer's English poetry or not?—is inadequate in our attempt to assess Anne's relationship with Chaucer and his work.

But if we move beyond the active/passive binary to embrace a more subtle model of cultural and religious mediation based on the examples of Esther and the Virgin Mary—in which notions of regal power and authority could coexist with humility and restraint—it becomes apparent that Anne's influence on Chaucer and others might have been exercised and understood in a similarly complex—and to our modern perception, contradictory—fashion. David Wallace's important analysis of how Italian humanist culture was channeled to England via Prague argues that Chaucer probably took Anne as an imaginary rather than as a real patron of his work based on his knowledge of her family's powerful reputation as patrons of vernacular culture. Wallace's hermeneutic model implies for Anne's cultural significance what Strohm's essay asserts for her political impact: that her participation cannot be reduced to an active/passive polarity. Imagining Anne as the recipient of *The Legend of Good Women* was not the same thing as imagining that she and her family were well educated: that, at least, is well attested by the sources. In other words, the reference to Anne as the recipient of the text in the F prologue of *The Legend of Good Women* cannot be reduced to an art/life, passive/active binary but rather dismantles this opposition: imagined recipience derives from the awareness of actual patronage.

Anne and International Court Culture

Following the lead provided by Strohm and Wallace, I shall argue that Anne's cultural and religious influence on English culture was far more extensive than most scholars realize. I shall suggest that for Chaucer and his English contemporaries Anne personified what Gervase Mathew has termed the "international court culture" of the late fourteenth century.[9] Anne's Bohemia had become almost as important as Paris for the international court culture. Its capital, Prague, was a vital crossroads in the heart of Europe where many cultures—Italian, French, German, and Czech—converged to create a dynamic center of the arts. Anne's grandfather, John of Luxembourg, had been elected king of Bohemia in 1310 after the extinction of the native Přemyslid dynasty. Although he spent little time in his new kingdom, preferring the itinerant life of the late medieval knight and the more sophisticated courts of the west, John's reign opened up the Bohemian court—hitherto German in its orientation—to French culture. His secretary Guillaume de Machaut, who accompanied the king on several diplomatic visits to Prague, was the greatest French composer and poet of his day, and his influence can be seen in the development of Bohemian polyphonic music and lyric poetry. Anne's father, Emperor Charles IV, transformed Prague into a beautiful city in the late Gothic style where he founded the first university north of the Alps in 1348 (figure 1).[10] Charles' court at Prague rivaled Paris and Naples in its cosmopolitanism. On a visit to Bohemia to petition the emperor to descend into Italy and bring unity to the peninsula, Petrarch himself was so impressed by Charles and his courtiers that he likened them to the ancient Greeks.

Anne's significance as a cultural and religious mediatrix was in large part inspired by the example of her family. Her female ancestors

---

[9] Gervase Mathew, *The Court of Richard II* (New York, 1968).
[10] See Iva Rosario, *Art and Propaganda. Charles IV of Bohemia 1346–1378* (Woodbridge, 2000).

Figure 1. Bust of Charles IV, King of Bohemia and Holy Roman Emperor (1316–78), ca. 1355. St. Vitus Cathedral, Prague. Erich Lessing/Art Resource, New York.

were particularly active as pious patrons of the arts. Her aunt, Bonne of Luxembourg, wife of John the Good of France, was an important owner of books as was Abbess Kunigunde, daughter of Přemysl Otakar II. In the Middle Ages royal consorts played an important role as transmitters of culture from their native to their adopted lands. The marriage in 1168 of Henry the Lion to Matilda of England, daughter of Henry II and Eleanor of Aquitaine, provided the context for the German translation of the *Chanson de Roland*. In the epilogue of the *Rolandslied* (ca. 1170) Duke Henry's desire to have the French version translated into German is attributed to his English wife: "the noble duchess requested it, / the daughter of a wealthy king" (9024–25).[11]

Recent scholarship has pointed to Anne's importance as a transmitter of the latest European cultural trends. It has even been suggested that she may have commissioned or inspired Chaucer's *The Legend of Good Women*, a work in which the influence of Machaut, Petrarch, and Boccaccio is clearly apparent.[12] This is not inconceivable, since Anne would have been familiar with courtly texts such as Boccaccio's *De claris mulieribus* that shed a favorable and positive light on women. Like Matilda of England's desire for a German translation of the *Chanson de Roland,* Anne may have encouraged Chaucer to compose a work that reflected the pro-feminine humanism of the court where she grew up.

There is no definitive evidence, however, that Anne actually commissioned *The Legend of Good Women*. A similar lack of evidence is apparent for Richard II's role as patron of the arts. This may have something to do with the fact that the king was deposed in 1399 and his effects, including his wife's library, were presumably dispersed after his death. Another major reason for the dearth of evidence concerning Anne's patronage is the late medieval practice of treating female patrons in an anonymous fashion. In the early and high Middle Ages writers frequently referred to their patrons by name, as in the case of Matilda of England and Marie de Champagne to whom Chré-

---

[11] "Des gerte die edele herzoginne, / aines richen chůniges barn." *Das Rolandslied des Pfaffen Konrad,* ed. Dieter Kartschoke (Frankfurt am Main, 1970), 390. For the importance of queens for the transmission of courtly culture in the High Middle Ages, see Joachim Bumke, *Courtly Culture. Literature and Society in the High Middle Ages,* trans. Thomas Dunlap (Woodstock, 2000), 76–77.

[12] For the claim that Anne may have commissioned *The Legend of Good Women,* see *Chaucer's Dream Poetry,* ed. Helen Phillips and Nick Havely (London, 1997), 283.

tien de Troyes dedicated his Arthurian romance *The Knight of the Cart*.[13] This was partly the case because early and high medieval royal women were empowered in a way that late medieval women were not. By making the names of their female patrons explicit, early medieval and high medieval authors acknowledged the power and influence of those ladies. But in the later Middle Ages the relationship between the writer and the female patron became more complex. It ceased to be fashionable to name one's male and female patrons, poets preferring such oblique strategies as acrostics or puns. In the first stanza of his Sixth Complaint, Guillaume de Machaut uses an acrostic to identify the names MARGEURITE/PIERRE, the latter referring to Pierre de Lusignan, king of Cyprus, whom Machaut memorialized in his long-verse chronicle *Prise d'Alexandrie*.[14] This discreet practice was initiated by the troubadours in southern France, who inaugurated an amorous, if unfulfilled, cult of high-born ladies, and was perpetuated by Jean de Meun's *Roman de la Rose* and Machaut's *Remede de Fortune*. In the *Remede* Machaut deliberately avoids identifying the lady for whom the work was composed, Bonne of Luxembourg. Machaut alludes to her as his patron by making puns on her name Bonne ("good"). Chaucer imitates this practice in his *Book of the Duchess* (1369), an elegy written on the death of Blanche, wife of John of Gaunt, by punning on her name: "And good faire White she het / That was my lady name right."[15]

But courtly discretion was only one aspect of the late medieval poet's complex relation to the lady. Religion also played a profound role in an age which saw an increased reverence for the Virgin Mary. In his discussion of the identity of the mysterious Margaryte in Thomas Usk's *The Testament of Love*, C. S. Lewis makes a valuable point about the ambiguity of medieval allegories of love in which the religious and profane representations of the lady become indistinguishable: "It is a mischievous error to suppose that in an allegory the author is 'really' talking about the thing symbolized, and not at all about the thing that

---

[13] See the introduction by William W. Kibler to *Chrétien de Troyes. Arthurian Romances* (Harmondsworth, 1991), 8.

[14] See James I. Wimsatt, *The Margeurite Poetry of Guillaume de Machaut* (Chapel Hill, 1970), 40–41.

[15] See Guillaume de Machaut, *Le Jugement du Roy de Behaigne and Remede de Fortune*, ed. James I. Wimsatt and William W. Kibler (Athens, 1998), 34.

symbolizes; the very essence of art is to talk about both. And for this particular conjunction, of divine and sexual love, Usk has a precedent in the two gardens of Jean de Meun, in the Beatrice of the *Divine Comedy*, and in the Song of Songs."[16] High and late medieval queenship was inextricably intertwined with the religious ideal of the Virgin Mary and the imagery associated with both were interchangeable: in the Coronation of the Virgin motif Mary is represented as a queen while queens were often depicted in terms of Marian iconography.

Thus the problem of assessing Anne of Bohemia's role as a cultural and religious mediatrix is not simply a question of recapturing facts that have been elided through the prejudice of insular chronicles or the manipulations of dynastic propaganda; it is also to recognize that courtly convention erases these traces, deliberately failing to draw a clear line between the real and the allegorical, the secular and the spiritual notion of womanhood. One of the difficulties inherent in establishing Anne's influence on English court culture is that her individual characteristics are often indistinguishable from those of the idealized lady of the love lyric or the religious ideal of the Virgin Mary. The need to acknowledge the complex relation of the particular to the universal and the secular to the religious in the interpretation of Anne's character thus inevitably complicates an exclusively positivist "biographical" approach to her life. But this recognition does not entirely preclude personal agency. Anne made a profound impression on English court poets less as an individual than as a representative of the international court culture. Inevitably, therefore, allusions to her become indistinguishable from the cosmopolitan culture she embodied.

Anne's Betrothal and Marriage

As was usually the case in the Middle Ages, the marriage of Anne of Bohemia and Richard II of England was determined by dynastic and political interests. The union was originally suggested by her father,

---

[16] C. S. Lewis, *The Allegory of Love. A Study in Medieval Tradition* (Oxford, 1936), 225. For the fusion of profane and religious elements in medieval lyric and romance, see also Derek Pearsall, *Gothic Europe 1200–1450* (Harlow, 2001), 40–41. For the importance of Marian iconography in fifteenth-century English queenship, see J. L. Laynesmith, *The Last Medieval Queens. English Queenship 1445–1503* (Oxford, 2004), 32ff.

Emperor Charles, in a letter sent to England in 1377. But it was only after the emperor's death in November 1378 and the ensuing schism in the Church that the proposal gathered momentum. On May 20, 1379, Charles's son and successor, Wenceslas IV, wrote to Richard proposing an Anglo-Bohemian alliance intended to support the Roman Pope Urban VI and to form the nucleus of a league against French hegemony and the Avignonese Pope Clement VII. A marriage agreement to cement the treaty was reached with Richard on May 2, 1381. Richard was to gain a prestigious connection with the imperial house of Luxembourg while the financially straitened Wenceslas was to be provided with an English loan of eighty thousand florins.[17]

In 1381, the year of the Peasants' Revolt in England, Bohemia was at the zenith of its international power and prestige. As the daughter of an emperor and as a member of one of the most cultivated dynasties in late medieval Europe, Anne of Bohemia must have made a dazzling impression on an English court still recovering from the trauma of Wat Tyler's rebellion. By contrast with England, Bohemia must have seemed stable, powerful, and sophisticated. This is certainly borne out by several court sources which contradict the negative opinion of the Westminster writer. Chaucer's friend and contemporary, John Gower, refers to the "guise of Beawme" ("the fashion of Bohemia") in his *Confessio Amantis*. This interesting reference comes in the poet-narrator's dream vision of the Parliament of Lovers (book 8), no doubt an idealized reflection of the youthful court of Richard and Anne. Significant is the connection between the Bohemian fashion and the cult of flowers and pearls which became virtually synonymous with Anne in English court poetry of the Ricardian era:

> I sih wher lusty Youthe tho,
> As he which was a Capitein,
> Tofore alle othre upon the plein
> Stod with his route wel begon,
> Here hevedes kempt, and therupon
> Garlandes noght of o colour,

---

[17] Anthony Tuck, "Richard II and the House of Luxemburg," in *Richard II. The Art of Kingship*, ed. Anthony Goodman and James L. Gillespie (Oxford, 1999), 205–29 at 218–19.

> Some of the lef, some of the flour,
> And some of the grete Perles were;
> The newe guise of Beawme there,
> With sondri thinges wel devised,
> I sih, wherof thei ben queintised.
> (8, 2462–72)[18]

In his *Boke of Cupid,* Sir John Clanvowe, a friend of the king, compliments "the queen at Woodstock." Woodstock was a royal lodge near Oxford and one of the queen's manorial estates. Anne's favorite manors were at Eltham and Sheen, the latter situated on the south bank of the Thames in present-day Richmond. As Clerk of the King's Works, a service he performed from July 1389 to June 1391, Geoffrey Chaucer was responsible for the day-to-day maintenance of seven royal manors, including Eltham and Sheen. The first reference to Anne as a literary patron comes in the prologue to *The Legend of Good Women* where Chaucer commands the narrator to send his completed book to the queen "on my byhalf, at Eltham or at Sheene" (F, 497). This raises the interesting question whether the poet ever met Anne. If he did so, it would not have been through the ready access of a high-born courtier but as an incident in the busy life of a clerk in royal service. If Chaucer and the queen ever spoke to each other, their common language would have been French rather than English, since there is no evidence that Anne ever became fluent in the language of her adopted people. And yet Chaucer wrote his major works in English; and it is in some of these works that Anne plays such an important role and where she receives so many compliments. How do we explain Anne's significance in Chaucer's English poetry?

The earliest work by Chaucer with a Bohemian connection is *The Parliament of Fowls* (ca. 1380).[19] Assuming the familiar form of a courtly dream poem in the manner of *The Romance of the Rose,* Dante's *Commedia* and Guillaume de Machaut, *The Parliament* describes how three tercel eagles compete for the hand of a formel eagle and are counseled in their wooing by a congregation of birds ("fowls"). The work alludes to the three principal suitors for the hand of the fourteen-year-old Anne

---

[18] John Gower, *Confessio Amantis,* ed. Russell A. Peck (Toronto, 1980), 473.
[19] For a discussion of this early work, see Derek Pearsall, *The Life of Geoffrey Chaucer* (Oxford, 1992), 121–27.

of Bohemia: a minor German prince, Friedrich of Meissen, to whom the Czech princess had been betrothed for six years; the dauphin of France (the future Charles VI) and the young King Richard II of England.[20] The formel eagle's deferral of her decision may help us to date the poem to the period immediately before the actual marriage contract was signed. According to Larry D. Benson, the *Parliament* was probably written sometime in 1380 to mark the betrothal of Richard and Anne:

> Late May of 1380 was a time when the proposed marriage of Richard and Anne must have been the principal topic of conversation in courtly and diplomatic circles. Michael de la Pole and John de Burley, who had begun the negotiations with Wenzel (Wenceslas), had just returned to London with a first-hand account of how the affair was proceeding, and an embassy, led by Simon de Burley and Bernard van Zetles, was preparing to leave (they left on June 18), empowered—if Richard's suit should prevail over those of Charles of France and Friedrich of Meissen—to contract the marriage. It is pleasant to speculate that *The Parliament of Fowls* was written for some gathering to bid good speed to the ambassadors.[21]

The Parliament of Fowls is principally a celebration of courtly love, but it also provides a humorous political commentary on the intricacies of international diplomacy. Benson has characterized the opening sequence of the poem, the *Somnium Scipionis*, as a "mirror for princes," a genre which—out of place in a love poem—would be appropriate if the poem were directed to the young King Richard who had come to the throne at the tender age of ten in 1377.[22]

The *speculum principis* was popular throughout Europe in the later Middle Ages and was deemed an especially important genre for young and inexperienced rulers like Richard II and his brother-in-law Wenceslas IV, both of whom had succeeded to thrones occupied for many

---

[20] See Donald R. Howard, *Chaucer. His Life, His Works, His World* (New York, 1987), 314–15.

[21] Larry D. Benson, "The Occasion of The Parliament of Fowls," in *The Wisdom of Poetry. Essays in Early English Literature in Honor of Morton W. Bloomfield*, ed. Larry D. Benson and Siegfried Wenzel (Kalamazoo, 1982), 123–44 at 144.

[22] Ibid., 129.

years by old and experienced rulers (Edward III and Charles IV). Charles IV's autobiography resembles a mirror for princes and was intended not merely to record the events of the emperor's life but to provide counsel for his son and heir who would occupy the two thrones of Bohemia and the Empire. A similar preoccupation with statecraft characterizes *The New Council* by the Czech nobleman Smil Flaška of Pardubice (1340s–1403), nephew of the Prague archbishop Arnošt of Pardubice. The original version of *The New Council* was written around 1385 but the surviving redaction dates from 1394 when the Bohemian nobility—of whom Smil was a prominent representative—was engaged in a protracted power struggle with the king. This second version combines positive and satirical counsels and expresses the author's profound ambivalence toward the king who had tried to deprive Smil of family property in southern Bohemia.

The New Council is not a love poem, like Chaucer's *The Parliament of Fowls*, but a political and moral allegory. Written in Czech and consisting of advice rendered by forty-four quadrupeds to the young Lion King (an allegorical reference to Wenceslas as king of Bohemia), it reflects the popularity of animal fables, largely for the purpose of moral edification, throughout medieval Europe. The tradition of using animals for moral and allegorical purposes is well represented by the Latin *Quadripartitus* of Gregorius de Hungaricali Broda and the famous encyclopedia of Bartholomeus Claretus de Chlumec, which includes a list of bird fables known as the *Physiologarius*.[23] Given Chaucer's well-known love of books and scholarly erudition, it is possible that he had heard of this list of bird fables.

The New Council is convened by the Lion King and is framed by two long speeches, those of the Eagle and the Swan. The Eagle may refer to Wenceslas' younger brother, Jošt, margrave of Moravia (whose symbol was an eagle) but it is more likely that it symbolizes Wenceslas's status as king of Germany (the eagle being the emblem of the German empire). The Swan, who concludes the counsel, represents Christ as well as Wenceslas's religious obligation as emperor-elect to protect Holy Church. The fact that Richard and Wenceslas were young and inexperienced rulers faced with the recent schism in the Church would

---

[23] See Alfred Thomas, *Anne's Bohemia: Czech Literature and Society, 1310–1420*, Medieval Cultures at Minnesota, vol. 13 (Minneapolis, 1998), 127.

explain the prominence of the *speculum principis* genre at the English and Bohemian courts, although in the case of Chaucer's *Parliament of Fowls* the emphasis is understandably less on statecraft and more on the king's betrothal and imminent marriage.

Anne's Patronage and Piety

After saying farewell to her family in Prague, Anne of Bohemia began the long and slow progress across Europe to England, interrupting her trip in Brussels for a month as a guest of her uncle, Wenceslas, duke of Brabant. On December 18, 1381, Anne's entourage made the crossing from Calais to Dover. On her arrival at Dover she was met by her fiancé, King Richard II. The royal couple headed north toward London and stayed overnight in the *camera regis* at the Royal Lodge at Ospringe, near Faversham in Kent. The Royal Lodge at Ospringe was the traditional place for medieval English kings to rest en route to their dominions in France. From Ospringe the royal couple continued to Leeds Castle where they spent Christmas and celebrated the New Year. Richard and Anne were married in Westminster Abbey on January 20, 1382. Two days later Anne was crowned Queen of England.[24]

The first direct allusion to Queen Anne in Chaucer's poetry occurs early in *Troilus and Criseyde* where the poet is describing his heroine's beauty ("Right as oure firste lettre is now an A.") By referring to Anne only by the first letter of her name, Chaucer was carefully and deliberately emulating international court practice. But tradition has it that the compliment backfired: by alluding to Anne in the same breath as his flawed Trojan heroine, Chaucer seems to have overlooked or underestimated the new humanist fashion for praising women's virtues. Whether the reprimand to the poet-narrator by the God of Love and his consort Alceste in the prologue to *The Legend of Good Women* reflects an actual conversation between Chaucer and Richard and Anne or whether it was a confrontation played out purely in his imagination is difficult to ascertain with any certainty. More significant is the fact that the commissioning of *The Legend of Good Women* as a palinode for the misogyny of *Troilus and Criseyde* was following a literary precedent

---

[24] Saul, *Richard II*, 89–90.

provided by Machaut's *Le Jugement du roy de Behaigne*. Less important than whether or not *The Legend of Good Women* was actually commissioned by Anne is the fact that, as the granddaughter of Machaut's patron alluded to in the title of his poem, she was the ideal arbiter of taste and the natural mediatrix between the irate God of Love and the chastened Poet. If the circumstances surrounding the composition of *The Legend of Good Women* were imaginary, the tradition of patronage in Anne's family was certainly not.

Another work by Machaut which seems to have provided an intertextual presence in Chaucer's mind as he composed *The Legend of Good Women* was *Remede de Fortune,* an elegy on the death of Bonne of Luxembourg composed for John the Good of France. By identifying Anne metonymically with her favorite manors of Eltham and Sheen, Chaucer was following the precedent provided by Machaut's poem whose only reference to the identity of the deceased Blanche is the park of Hesdin, where the lover makes his complaint after leaving his lady's château in confusion. This great castle in northwest France has been referred to as "the Versailles of the Middle Ages."[25] It was here that Bonne frequently maintained a household for her husband, John the Good. Chaucer was probably imitating Machaut's topographical allusion in paying his own compliment to Bonne's niece, Anne, whose favorite residence was situated on the south bank of the Thames. As Clerk of the King's Works, Chaucer would have been familiar with life at the queen's palace at Sheen; and even if he did not play an active part in the literary life of the court there, he would have had the opportunity to observe it at close quarters.

So did Anne actually commission *The Legend of Good Women*? The fifteenth-century poet John Lydgate said in his *Fall of Princes* that Chaucer wrote "at the request off the queen, / A legende off parfit hoolynesse / Off Goode Women" (lines 330–32). As Helen Phillips points out, he might have surmised that from the poem itself, but it equally may be true.[26] Crucially, it is not Chaucer the author who gives the book to the queen but his poetic surrogate: art's mediating role here mirrors Chaucer's indirect or distant relation to the Ricardian court and the sovereign he served. Just as the narrator mediates between re-

---

[25] Machaut, *Le Jugement*, 33–34.
[26] Phillips and Havely, *Chaucer's Dream Poetry,* 283.

ality and fiction, so does the figure of Alceste mediate between the "real" Anne and Chaucer's poetic ideal of womanhood as well as between the narrator himself and the irate God of Love, whose sun-connoted imagery suggests the tyrannical proclivities of the young Richard II.

Analogously, Chaucer's Bohemia represents a liminal space between reality and the imagination. For Wallace, it becomes a "congenial cultural and political" alternative to the terrifying prospect of an England that—like Lombardy—has assumed the absolutist trappings of political tyranny.[27] According to Wallace, Bohemia served as a conduit for the transmission of Italian humanist culture to England. Indeed, the Bohemian lands were among the most important centers of humanist learning outside Italy, and the personal and intellectual links between the two countries were extremely strong.[28] Cola di Rienzo and Petrarch were both guests at the court of Charles IV in Prague, and counted several courtiers among their friends, such as Chancellor John of Středa whose bishopric of Olomouc in Moravia (1364–80) became a leading center of the new learning.[29] John's distinguished library at Olomouc contained several works by Petrarch as well as a copy of Boccaccio's *De claris mulieribus*.[30] Petrarch visited Prague where he met the emperor's third wife, Anne of Schweidnitz, and wrote an epistolary encomium for her, *De laudibus feminarum*, in which he praises Anne's intellectual powers as well as her biological importance as the mother of the future emperor.[31]

As Wallace suggests, more important than whether Anne of Bohemia actually commissioned *The Legend of Good Women* is the fact that Chaucer imagines that she did so. But this is not to say that Anne's patronage is simply a figment of his imagination. By making the queen the recipient of his text, Chaucer is telling us something about the way he perceives her: this is clearly a woman interested in books and per-

---

[27] David Wallace, *Chaucerian Polity. Absolutist Lineages and Associational Forms in England and Italy* (Stanford, 1997), 338.
[28] See the essays in *Studien zum Humanismus in den böhmischen Ländern*, ed. Hans-Bernd Herder and Hans Rothe (Cologne, 1988).
[29] Anežka Vidmanová, *Laborintus. Latinská literatura středověkých Čech* (Prague, 1994), 144–49.
[30] Ibid., 145. See Giovanni Boccaccio, *Famous Women*, trans. Virginia Brown (Cambridge, Mass., 2003).
[31] Wallace, *Chaucerian Polity*, 362.

haps especially in books about the lives of holy women. Chaucer seems to have intended his work to have the style of a collection of saints' lives as illustrated by the use of Latin rubrics at the head of each legend, a practice also adopted by Boccaccio in his *De claris muleribus*.[32] In five of these rubrics the heroine is described as a "martyr." In following the precedent provided by Boccaccio, Chaucer may well have been attempting to conform to the pious atmosphere of a court presided over by a young woman whose literary interests, like those of her father, were directed more toward saints' lives than chivalric romances. The reference to "the suster of Cesar" (line 592) in "The Legend of Cleopatra" was probably intended as a compliment to Anne, whose half-brother Wenceslas was frequently styled Caesar in official documents, although he was never crowned as such in Rome.

In presenting Anne as the recipient of *The Legend of Good Women*, Chaucer was simply acknowledging her family's prominence as patrons of European vernacular culture, the kind of patronage of which he could only have dreamed in a country like England where courtly literature was still predominantly French. By contrast, literary patronage was practiced on both the Franco-Luxembourg and Bohemian sides of Anne's family. Anne's father, Emperor Charles, commissioned works of pious devotion in Czech and German. According to the anonymous Dominican translator and redactor of the so-called prose *Passional*—an important prose compilation of saints' lives translated from Latin into Czech and based on the *Golden Legend*—Charles personally commissioned the project. His son Wenceslas was an enthusiastic bibliophile deeply impressed by the great library of Charles V at the Louvre, which he had seen on a visit to Paris with his father in the winter of 1377–78. In the 1390s Wenceslas ordered a richly illuminated German translation of the Bible and a gorgeous illustrated version of Wolfram von Eschenbach's pious courtly romance *Willehalm*. Wenceslas's consort, Queen Sophie, was also an avid reader: her posthumous library included at least eleven books, one in German, the rest in Czech, among them a psalter and a romance of Alexander the Great.[33]

The later Luxembourg rulers seem to have had a particular penchant for pious and mystical reading. According to the inventory of St.

---

[32] Phillips and Havely, *Chaucer's Dream Poetry*, 352.
[33] Thomas, *Anne's Bohemia*, 46.

Vitus Cathedral for the year 1354, Charles IV presented the cathedral with a copy of the *Scivias* by the twelfth-century nun and mystic Hildegard von Bingen.[34] A second copy of the same text, which Charles had given to Arnošt of Pardubice, came to the cathedral the following year. As Barbara Drake Boehm remarks, Charles was probably drawn to Hildegard's writings because of her religious visions and his own mystical tendencies that he describes in his autobiography. But another reason for Charles's enthusiasm for Hildegard was probably his fascination with female holiness. Charles would have been keenly aware of an illustrious tradition of female piety and learning among his Bohemian ancestors. Agnes of Bohemia, who founded the first Franciscan house for women in the Czech lands in 1233, had corresponded in Latin with St. Clare of Assisi and with Pope Gregory IX to solicit advice for her foundation in Prague.[35] Agnes's niece, Kunigunde (Kunhuta in Czech), was also a learned patron of the arts. After divorcing her Polish husband, Bolesław Mazovius, she returned to Prague and entered the St. George Convent at the Castle where she became its most distinguished abbess and a great patron of literature. The so-called *Passional of Abbess Kunigunde* is a miscellany of devotional works written by the Dominican friar and court theologian Kolda of Koldice and lavishly illuminated by a monastic workshop headed by the Benedictine monk Beneš. The title page of the *Passional* depicts Kunigunde seated on a throne and crowned by angels. Kolda presents the abbess with his book, while a miniature Beneš kneels to the left. To the right of the princess stand nine nuns of the St. George Convent, each of them holding a clasped book in her left hand, an eloquent indicator of the convent's fervent commitment to female literacy and learning.

Kunigunde's sister-in-law, Elizabeth Rejčka, widow of Wenceslas II, was also a major patron of the arts who presided over a brilliant court at Brno. There she maintained a scriptorium from 1316 to 1323 that produced eight illuminated Latin codices.[36] By the second half of the fourteenth century devotional works in Latin were being adapted or translated into the vernacular for the edification of an increasingly pious laity, many of whom were women. A diminutive codex containing

---

[34] Boehm, "Charles IV," 24.
[35] See Joan Mueller, *The Privilege of Poverty. Clare of Assisi, Agnes of Prague, and the Struggle for a Franciscan Rule for Women* (University Park, 2006) chaps. 3 and 4.
[36] Thomas, *Anne's Bohemia*, 40–41.

the Hours of the Virgin or Little Office of the Blessed Virgin (*cursus horae sanctae Mariae*) is one of two surviving manuscripts of hours written in Czech from the end of the fourteenth century. The queen depicted on folio 77r, presumably the patron of the manuscript, has not been identified. But an intriguing clue (the monogram AB) appears next to the saint before whom the royal figure is kneeling.[37] Given the diminutive size of the codex (10 × 8 cm), it may have been made for a royal infant or for easy travel. Whether or not the book was made for Anne, this beautiful miniature codex clearly reflects the importance of female piety and patronage in the Bohemian royal family. Works in Czech belonging to women in the royal family date back to the end of the thirteenth century. One of the oldest surviving religious poems in Czech—the so-called "Prayer of Kunigunde" (1290)—was composed for Kunigunde, probably as a child or young woman before she was able to read in Latin. Presumably the princess was extremely fond of the poem for it has survived in her Latin breviary.

Indirect evidence of bilingualism among royal women is provided by the court art of the period, in particular, the motif of the Virgin Annunciate. Although scenes of the Virgin reading from an open book are common in late medieval representations of the Annunciation, it is rare to find her reading two books, as in the Vyšší Brod Altarpiece (ca. 1350s) or in the missal of John of Středa, where the Virgin is seated before an open book standing on a lectern while clasping a closed book to her swollen belly. The juxtaposition of the closed book to the Virgin's womb probably symbolizes the Savior as the incarnation of the Logos or Word, recalling the beginning of St. John's Gospel: "In principio erat Verbum et Verbum erat apud Deum, et Deus erat Verbum."[38]

But the presence of two books may equally reflect the bilingualism of the royal court at Prague. The owner of the missal described above, Chancellor John of Středa, translated Latin devotional works into German, for example, *Das Buch der Liebkosung,* based on the thirteenth-century pseudo-Augustinian *Soliloquaie animae ad deum.* Although German had been the main spoken and literary language of the Bohemian court since the thirteenth century when the Czech kings began to cultivate German poets, Charles IV gave equal cultural and political

---

[37] See Boehm and Fajt, *Prague, The Crown of Bohemia,* 218–19.
[38] Thomas, *Anne's Bohemia,* 28.

weight to his mother's native language and associated it with the powerful tradition of female saintliness in the Přemyslid royal family. Charles required the sons of the imperial electors to learn Czech as well as German. Many of the devotional works commissioned by the emperor, such as the prose *Passional* based on the *Golden Legend* and the exquisite verse *Life of Saint Catherine*, were written in Czech. And it is perhaps significant that his son Wenceslas spoke to his court chamberlain in German and to his chaplain in Czech.

Thus Czech seems to have been closely identified not only with the native Přemyslid dynasty but also with the saintliness and piety characteristic of so many of its members. The fact that English came to play a far more prominent role as a medium of courtly literature during the reign of Richard II raises the question whether the coexistence of French and English as court languages and literatures reflected the bilingual example provided by German and Czech at the royal court of Prague. If this was so, Chaucer's decision to write his courtly works in English rather than French should be seen less as a personal choice and more as a response to a foreign precedent and an international trend.

The queen's name is also significant for our understanding of Anne of Bohemia's literacy and commitment to female learning. In the later Middle Ages the Virgin Mary's mother, St. Anne, was closely identified with the practice of female reading. In paintings, statues, and stained glass Anne is often depicted teaching her daughter to read. The cult of St. Anne was particularly well developed in fourteenth-century Bohemia where many churches were named in her honor, including the church adjacent to the Dominican church at Prague. She also features in the illuminated Bohemian manuscript of the *Travels of Sir John Mandeville* in the British Library, where she lies in effigy next to St. Luke the Evangelist and St. John Chrysostom in Constantinople, a city which was of profound political and cultural significance for Charles IV and the Luxembourg dynasty. A painting by the court painter Master Theodoricus in the imperial Chapel of the Holy Cross at Karlstein Castle depicts St. Anne supporting the Virgin and Child with her left arm and holding a large closed book in her right hand, suggesting the compatibility of domesticity and literacy. It is interesting that the Czech *Life of Saint Catherine* refers to St. Anne as the Virgin's mother in his description of the Virgin and Child in the first celestial vision:

"Among those precious sights was enthroned Mary, that blossoming maiden, whose mother is St. Anne, holding her precious one, Christ, her dear little son and loving him most fervently."[39] This reference may have been intended not only to emphasize Jesus' matrilineal ancestry but also to foreground the female literacy associated with his grandmother as well as with Catherine of Alexandria.

Shortly after her marriage, Anne of Bohemia asked the pope that the feast of St. Anne be "more solemnly" observed; and in 1383 Urban VI granted her request in honor of her marriage.[40] This was more than a pious gesture: it was an acknowledgment that Anne regarded literacy as an integral feature of female devotional practice.[41] It is probable that a great deal of the devotion shown to St. Anne in England in the fifteenth century can be attributed to Queen Anne's mediation with the pope. Margery Kempe's meditation on St. Anne pregnant with the Virgin Mary is consistent with the popularity of the saint's cult in East Anglia in the early fifteenth century: "And than anoon sche sawe Seynt Anne gret wyth chylde, and than sche preyd Seynt Anne to be hir mayden and hir servawnt."[42]

Although *The Legend of Good Women* was written in a pro-feminine and humanist climate prevalent in the international courts of Europe, it is equally true that the work exemplifies the ambivalence of the age's attitudes to women. In fact, scholars have long debated whether Chaucer was being serious in writing a series of legends ostensibly praising virtuous women. One persuasive theory is the idea of the work as a courtly game in which the nature of Woman becomes the subject of a humorous debate.[43] Florence Percival locates *The Legend of Good Women* in the courtly context of the late fourteenth and early fifteenth centuries when clerical antifeminism was pitched against the pastime of *la louange des dames* made fashionable at the French court of

---

[39] "The Old Czech Life of St. Catherine of Alexandria," trans. Alfred Thomas, in *Medieval Hagiography. An Anthology,* ed. Thomas Head (New York, 2000), 773.

[40] Saul, *Richard II*, 324.

[41] For the importance of St. Anne's cult for female literacy, see Pamela Sheingorn, "'The Wise Mother'. The Image of St. Anne Teaching the Virgin Mary," in *Gendering the Master Narrative. Women and Power in the Middle Ages,* ed. Mary C. Erler and Maryanne Kowaleski (Ithaca, 2003), 105–34.

[42] *The Book of Margery Kempe,* ed. Barry Windeatt (Harlow, 2000), 75. For the cult of St. Anne in East Anglia in the fifteenth century see Gail McMurray Gibson, *The Theater of Devotion. East Anglian Drama and Society in the Late Middle Ages* (Chicago, 1989).

[43] Florence Percival, *Chaucer's Legendary Good Women* (Cambridge, 1998), 325.

Charles VI.[44] As Percival points out, the ludic element was sometimes already present in clerical antifeminism but the notion of a game becomes even more pronounced when it "moved into the vernacular and was accompanied by a higher consciousness of women in the audience."[45]

It may be assumed, therefore, that female patronage is a major factor in Chaucer's decision to compose *The Legend of Good Women*. Whether or not Anne actually commissioned or received it, it was clearly intended for a courtly audience in which women were imagined to be present. And given Anne's pedigree as a member of a family with sophisticated tastes in literature, it is reasonable to conclude that she formed part of that ideal audience. Here too there may have been a significant precedent in Anne's family. The debate concerning women's virtues and vices also found literary expression in the prose disputes *Der Ackermann* (*The Plowman*) (1401) and its Czech analogue *Tkadleček* (*The Weaver*, ca. 1406–7), both of which were written in Bohemia. Both of these works assume the standard form of a scholastic dispute between faith and reason, heart and mind. In *The Plowman* the eponymous plaintiff, whose beloved wife has died, complains to Death, while in *The Weaver* the jilted lover Ludvík (a "weaver" of words, in fact a writer) complains to Misfortune about the loss of his girlfriend. A key feature of both texts is the veiled identity of the beloved. Only at the very end of *The Plowman* is the name of the plaintiff's wife (Margaret) spelt out, while in *The Weaver*, Ludvík's lover Adlička is identified by cryptogram. One of the major differences between *The Plowman* and *The Weaver* is that the latter is more humorous, since the plaintiff's lover is not dead but rather has jilted him. Given his allegorical status as a courtly writer, Ludvík is caught on the horns of a comic dilemma, at once praising his beloved in courtly language while forced to admit that she has abandoned him for another. The gap between Ludvík's courtly ideal of Woman and Misfortune's antifeminine characterization of Adlička as a whore renders the entire work less an eschatological debate on life and death than a courtly disputation on the vices and virtues of Woman.

The Weaver is a good illustration of the transition from Latin to ver-

---

[44] Ibid., 299.
[45] Ibid., 300.

nacular writing and the concomitant shift from an exclusively male to a courtly audience in which women were included. Its scholastic sources were Latin, including *De vita et moribus philosophorum antiquorum* by the Oxford-trained Englishman Walter Burley (1275–1343). Such works were primarily intended for male clerics. Unlike Burley's treatise *The Weaver* was probably composed for a mixed courtly audience of men and women. The reference to Adlička as a maid at the regional court at Hradec Králové ("the Queen's Castle") in northeast Bohemia suggests that Wenceslas's consort, Queen Sophie, and her entourage formed the intended audience of the Czech dispute.

An important feature of the courtly game was the symbolic significance attached to flowers and their meaning. In the prologue of *The Legend of Good Women* Chaucer plays upon the prominence of the daisy (*marguerite* in French) in connection with Alceste, Anne's poetic surrogate. As Florence Percival has pointed out, the cult of the daisy had been made famous by Machaut and was mediated to Chaucer via the poetry of Jean Froissart, court poet to Philippa of Hainault, in the late 1360s.[46] In the right-hand panel of the Wilton Diptych the daisy is prominent in the flowery meadow where the Virgin and Child stand surrounded by angels, suggesting a further association with Queen Anne. Another flower connected with Anne's memory was the periwinkle, a blue flower with dark green leaves, which appears to the right of the Virgin under the extended arm of an angel. On the outside of the diptych the king's personal device, the white hart, rests on a bed of rosemary, one of the queen's personal devices along with the fern which is also present in the flowery meadow. Three collars in the form of ferns have recently been identified as a device of Anne of Bohemia.[47]

Flower symbolism was also important in Bohemian court culture. In chapter 3 of *The Plowman* the grieving plaintiff compares the loss of his happiness without his beloved to a summer flower torn from the garden of his heart.[48] Invoking the clerical motif of *contemptus mundi*,

---

[46] Ibid., 23–42. For Machaut's use of the *marguerite* motif, see Wimsatt, *The Margeurite Poetry of Guillaume de Machaut*.

[47] See Celia Fisher, "A Study of the Plants and Flowers in the Wilton Diptych," in *The Regal Image of Richard II and the Wilton Diptych*, ed. Dillian Gordon, Lisa Monnis, and Caroline Elam (London, 1997), 155–63 at 161.

[48] "Ir habt meiner wünnen lichte sumerblumen mir aus meines herzen anger jemerlichen ausgereutet." Johannes von Tepl, *Der Ackerman*, ed. Willy Krogmann (Wiesbaden, 1954), 102–3.

Death later refers to the ephemeral courtly practice of flower symbolism. In a brilliant rhetorical sleight of hand, the author conflates the mowing down of flowers with Death as the Grim Reaper cutting down souls: "White, black, red, brown, green, blue, grey, yellow, indeed, flowers and grasses of every glistening hue, We mow them down regardless of their splendor, strength, or other virtues. We do not spare the violet for its beautiful color or its full fragrance."[49] The author of *The Weaver* amplifies the German passage by listing more flowers and by glossing their significance in terms of the courtly code. This amplification reinforces the likelihood that flower symbolism was highly developed at the royal court:

> The violet will not hide from us even with its luxuriant color which denotes permanence. The lily with its beauty and whiteness will not fell us even in bright hope. The red rose with its scarlet color will not be veiled from us in burning love. The clover, the ivy, the juniper, the periwinkle, which is the leader of all incipient love, cannot hide from us. The field rose with its russet color, sign of all mystery, cannot escape us. Even the invented, stolen color of gray, ingeniously composed from many colors, will not escape us. The blue cornflower of evil hope or perfection will not resist us. The dandelion with its vigor and its yellow color, a flower much abused, will not profit against us.[50]

Included in this list is the periwinkle (*barvínek*), which the Czech author identifies "as the leader of all incipient love." This flower appears to have been a favorite motif in the international court culture. As mentioned earlier, it appears in the Wilton Diptych to the right of the Virgin Mary, perhaps as a token of the love between Richard and Anne. Periwinkles also alternate with parrots on Sir Gawain's *hourson* (a band of embroidered silk attached to the helmet) in *Sir Gawain and the Green Knight* (II, 611).

The blue color of the periwinkle is also significant for our under-

---

[49] "Weiß, swarz, rot, braun, grün, blau, grau, gel und allerlei glanzes blumen unde gras heuet sie vür sich nider, ires glanzes, irer kraft, irer tugend nicht geachtet. Da geneußet der veiol nicht seiner schönen farbe, seines reichen ruches, seiner wolsmeckender safte." Tepl, *Der Ackerman*, 115.

[50] Quoted from *Czech Prose. An Anthology*, ed. William E. Harkins (Ann Arbor, 1983), 30–31. For the Czech original, see *Tkadleček*, ed. František Šimek (Prague, 1974), 27.

standing of the complex iconography of the Wilton Diptych. Blue is the emblematic color of the Virgin Mary, and it is in a vivid blue robe that she and her attendant angels appear in the flowery meadow in the right-hand panel. In the fourteenth-century Czech courtly love lyric "The Song of Colors" blue is identified with virginity:

> The wise praise the color blue,
> For she never sullies herself.
> Whatever she does remains the same;
> Therefore she is worthy of a king.[51]

References to Anne in Chaucer's work disappear after 1388, the year of the Merciless Parliament. Chaucer was astute enough to distance himself from royal circles during this crisis in the fortunes of Richard and his wife. The Lords Appellant took murderous revenge on the king's closest friends and advisers. Queen Anne interceded with these lords to spare the life of the king's tutor, Sir Simon Burley, who had visited Prague in order to negotiate the royal marriage in 1380. Following ancient queenly precedent, she kneeled before the lords for several hours, much to her husband's humiliation. But all appeals for mercy fell on deaf ears: Burley was beheaded along with several of the king's men. Among these victims of factional violence was Thomas Usk whose *Testament of Love* was presumably written in jail prior to the execution. Although it is conventionally modeled on Boethius' *Consolation of Philosophy*—and might even have relied on Chaucer's translation of Boethius rather than the Latin original—this work is unusual in using prose rather than verse to articulate courtly ideas.

The Testament of Love takes the form of a first-person experience of incarceration in which the prisoner appeals to his beloved lady Margaret. In the first book Lady Love appears to the speaker and consoles him on his plight. This practice clearly recalled a tradition established by Machaut, Froissart, and Chaucer in which the lady becomes an intercessory figure for the poet: "Neverthelater, yet hertly, lady precious Margarit have mynde on thy servant and thynke on his disease how

---

[51] My translation. For the original Czech, see *Staročeská lyrika*, ed. Jan Vilikovský (Prague, 1940), 63.

lyghtless he lyveth, sithe the beames brennende of thyn eyen are so bewent that worldes and clouds atwene us twey wol nat suffre my thoughtes of hem to be enlumyned."[52] According to the editor of *The Testament of Love*, the mysterious figure of Margaret addressed in the work was intended as an allegorical homage to Queen Anne.[53] Although there are precedents in the French *marguerite* tradition, the name Margaret seems to have become particularly common in association with Anne. In *The Legend of Good Women* Chaucer's identification of Alceste with the daisy exploits the double meaning of the French word *marguerite:* "daisy" and "pearl." Margaret is also the name of the plaintiff's deceased wife in *The Plowman*. Probably inspired by Chaucer but perhaps also aware of European courtly tradition, Usk deploys the name Margaret to identify Anne as his personal protectress. Important here is the long-established association of pearls and other gems with virginity, especially since Anne appears to have espoused a life of chastity in marriage. In this respect Anne followed a long-established precedent of virginity on the Slavic side of her family and in central Europe as a whole.

The first female saint in the medieval Slavic world was Anne's distant ancestor, St. Ludmila, grandmother of the martyred Duke Wenceslas. Ludmila is associated with precious gems by the tenth-century monk Christian, who describes her as "adorned with the jewels of virtue."[54] The Bohemian protomartyr Ludmila is prominent, alongside Wenceslas, Adalbert, and Procopius, in the bottom right corner of an illumination of the celestial Jerusalem from a thirteenth-century manuscript of St. Augustine's *De Civitate Dei* (figure 2). A thirteenth-century Latin hymn, which forms part of the office of St. Ludmila ("Hymnus Lux vera lucis radium") presents the saint as the intercessor between God and the Czechs:

---

[52] Thomas Usk, *Testament of Love,* ed. R. Allen Shoaf (Kalamazoo, 1998), 56.

[53] Ibid., 22–25. For the same claim, and the conclusion that there existed an entire body of English Margaret poems written in praise of Queen Anne, see Ramona Bressie, "The Date of Thomas Usk's 'Testament of Love'," *Modern Philology* 26 (1928): 17–29 (26–28).

[54] Christian, *Legenda Christiani*, ed. Jaroslav Ludvíkovský (Prague, 1978), 30. For the close association of female virginity with gems and precious stones in Anglo-Norman literature, see Jocelyn Wogan-Browne, *Saints' Lives and Women's Literary Culture. c. 1150–1300. Virginity and Its Authorizations* (Oxford, 2001), 73.

Figure 2. The Bohemian saints Ludmila, Wenceslas, Adalbert, and Prokop appear at bottom right. Thirteenth-century Bohemian manuscript of Saint Augustine's *De Civitate Dei*. Archives of Hradčany Castle, Prague. Erich Lessing/Art Resource, New York.

Bohemia, praise God,
Sing, rejoice, celebrate,
Have hope in the heavenly kingdom
Through Ludmila's intercession.[55]

The compiler of the office is identified in the manuscript as "the preacher Domaslas," confirming the important role of the Dominican Order in propagating female piety in the Bohemian Lands.[56] In his courtly *Life of Saint Wenceslas* Emperor Charles refers to Ludmila as the "protectress of the Czechs" and the "first pearl and the first flower plucked in Bohemia."[57] Emperor Charles was an important supporter of the Bohemian Dominicans.[58] Like them, he venerated St. Ludmila's memory and mentions her with great respect in his autobiography.

Another celebrated holy woman from the region was the Blessed Hedwig of Silesia (1174–1243), who was canonized in 1267. A beautifully illustrated life of Hedwig—the *Vita beatae Hedwigis*—was commissioned in 1353 by her grandson Duke Ludwig of Legnica and Brzeg, a vassal of Charles IV and grandson of King Wenceslas II of Bohemia.[59] Hedwig was a mother of seven but later renounced sex within marriage in order to espouse "conjugal chastity."[60] Although not canonized until the twentieth century (by Pope John Paul II), Agnes of Bohemia was another example of a royal lady who chose chastity over marriage. Emperor Frederick II himself asked Agnes's brother, King Wenceslas I, for her hand in marriage but Agnes was determined not to marry. Such was Agnes's reputation for holiness that not only her brother but also the emperor himself accepted the rejection graciously.[61] Ludmila, Agnes of Bohemia, Abbess Kunigunde, and Hedwig of Silesia represent an illustrious genealogy of pious royal women

---

[55] "Lauda Deum Bohemia, / Psalle, gaude, tripudia, / Ludmille per suffragia / Regna sperans celestia." State Library, Prague, Pu IV C 17.

[56] See Thomas, *Anne's Bohemia*.

[57] *Die St. Wenzelslegende Kaiser Karls IV. Einleitung/Texte/Kommentar*, ed. Anton Blaschka, Quellen und Forschungen aus dem Gebiete der Geschichte, 14 (Prague, 1934), 61–80.

[58] Thomas, *Anne's Bohemia*, 91–92.

[59] See Boehm and Fajt, *Prague. The Crown of Bohemia*, 138–39.

[60] See André Vauchez, *The Laity in the Middle Ages. Religious Beliefs and Devotional Practices*, ed. Daniel E. Bornstein (Notre Dame, 1993), 185–90.

[61] Mueller, *The Privilege of Poverty*, 54.

to whom Anne of Bohemia could look as a role model for her own chaste marriage to Richard II.

Charles IV also venerated the female saint of eastern provenance, Catherine of Alexandria. She had become his personal protectress after his victory at the Battle of San Felice in northern Italy, fought on the saint's feast day (November 25, 1332). Charles built a church in Catherine's honor in the New Town in Prague (1356) and dedicated his private oratory to her in his castle at Karlstein near Prague (after 1347). It is possible that he also commissioned the Czech verse *Life of Saint Catherine*. The description of Catherine's peerless beauty and learning is unashamedly elitist; and it is likely that the importance attached to her erudition reflected the kind of education that the emperor envisaged for his own children: "She was instructed in much wondrous learning, familiar to the most erudite scholars: wisdom, the meaning of literal and allegorical texts, about the essence of everything, as best it can be reached by all kinds of philosophical enquiry. All that the maiden mastered in just a few years, surpassing in learning all the learned students in the world."[62] The Czech *Life of Saint Catherine* also emphasizes the saint's insistence on preserving her virginity at all costs. It is possible that Anne of Bohemia heard this legend as a child at her father's court and that it influenced her in later life. Like Agnes of Bohemia, Catherine refuses to accept the hand of the emperor's son: "I would be mad to take a husband whom I have never set eyes on and whom I do not know, whether he is hunchbacked or handsome, whether he has castles or run-down houses, whether he is blind or can see, hideous or lovely, generous or stingy, beautiful or ugly, foolish or wise, false or true, sickly or healthy, or what his manners are like. I would rather preserve my chastity forever until I die, since no one alive is equal to my wisdom or my beauty."[63]

Female piety and saintliness enjoyed something of a vogue in Bohemia in the second half of the fourteenth century. The Czech nobleman Thomas of Štítné (ca. 1331–1401), who wrote works of devotion for the edification of his two daughters, translated a selection of *The Visions of Saint Bridget* sometime after 1391. His own preface to the selection exalts some women as channels of God's grace: "And have not

---

[62] Head, *Medieval Hagiography*, 769.
[63] Ibid., 771.

women been prophets through whom God has worked wonderfully and done great things: Judith, Esther, the widow Anna, the Sibyls? Hence, though one should not believe any spirit, still not all simple folk, uneducated, or women should be excluded when they speak so, but it is proper to put it to the test to see if it be from God."[64]

Thomas's *Six Books on General Christian Matters* (1376) includes an important section on virginity. Folio 45b of the manuscript represents two young lay women with free-flowing hair kneeling before an altar and placing crowns, symbolic of their virginity, on an altar. The maidens are attended by an older woman who cuts the long flowing locks of one of the girls as if preparing her for entry into a cloister, while a group of four other women are kneeling and praying to the left. What is striking about this church scene is the complete absence of priests or clerics and the fact that none of the women are actually nuns: it is laywomen who preside in this scene of women dedicating their virginity to Holy Church.

Typical of this fashion for female virginity is Chaucer's *Life of Saint Cecilia*, which was later included in the *Second Nun's Tale* in the *Canterbury Tales* and dates from the early to mid-1380s. It tells of the Roman virgin-martyr's desire to lead a life of chastity within marriage. Cecilia is a powerfully active character rather than a passively suffering martyr who confronts the pagan Almachius with strength and fortitude. Similarly the Czech *Life of Saint Catherine* emphasizes the saint's defiance and intellectual qualities in her confrontation with Maxentius and the pagan wise men who try to convert her. Symbolic of this empowerment of women is a painting of three female saints (Catherine, Mary Magdalene, and Margaret) in an altar painting from Třeboň in southern Bohemia (ca. 1380). Saint Catherine stands on the far left, the wheel of her martyrdom in her right hand and an upraised sword (with which she was beheaded) in her left. Although the sword is an instrument of Catherine's martyrdom, its upright phallic position serves to empower her as a symbol of orthodoxy and learning.

The lives of the virgin martyrs were popular in Czech literature as well as in Bohemian art in the second half of the fourteenth century. Forming part of what is known as the Second Cycle of Legends (to dis-

---

[64] Harkins, *Czech Prose. An Anthology*, 18. For the Czech original, see *Počátky staročeské mystiky* (Prague, 1948), ed. Jan Menšík, 80–81.

tinguish them from an earlier cycle written at the end of the thirteenth century based on the *Golden Legend*), these saints' lives witness both to the growth of a pious laity in Bohemia and to the powerful role model of holy women for female members of the laity.

Chaucer's tale of the virginal union of Cecilia and her husband Valerian has led some scholars to speculate that it was written explicitly to extol the chaste marriage practiced by Anne of Bohemia and Richard II.[65] The *Life of Saint Cecilia* begins with an invocation to the Virgin Mary. Devotion to Mary is also an important feature of Usk's veneration for his protectress. In the early and high Middle Ages powerful queens were often compared with Esther but in the later Middle Ages they were more frequently identified with the Blessed Virgin Mary.[66] Devotion to Mary was especially prominent at the royal court of Prague under King Wenceslas II, who was also a notable *Minnesinger*. At his court the cult of Mary fused with courtly love poetry (*Minnesang*) to create one of the most unusual and outstanding articulations of religious devotion in the Middle Ages: the so-called *Frauenleich* by the German poet Heinrich von Meissen more usually known as Frauenlob ("Praise of Women") (ca. 1260–1318). Frauenlob's masterpiece is an ecstatic mystical hymn to the Virgin Mary based on the *mulier amicta sole* (Woman Clothed with the Sun) of Revelation 12.1.[67] It is not known for certain whether this great poem was written during Frauenlob's residence at the court of Prague. But its daring synthesis of religious devotion and courtly love eroticism is certainly consistent with the profoundly mystical atmosphere that prevailed at the Prague court:

> I am chosen to be great;
> My will is both mighty and gentle.
> For love I lovingly arose;
> At the window of my cloister-door
> My love all filled with love came in;

---

[65] Bowers, *The Politics of Pearl*, 170.

[66] See Lois L. Huneycutt, "Intercession and the High Medieval Queen. The Esther Topos," *Power of the Weak. Studies on Medieval Women*, ed. Jennifer Carpenter and Sally-Beth MacLean (Urbana, 1995), 126–46.

[67] Heinrich von Meissen, *Leiche, Sangsprüche, Lieder*, ed. Karl Stackmann and Karl H. Bertau, vol. 1 (Göttingen, 1981), 126–46.

> His hand touched me, I feel it yet!
> It was wet with sweet dew,
> And seemed to me a honey-jar.
> (I, 9, lines 1–8).[68]

The authoritative female speaker of these lines merges with the humble figure of the enclosed nun who, as *sponsa Christi*, awaits the arrival of her celestial bridegroom. Elsewhere in the poem the bridegroom is described as the *Minnefreund* (the courtly lover). We see evidence of a similar conflation of Marian and courtly love motifs in the Latin "Parable of the Invincible Knight" (*De strenuo milite*) composed for Wenceslas II's sister, Abbess Kunigunde, by the court theologian, the Dominican Kolda of Koldice. Important in the strophe just quoted is the way femininity combines ostensibly contradictory qualities of regal authority ("mighty") with humble submissiveness ("gentle"). This fusion of regal power and humility in Frauenlob's representation of the Virgin reflects the empowered status of royal women in high and late medieval Europe.

The Bohemian cult of Mary reached its high-water mark in the reign of Charles IV. Both the art and the literature of the period reflect this trend. The court poet Heinrich von Mügeln wrote poetry in praise of the Virgin; and Marian elements are an important feature of *Das Buch der Liebkosung*. The Marian motif of the *mulier amicta sole* is also prominent in the wall paintings in the Lady Chapel at Karlstein Castle by the court painter Master Theodoricus, as well as in those at the Na Slovanech Monastery in Prague by Nikolaus Wurmser of Salzburg (ca. 1360). Devotion to Mary is also apparent in Czech literature of the Caroline period. In the Czech version of the German minstrel epic *Duke Ernest* (ca. 1350s), the close relationship between the banished hero and his devoted mother, Adlička, is frequently described in the affective language of Christ's love for His mother. The description of the beautiful Indian princess encountered by Ernest and his companions during their Otherworld Voyage also employs Marian topoi, including the *pulchra ut luna, electa ut sol* (the beloved, described as "fair as the moon,

---

[68] Ibid., 252: "ich bin ez die groze von der kür, / min wille ist kreftig und ouch mür. / gein liebem liebe ich mich erbür. / daz venster miner klosentür, / da gieng min lieb so triutlich vür. / sin hant mich rurte, des ich spür, / sie was von süzem touwe naz, / ez duchte mich ein honigvaz."

clear as the sun") from the Song of Songs 6:10: "She was similar to the moon / when it achieves its greatest luminosity / and clothes itself in sunlight."[69]

The fusion of Marian devotion and courtly love convention we find in the Bohemian court culture of the Caroline period also informed English Ricardian literature. In *Sir Gawain and the Green Knight* the inside of the hero's shield displays a painted image of the Virgin Mary, his protectress during the dangerous journey through the frozen wastes of northern Wales and the Wirral. In Book 1 of *Troilus and Criseyde* (1382–85), where Chaucer offers a veiled compliment to Anne of Bohemia when extolling the peerless beauty of his eponymous heroine, the word "makeles" ("pure" and "peerless") suggests the language of Marian devotion:

> Among thise othere folk was Criseyda,
> In widewes habit blak; but natheles,
> Right as oure firste lettre is now an A,
> In beaute first so stood she, makeles. (Book 1, 169–72)[70]

Significant is the fact that Chaucer does not spell out the queen's full name, this being completely in accordance with the etiquette of the international court culture. The use of the first letter to identify the beloved lady is also attested in *The Plowman,* where the plaintiff alludes to his dead wife by the twelfth letter of the alphabet ("M"); her name is revealed as "Margaret" only in the final prayer in chapter 34. Further evidence of the widespread popularity of this *marguerite* tradition in Bohemia is the anonymous Czech lyric "Slovce M" ("The Letter M") with its characteristic tension between Marian and courtly love elements:

> None else on earth shall ever be
> Whom I would serve with constancy
> In joy and bliss.
> Sole my beloved M
> That can reward and can condemn
> My master is.[71]

---

[69] See Alfred Thomas, *The Czech Chivalric Romances Vévoda Arnošt and Lavryn in their Literary Context, Göppinger Arbeiten zur Germanistik* 504 (Göppingen, 1989), 143.

[70] *The Riverside Chaucer,* ed. Larry D. Benson 3d ed. (Oxford, 1988), 475.

[71] *An Anthology of Czech Verse,* ed. Alfred French (Ann Arbor, 1977), 37.

One of the most famous and widely anthologized English lyric poems of the later Middle Ages is the Marian "I syng of a myden." In highly terse strophes the anonymous poet evokes the mystery of the Incarnation in terms of the lover's hushed arrival at the lady's flowery bower. The term "makeles" puns on the religious and courtly associations of womanhood previously encountered in Chaucer's delineation of Criseyde:

> I syng of a myden
> That is makeles:
> Kyng of alle kynges
> To here sone che ches.
>
> He cam also stylle
> Ther his moder was
> As dew in Aprylle
> That fallyt on the gras.
>
> He cam also stylle
> To his moderes bowr
> As dew in Aprille
> That fallyt on the flour.
>
> He cam also style
> Ther his moder lay
> As dew in Aprille
> That fallyt on the spray.
>
> Moder and mayden
> Was never non but che;
> Wel may swych a lady
> Godes moder be.[72]

Anne's Death and Apotheosis

Unlike the texts we have considered so far, the anonymous poem *Pearl* provides no explicit connection with Anne of Bohemia. One reason for

[72] *Middle English Marian Lyrics*, ed. Karen Saupe (Kalamazoo, 1998), 61.

this fundamental difference is that the poem was probably written after the queen's death rather than during her lifetime. It has recently been suggested that *Pearl* was conceived as an elegy for the queen, who died of the plague in 1394 at the poignantly young age of twenty-eight.[73] It is worth recalling in this connection that Machaut's *Remede de Fortune* was written for King John the Good of France to commemorate the death of his wife, Bonne of Luxembourg, who died of the plague in 1349. This great poem of French medieval literature was, of course, an important influence on Chaucer's *Book of the Duchess*, an elegy for Blanche of Lancaster who died in 1369. But it may also have influenced the *Pearl*-poet and, if so, would have been a especially appropriate source for an elegy on the death of Bonne of Luxembourg's niece.

Remede and *Pearl* are both examples of the popular medieval genre of the dream vision; both express the love of a social inferior for his lost lady, and both articulate the lover's loss in a natural setting away from the castle or château where his services are engaged. Machaut's distraught lover flees to the park at Hesdin whereas the Dreamer in *Pearl* awakes in a flowery meadow and stumbles along in unknown terrain as if trespassing in the grounds of a castle. Both authors are products of a court culture in which the role of cleric is combined with the role of courtier. Machaut was a forty-year-old canon at the cathedral of Rheims when he wrote *Remede*, but for many years previously he had served as secretary to Bonne's father, King John of Bohemia, and had even accompanied his royal master on diplomatic trips to Prague. It was probably while in John's retinue that he visited the estate at Hesdin where Bonne maintained a household for her husband, John the Good, the future King of France.

We do not know the identity of the author of *Pearl*, but it is likely that he, like Machaut, was a cleric attached to a noble household, perhaps as a confessor. This ambiguous status of cleric-courtier would help to explain the Dreamer's ambiguous position as an instructive father figure (in so far as he refers to the Maiden as his deceased daughter) and as a social inferior. This combination of instructive and submissive roles also correlates with the ambiguous identity of the Maiden who mediates between authoritative virgin-queen and child-

---

[73] Bowers, *The Politics of Pearl*, chapter 8.

like innocent in the *consolatio* tradition. If the significance of the latter would explain the paternal function of the narrator's clerical persona, Queen Anne's identification with the Pearl Maiden would explain his inferior status as a courtier. The double role of cleric-courtier would certainly illuminate the tension between the authoritative role of father figure and the deferential role of servant. This is the conclusion Nicholas Watson comes to in his reading of the poem: "Involving the poet as it does in a relationship with his audience which is both deferential and authoritative, some such situation may explain the unusual interplay in the poem between its consolatory and instructive functions."[74]

Although *Pearl* is influenced by the French tradition of the dream vision, the debate between the Maiden and the Dreamer owes a great deal to the scholastic dispute between reason and emotion which was especially popular in Bohemia where many examples are attested in Latin, German, and Czech. The most famous of these are the German *Plowman* and its Czech analogue *The Weaver*. The tension in the persona of the Dreamer between cleric and courtier also informs *The Plowman* and *The Weaver* in which the plaintiffs resemble courtiers in praising their lost lovers in the language of courtly love while Death and Misfortune (respectively) respond with the anti-feminine virulence of the cleric. The plowman refers to his lady in the courtly language of *Minnesang* as his lost "falcon" while Death employs the clerical discourse of *contemptus mundi*: "And take away and pull off the clothes of the tailor's glamor from the fairest woman, and you see nothing but a pitiful puppet, a quick-wilting flower of short-lived appearance and a soon-crumbling clod of clay."[75] Like *The Plowman* and *The Weaver*, *Pearl* takes the form of a scholastic dispute between reason and emotion, the Maiden assuming the role of reason and the Dreamer the role of emotion. As in the Bohemian analogues, the Dreamer is a desolate lover unable to reconcile the magnitude of his earthly loss

---

[74] Nicholas Watson, "The Gawain-Poet as a Vernacular Theologian," in *A Companion to the Gawain-Poet*, ed. Derek Brewer and Jonathan Gibson (Cambridge, 1997), 293–313 at 299. For a useful discussion of the fusion of chivalric and clerical voices in the work of the *Gawain*-poet, see Ad Putter, *Sir Gawain and the Green Knight and French Arthurian Romance* (Oxford, 1995), chap. 5.

[75] "Benim und zeuch ab der schönsten frauen des sneiders farbe, so sihestu ein schemliche tocken, ein schiere swelkende blumen von kurze taurendem scheine und einen balde faulenden erdenknollen." Johannes von Tepl, *Der Ackerman*, 126.

with his desire for reunion with his beloved. There is an interesting coincidence in the fact that in all three texts the male protagonist personifies emotion rather than reason, a reversal of the standard Aristotelian association of masculinity with intellect and femininity with passion. The personification of reason as a young woman in *Pearl* probably derives from the allegorical figure of philosophy as a woman (*Philosophia*) in Boethius' *Consolation of Philosophy* but it may equally reflect the elevated status of learned and pious women in fourteenth-century court culture. This was, of course, the role assumed by Queen Anne in her real-life mediation between her irate husband and the citizens of London.

The fusion of two distinct genres in *Pearl*—the dream vision derived from the French tradition, and the debate form widely attested in Bohemia—corresponds to the two sides of Anne's family, the Luxembourg line and the Slavic line. Combining the courtly form of the dream vision and the religious form of the scholastic debate, through which the rift between reason and emotion is reconciled through faith in God's mercy and the promise of redemption, *Pearl* can be read as a testament both to the literary and to the pious tastes of Anne and her family.

The notion that Anne's death may have provided the instigation for the writing of *Pearl* has intrigued John Bowers, who has pointed out the connection between the seasonal setting of "Augoste in a hyȝ seysoun," (I, 39),[76] when the Dreamer loses his beloved pearl, and the date of the queen's funeral which took place at Westminster Abbey on the octave of St. Anne's day, August 3, 1394.[77] The reference to the month of Anne's obsequies is intriguingly suggestive of an elegy written on her death. Other details in the same passage reinforce this impression. The heraldic imagery and terminology associated with the grave mound ("huyle"), where the pearl rolls down and is lost, bring to mind Anne's resting place at Westminster. One year after Anne's death, in 1395, Richard commissioned a splendid double tomb for himself and his wife, including two lifelike effigies "powdered" with their personal badges and studded with precious jewels. "Powdered" is the word used by the *Pearl*-poet to describe the peonies scattered on

---

[76] *Pearl. An Edition with Verse Translation*, ed. William Vantuono (Notre Dame, 1995), 10.
[77] Bowers, *The Politics of Pearl*, 156.

the mound, but it is also a technical term referring to the badges and decorations on coats of arms and tombs. As Mary Carruthers points out, "jewels—often pearls, rubies, and other stones mentioned in the Bible—were commonly painted into the margins of Books of Hours at the end of the Middle Ages, an allusion to their nature as memorial shrines and thesauri."[78]

The flowers which cover the grave mound may also allude to Anne of Bohemia. The gillyflower in line 43, along with ginger and gromwell, was probably associated with the cult of the Virgin Mary although it also seems to have had a secular significance as a queenly device. Gillyflowers alternate with roses in the Marian-style portrait of Queen Elizabeth Woodville, consort of Edward IV, in the *Book of the Fraternity of the Assumption* (ca. 1472). The same tension between religious and secular symbolism is apparent in the seasonal imagery in *Pearl*. If August refers to the date of Queen Anne's funeral, as Bowers suggests, it equally alludes to the liturgical and theological significance of the high religious holidays cited by established scholarship on the poem: Lammas Day (August 1), the Transfiguration (August 6) and, especially, the Assumption of the Blessed Virgin Mary (August 15). Unlike Bowers I do not regard these details as biographical "clues" but rather as mutually reinforcing theological and personal elements.[79] The biographical interpretation is particularly problematic given the *consolatio* tradition to which *Pearl* belongs, since the identity of the lost beloved does not necessarily reflect the author's marital or familial status. It is significant in this connection that the wife of Johannes von Tepl was not Margaret, as indicated in the text, but Clara; moreover, legal documents drawn up at the time of Johannes' death indicate that far from predeceasing her husband, she actually survived him by several years.[80]

The imagery of precious jewels in the description of the Pearl Maiden may also suggest that the poem was composed to commemorate Anne's death. We have already seen how Chaucer and Usk em-

---

[78] Mary J. Carruthers, *The Book of Memory. A Study of Memory in Medieval Culture* (Cambridge, 1990), 41.

[79] Bowers, *The Politics of Pearl*, 165.

[80] See Christian Kiening, *Schwierige Modernität. Der Ackermann des Johannes von Tepl und die Ambiguität historischen Wandels* (Tübingen, 1998), 22. For the Latin consolation tradition, see Peter von Moos, *Consolatio. Studien zur mittellateinischer Trostliteratur über den Tod und zum Problem der christlichen Trauer*, 2 vols. (Munich, 1971), vol. 1.

ployed the *marguerite* tradition in connection with Anne. As David Wallace has pointed out, Chaucer was probably recycling and refining a previously established association of pearls with Anne. Two years after her death the pearl was being identified with her more than it had been in life. When in October 1396 Richard traveled to France to receive his second wife, the infant Isabelle, from her father Charles VI, he wore a hat of hanging pearls and gave a collar of pearls to his new father-in-law, while his attendants were dressed in the livery of his deceased queen.[81]

The crown worn by the Pearl Maiden recalls the coronal (now in Munich) with its high flower-shaped pinnacles and ornate jewels which Anne had brought with her from Bohemia and which later formed part of the dowry of Henry IV's daughter Blanche when she married Ludwig III of Bavaria in 1401: (figure 3)[82]

> A pyȝt coroune ȝet wer þat gyrle,
> Of marjorys, and non oþer ston,
> Hiȝe pynakled of cler quyt perle,
> Wyth flurted flowreȝ, perfet vpon.
> To hed hade he non oþer werle.
> Her lere-leke al hyr vmbegon,
> Her semblaunt sade for doc oþer erle;
> Her ble more blaȝt þen whalleȝ bon.
> As schorne golde schyr her fax þenne schon,
> On schyldereȝ þat leghe vnlapped lyȝte.
> Her depe colour, ȝet, wonted non
> Of precios perle in porfyl pyȝte.
>
> An ornate crown yet wore that girl,
> Of margarites, and no other stone,
> Pinnacled high with clear white pearl,
> With flowers fashioned there, full-blown.
> No other circlet was set awhirl;
> On face was cambric, finely sewn.
> Her semblance suited a duke or earl,

---

[81] Wallace, *Chaucerian Polity*, 372–73.
[82] Bowers, *The Politics of Pearl*, 106–7.

Figure 3. Crown of Anne of Bohemia, ca. 1350. Residenzmuseum, Munich. Scala / Art Resource, New York.

> That ivory visage, whiter than whale's bone.
> Like shorn gold sheer her hair then shone,
> Lying on shoulders in stylish state.
> Her collar wide lacked not the tone
> Of precious pearls on borders ornate. (IV, 205–16)[83]

The stylized description of the Pearl Maiden recalls the international court style of literature, painting, and statuary well represented in Bohemian Gothic art of the late fourteenth century. The Pearl Maiden's unbound hair like bright cut gold resembles the description of St. Catherine's hair in the Czech legend of her life and of the Virgin Mary in the *mulier amicta sole* from the Apocalypse cycle by Master Theodoricus at Karlstein. Strangely, the Pearl Maiden is described as wearing a wimple which entirely encompasses her face ("Her lere-leke al hyr vmbegon") (IV, 210). In fourteenth-century Bohemian art noble

[83] Vantuono, *Pearl*, 22.

women have their hair loose and flowing—as in the case of Charles IV's third wife, Empress Anne, in the triforium in St. Vitus Cathedral—or they wear elaborate wimples and head scarves. Generally speaking, maidens or young women have free-flowing hair and older women have head scarves and wimples. The combination of long flowing hair and a wimple in the description of the Pearl Maiden suggests that for the author she personifies the sexual ideal of maidenhood and the wisdom of maturity. To my knowledge, the only example in late medieval art of a woman wearing long hair and a wimple is the depiction of the coronation of a king and queen in the *Liber Regalis* (fol. 20) (See figure 9, p. 58). The style of the four illuminations in this English manuscript has been linked with the influence of Bohemian art at the Ricardian court (see chapter 2). It is not inconceivable that the author of *Pearl* had seen the *Liber Regalis* and was influenced by it, especially if he was attached to the royal court in some clerical capacity. (The manuscript is not mentioned in any of the inventories of Westminster Abbey, since it was probably kept with the royal regalia.) Even the ivory pallor of the queen's face in the manuscript recalls the stylized description of the Pearl Maiden in the poem. If the manuscript was indeed made to commemorate the coronation of Anne of Bohemia in 1382, the influence of the *Liber Regalis* on an elegy on her death twelve years later would be particularly appropriate.

    The Pearl Maiden's dress, embroidered entirely of pearls, is in the latest courtly style and recalls the tight-fitting costumes worn by biblical characters in the Bible of Wenceslas IV, for example, folio 17, where an angel announces the birth of Samuel to his father and mother. The latter is dressed in the high-fashion of the Luxembourg court: a tightly fitting surcoat embroidered with pearls along the collar, front and hem as well as on the borders of the long, fur-lined sleeves. Precious gems—among them pearls—figure prominently in the description of the celestial hall where St. Catherine receives her second vision of Christ and His mother in the Czech life of the virgin-martyr: "The floor was made from beryls, the walls from diamonds set in gold, many windows were fashioned from emeralds and sapphires and, instead of glass, were glazed with precious stones: hyacinths, rubies, turquoises, carnelians, spinels set in ivory; there were jaspers, chalcedons, topazes, garnets, olivines, amethysts, and pearls, all most beautifully cast and assembled."[84] This imaginary evocation of paradise derives from the description of the celestial Jerusalem in the Book of Revelation and finds a striking analogue in the description of the Apocalypse in the Dreamer's vision in *Pearl* (XVII). The imagery of the Apocalypse is an important feature of international court art in the late fourteenth century. The private oratory of the Emperor Charles in Karlstein, which he dedicated to St. Catherine, is studded with semiprecious stones and was intended to evoke the wonders of the celestial Jerusalem. The imperial oratory can be seen as an architectonic analogue both to the description of the heavenly hall in the Czech *Life of Saint Catherine* and to the vision in *Pearl*. The list of gems and their corresponding color symbolism are clearly indebted to medieval lapidaries. Color symbolism is also an important feature of the flagellation scene in the Czech *Life of Saint Catherine:*

> She bore on her body ribbons of six colors, signs of true love for her beloved as a lady should for her beloved. The first color quickly appeared in her cheeks, which used to blossom white and red, but these two were changed by her suffering. Her cheeks did not lose their blood but lost their beauty and became *green* with shame as she stood naked in front of these insensitive pagans. . . . A second color she wore was of purest *white,* the color of hope. Indeed, whenever had there been a spouse more loved than this precious one, whose pure white body shone before the pagans, on which blossomed the *red* color from her holy blood with which the accursed henchmen sprinkled such gleaming whiteness? Many a flowering rose appeared among the skin and flesh, which the hooks had ripped from the bones. These wounds congealed and turned painfully *black*. A fifth color she next bore from fidelity to her beloved husband, like a steadfast, faithful handmaiden. Many bruises made by the tails, sore and swollen with blood under the skin, were turning dark *blue* and contracted among the wounds wherever the tormentor had aimed with his scourge. . . . Now her body assumed a sixth color, that of her desirable hair which had also to suffer and which shone more preciously than all the *gold* in the world. . . . Thus these colors shone, one next to the other, here in the skin, here in

---

[84] Head, *Medieval Hagiography,* 774.

the bruise: white, black, green, blue, gold, and red, each in its own substance . . .[85]

It is striking that the colors listed in the description of the celestial Jerusalem in *Pearl* follow the same order as in the flagellation of Catherine (green, white, purple/red, gold), although black and blue are missing. This sequence is of great symbolic importance in both descriptions. In the flagellation green denotes incipient love and gold defines the culmination of that love in the mystical union with Christ. In *Pearl* green and gold are the colors that frame the description of the celestial Jerusalem. The city and the female body are here both seen in terms of transcendental purity. This is not accidental, since in *Pearl* it is the purity of the Pearl Maiden which permits the Dreamer access to the vision of the Apocalypse in the first place.

Green, gold, and white are also the colors sported by Alceste as she makes her entry alongside the God of Love in the prologue of *The Legend of Good Women*:

> The God of Love, and in his hand a quene,
> And she was clad in real habit grene.
> A fret of gold she hadde next her heer,
> And upon that a whit corowne she beer
> With flourouns smale, and I shal nat lye . . . (F 213–17)[86]

As James Wimsatt has pointed out, Chaucer's palate of colors (green, gold, and white) deviates from Machaut's depiction of the lady with a girdle of white and a crown of red in *Lis et Margeurite*.[87] Unlike Machaut, Chaucer presents the Daisy Queen as a real female figure rather than as an allegorical flower. Moreover, his choice of colors is consistent with those selected in *Pearl* and the Czech *Life of Saint Catherine* to emphasize the virginal purity of the lady.

The association of the geographic Other with the feminine is also evident in the first part of the vision. The narrator's discovery of the terrestrial paradise immediately precedes his encounter with the Pearl Maiden. As in the subsequent description of the celestial Jerusalem, the

---

[85] Ibid., 776.
[86] *The Riverside Chaucer*, 593.
[87] Wimsatt, *The Margeurite Poetry of Guillaume de Machaut*, 36.

imagery evoking the terrestrial paradise and the maiden is artificial rather than natural, material rather than abstract. In fact, the entire description of the Pearl Maiden and the terrestrial paradise is the product of a court culture in which material artifacts (precious gems, tapestries, painting) play a prominent role. Even seemingly naturalistic details of the landscape turn out—on closer inspection—to proceed from the world of art rather than life:

> I welke ay forth in wely wyse,
> No bonk so byg þat did me dereȝ.
> Þe fyrre in þe fryth þe feier con ryse
> Þe playn, þe plontteȝ, þe spyse, þe pereȝ,
> And raweȝ, and randeȝ, and rych reuereȝ;
> As fyldor fyn her bukes brent.
>
> I wandered onward in happy wise,
> No hill so high, no path with snares.
> Farther in the forest fairer did rise
> Plains and spices, and trees with pears,
> Hedgerows on lands, and rivers through lairs;
> Their currents gleamed like fine gold filament. (II, 101–6)[88]

This idealized landscape recalls courtly representations of paradise as a walled garden full of singing birds and blossoming fruit trees. A beautiful example of this *hortus conclusus* is to be found in the depiction of Seth at the Gate of Paradise in the illuminated Bohemian manuscript of the *Travels of Sir John Mandeville*, which was made for the court of Wenceslas IV around 1400 at about the same time as the *Pearl* manuscript.[89]

For the Dreamer, the terrestrial paradise is not ineffable but deeply palpable. As in the opening section of *Pearl*, which is set in a late summer landscape, the virgin Catherine's first vision in the Czech *Life of Saint Catherine* is similarly reflective of this world rather than the next: "At that moment she had a wondrous, lovely, and vivid dream. She dreamt that she was sleeping in a long and wide, perfect and pleasur-

---

[88] Vantuono, *Pearl*, 14.
[89] See Josef Krása, *The Travels of Sir John Mandeville* (New York, 1983), plate 9.

able meadow. It gleamed with fresh summer grass and was in full, gorgeous bloom."⁹⁰ Here the virgin's pure body finds an appropriate setting in a beautiful meadow. Similarly, in *Pearl*, the wondrous land that lies beyond the impassable stream forms an imagistic unity with the maiden seated in its midst:

> More meruayle con my dom adaunt.
> I segh byȝonde þat myry mere
> A crystal clyffe ful relusaunt.
> Mony ryal ray con fro hit rere.
> At þe fote þerof þer sete a faunt,
> A mayden of menske, ful debonere.
> Blysnande whyt watȝ hyr bleaunt.
> I knew hyr wel; I hade sen hyr ere.
>
> More marvels now amazed my mind,
> As I gazed beyond those currents clear
> To a crystal cliff with rays refined,
> Each royal beam a radiant spear.
> At the base a child sat enshrined;
> A maiden of dignity in glowing gear,
> Her attire by dazzling white defined;
> I had seen her before in different sphere. (III, 157–64)⁹¹

The equation of sacred space with the feminine is not unique to *Pearl* or the Czech *Life of Saint Catherine*. Iain Higgins has detected a similar trope of the Holy Land as a lady in the exordium of the *Travels of Sir John Mandeville*, a text with which the anonymous English poet was certainly familiar: "Excellent and worthy, the land is not simply female, but a lady and a sovereign. It is even possible, given the following references to Jesus and Mary, that the land is being indirectly characterized as the Mother of God, thus making it virgin land—if not quite in the sense familiar from exploration and colonialist discourses."⁹² The binary opposition between here and there, profane and

---

⁹⁰ Head, *Medieval Hagiography*, 773.
⁹¹ Vantuono, *Pearl*, 18.
⁹² Iain Macleod Higgins, *Writing East. The "Travels" of Sir John Mandeville* (Philadelphia, 1997), 35.

spiritual, both important distinctions for the *Mandeville*-writer, also structures the dream genre of *Pearl* with its contrast between the terrestrial and the transcendental. In section IX of the poem the narrator refers to the death of the Maiden (at the age of two) in terms not of death and life but of home and abroad: "Þou lyfed not two ȝer in oure þede" ("You did not live even two years in our land") (IX, 483).[93] This geographical metaphor for death is significant not only in terms of allegory but also in terms of the poem's status as elegy. The formulation "in our land" may be an allegorical image but it may also allude to the status of the deceased beloved as a foreigner.

Parallels between the historical Anne and the Pearl Maiden can be taken further but these invariably merge with theological and allegorical convention so that it becomes difficult to distinguish at what point life ends and art takes over. This is especially true of the Marian imagery in section VIII of the poem. Although the references to "Emperise" (441) and "empire" (454) resonate with Anne's status as the daughter of an emperor and sister of an emperor-elect, they are also part of the conventional iconography of Mary as Queen of Heaven. The elegiac/biographical and the allegorical/theological references here are not mutually exclusive but mutually reinforcing: the horticultural imagery associated with Anne (such as herbs and flowers) is also emblematic of traditional Marian devotion. For example the flowery meadow invoked at the beginning of the poem, where the pearl rolls down and is lost, suggests the *hortus conclusus* from the Song of Songs 4:12 with its close association with the Virgin Mary and the Church. Later in the poem, when the Dreamer looks across the stream at the Pearl Maiden behind the wall of the New Jerusalem, the audience of courtly initiates might have been conscious not only of the scene's theological and eschatological associations but its biographical implications as well, since Anne of Bohemia's homeland lay across the English Channel on the European mainland.

Conclusion

Although Queen Anne may not have actively patronized Chaucer, Usk, or the *Pearl*-poet, her life and death provided the inspiration for

---

[93] Vantuono, *Pearl*, 42.

the composition of some of their major works. *The Parliament of Fowls* was most likely intended as an occasional poem to celebrate Anne's betrothal to Richard II; *The Legend of Good Women* reflects Anne's reputation for learning and piety; *The Testament of Love* witnesses to Anne's apotheosis as an intercessory figure, while *Pearl* offers compelling, if circumstantial, evidence that it was written to commemorate the queen's untimely death of the plague in 1394. Like the Virgin Mary, on whom her life of conjugal chastity was modeled, Anne defies the active-passive binary associated with crude modern constructions of femininity. Regal power and prestige could—and did—coexist harmoniously with female models of modesty and restraint. This is precisely the tension we find in the popular lives of the virgin martyrs. I have argued elsewhere that these saints' lives formed a powerful role model for late medieval Catholic women like Perchta of Rožmberk, a fifteenth-century Bohemian noblewoman whose defiance of her husband's tyrannical household and her use of the epistolary genre to advertise her domestic plight reflect the influence of independent-minded saints like Catherine of Alexandria, Margaret and Cecilia.[94] Demonstrating the same combination of strength and humility, defiance and submission, Anne of Bohemia was able to reconcile the traditionally passive role of intercessor with the more active and affirmative role of patron of the arts.

---

[94] See my review of John Klassen's *The Letters of the Rožmberk Sisters. Noblewomen in Fifteenth-Century Bohemia* in the *English Historical Review* 118/478 (September 2003): 1051–52.

Chapter 2

Imperial Designs

Art and Ideology at the Ricardian and Luxembourg Courts

In the late 1390s Anne of Bohemia's half-brother Wenceslas IV seemed increasingly unlikely to be elected emperor. His inability to control his feuding magnates in Bohemia and his vacillating policies toward the Church rendered him unworthy in the eyes of the electors to succeed his illustrious father as Holy Roman Emperor. He was deposed as king of the Romans in September 1399—by a strange coincidence, the same month in which Richard II was deposed as king of England. Wenceslas' deficiencies as a ruler had played a crucial role in Richard II's ambitions to succeed his father-in-law as emperor. The key to such ambitions was securing the support of the seven German electors. Richard's primary claim to the imperial title was not through blood but through his marriage to Anne of Bohemia. Although concrete efforts to woo the electors began in earnest only after Anne's death, Richard's promotion of his wife's imperial pedigree goes right back to the beginnings of his reign when in 1383 the royal couple visited the chancel of the Great Hospital in Norwich and admired the wooden roof carved with imperial eagles. The king's imperial ambitions were given artistic expression in the carved head of an emperor, wearing a triple crown, still visible in the southeast pier of York Minster.¹ The imperial eagles at Norwich date from the beginning of Richard's reign, while the emperor's head anticipated his campaign to be elected emperor in the 1390s. Richard never overlooked an opportunity to strengthen his links with the house of Luxembourg. When news of the death of Queen Anne's mother, Elizabeth of Pomerania, reached England, he gave instructions for a Requiem Mass to be performed in St. Paul's Cathedral on 21 June, 1393, and ordered the construction of a "very unusual shrine, the like of which had nowhere been seen before."²

As the apocalyptic year 1400 approached, Richard's efforts to secure the imperial crown gathered greater momentum. The spring and summer of 1397 saw a flurry of diplomatic activity with ambassadors shuttling between England and Germany. The earls of Rutland and Nottingham and the bishop of Carlisle were dispatched to the continent to secure the support of the German electors. They met Richard's new vassal, Rupert of Bavaria, count palatine of the Rhine, at Bacharach on June 16. Rupert was not the only German elector whom Richard bribed to advance his political ambitions. In late June Hugh Hervorst, archdeacon of Cologne, arrived in England and on July 7, in complementary ceremonies at Westminster and Godesberg, Frederick, archbishop of Cologne, performed homage to the king in return for an annual pension of one thousand pounds.³ As Michael Bennett has demonstrated in his careful analysis of the chronology of the last years of Richard's reign, the king's coup against the duke of Gloucester and the earls of Arundel and Warwick not only coincided with these diplomatic initiatives but may have even been prompted by them. Richard's problems with his unruly subjects were known in Germany, a fact confirmed by a letter sent by Richard's rival, Wenceslas, from Nuremberg on September 24, 1397, which commiserated with Richard and offered him help against his rebellious subjects. We can only presume that this letter, which was probably intended to advertise Richard's problems as much as to solve them, made Richard all the more determined to crush political dissent within his realm. On May

---

¹ John H. Harvey, "Richard II and York," in *The Reign of Richard II: Essays in Honour of May McKisack*, ed. F. R. H. du Boulay and Caroline M. Barron (London, 1971), 202–17 (214).
² Michael Bennett, *Richard II and the Revolution of 1399* (Stroud, 1999), 59.
³ Ibid., 90.

23, 1398, the king arranged for the archdeacon of Cologne to go to Rome to enlist papal support for his candidacy. In September of the same year, Wenceslas' younger brother, Sigismund, king of Hungary, referred to Richard's ambitions when exhorting Wenceslas to go immediately to Rome to be crowned by the pope.[4]

The Wilton Diptych

Central to Richard's imperial ambition was the ideological function of the court art and architecture associated with his patronage, which, as we shall see, deliberately emulated Bohemian court style and practice. Perhaps the most important and beautiful work of court art to articulate Richard's imperial ambitions, as well as his devotion to the memory of his beloved spouse, is the Wilton Diptych, commissioned around 1395 or shortly thereafter. One of the most unusual features of this small moveable altarpiece is the lovely painting of a delicate white hart (the king's personal device) kneeling on a bed of rosemary (one of Anne of Bohemia's devices) (figure 4). This representation is a moving testament to the deep love which existed between the king and his wife. But it also points to the king's extraordinary political ambitions.

In the left-hand panel inside the altarpiece Richard kneels accompanied by three saints, Edmund the Martyr, Edward the Confessor, and John the Baptist holding the Lamb of God. The king's gorgeous robes, on which white harts alternate with imperial eagles, reveal Richard's close identification with his wife's family. In the right-hand panel the Virgin and Child are accompanied by eleven angels, all dressed in blue chaplets sporting badges of the white hart on their chests (frontispiece). One of the angels holds a banner emblazoned with the emblem of St. George, a red cross on a white background. George was the patron saint of England but he was also an important royal saint in Bohemia. The saint's heart was preserved as a relic at the St. George Convent at the Prague Castle before it was brought to England by Emperor Sigismund in 1414 as a gift for Henry V.

Behind Richard stand his three patron saints. Important here is the king's implied descent from a line of holy English kings stretching

[4] Ibid., 125.

Figure 4. A white hart resting on a bed of rosemary. Outside panel of the Wilton Diptych. Erich Lessing/Art Resource, New York.

back to the Confessor. Whereas his Plantagenet ancestors tended to look back to the mythical warrior-king Arthur as their hero, Richard's focus was on pre-Conquest saints of the Anglo-Saxon royal house such as Ethelred of Kent, Edward King and Martyr, Edmund King and Martyr, and Edward the Confessor.[5] Richard's preference for royal saints like Edward the Confessor over military heroes like King Arthur can partly be explained in terms of the king's antimilitaristic temperament; but it also had an underlying ideological motivation: Richard was attempting to create a new vision of kingship modeled on the example of his Luxembourg relatives. Whereas his grandfather Edward III had ruled in traditional feudal fashion with the support and collaboration of his magnates, Richard sought to emulate his murdered great-grandfather Edward II (whom he tried to have canonized) in creating a new class of royal servants who would provide the crown with greater independence from the nobility. This was a practice successfully pursued by Charles IV and less successfully by Wenceslas IV.

Richard's inclusion in the triad of holy kings recalls the cult of the Epiphany. Richard was born on the Feast of the Epiphany (January 6) and greatly honored his natal feast day throughout his life. The center of this cult was the shrine of the Three Kings at Cologne Cathedral, built between 1197 and 1225 by the goldsmith Nicholas of Verdun to house the relics brought from Milan by Reinald von Dassel, archbishop of Cologne, in 1164. The translation of the Three Kings' bodies to Milan from Constantinople was attributed to Eustorgius I, bishop of Milan (315–31), and the earlier translation of the relics to Constantinople was ascribed to St. Helena, the mother of Emperor Constantine. The shrine of the Three Kings at Cologne was well known in fourteenth-century England, forming part of the three most important European sites of pilgrimage along with Rome and Santiago de Compostela in Galicia. Chaucer's Wife of Bath had been to all three places:

> At Rome she hadde been, and at Boloigne,
> In Galice at Seint-Jame, and at Coloigne.
> (I 465–66)[6]

---

[5] See W. M. Omrod, "Richard II's Sense of English History," in *The Reign of Richard II*, ed. Gwilym Dodd (Stroud, 2000), 97–110 at 101.

[6] *Riverside Chaucer*, 31.

A Latin account of the Three Kings by John of Hildesheim known as the *Historia Trium Regum* was adapted into Middle English around 1400. The popularity of the legend in England may have owed something to Anne of Bohemia's presence. It is even possible that the queen and her entourage had stopped in Cologne en route from Prague to England and that she encouraged the dissemination of the cult of the Three Kings in her adopted homeland. Certainly, her husband Richard seems to have identified with them, as the Wilton Diptych suggests. If Olga Pujmanová is correct in her assertion that Richard's inclusion of himself in a triad of kings in the Wilton Diptych is intended as an allusion to the Magi, this identification with the cult at Cologne would have strengthened Richard's candidacy for election as emperor.

Emperor Charles displayed a special interest in the cult of the Three Kings, perhaps because of its historical connection with Constantinople, the ancient capital of the Empire with which he identified as Holy Roman Emperor, and Cologne, a German city over which he nominally ruled. During a state visit to France in the winter of 1377–78, the ailing emperor chose the feast of the Three Kings to climb up the Grande Chasse in the Sainte-Chapelle to inspect the relics of the Passion, most notably the Crown of Thorns, preserved there. As Barbara Drake Boehm has commented, Charles "and his secular royal contemporaries saw themselves as quite literally the living heirs of this regal tradition and paid homage, as earthly kings, to the infant Jesus, as the King of Kings."[7] Charles had himself depicted as one of the Three Kings in the Morgan Diptych and in the wall painting of the Adoration of the Three Magi in the Chapel of the Holy Cross at Karlstein Castle. This Luxembourg practice was emulated by Richard II in the left panel of the Wilton Diptych, where he appears with two other saintly kings.[8] Richard's political ambition to become emperor would also explain the

---

[7] Barbara Drake Boehm, "Charles IV. The Realm of Faith," in *Prague, The Crown of Bohemia 1347–1437*, ed. Barbara Drake Boehm and Jiří Fajt (New York, 2005), 23–33 at 25–26.

[8] Ibid., 26. For the influence of this Luxembourg practice on the Wilton Diptych, see Olga Pujmanová, "Portraits of Kings depicted as Magi in Bohemian Painting," in *The Regal Image of Richard II*, ed. Dillian Gordon, Lisa Monnis, and Caroline Elam (London, 1997), 27–32 at 28–29. The motif of the Three Kings is also attested in other works of Ricardian court culture apart from the Wilton Diptych. Among the list of royal tapestries in the reign of Henry V there are religious scenes like the Three Kings of Cologne. According to Gervase Mathew, this tapestry was most likely commissioned by Richard II. See Mathew, *The Court of Richard II* (New York, 1968), 50.

presence of the heraldry of the Three Kings at York Minster, where, as previously mentioned, we find the head of an emperor wearing a triple crown.

Although the image of Queen Anne is absent from the Wilton Diptych, her important social status as the daughter of an emperor and as a beloved consort is very much in evidence through numerous heraldic and familial clues. Significantly, the posture of the Virgin and Child on the right side of the diptych resembles Bohemian sculptural treatments of the motif (in particular the Krumlov Madonna), leading the art historian Dillian Gordon to suggest that it may have been modeled on an actual statue in the queen's possession (figure 5).[9] If this is the case Richard's veneration for the Holy Family becomes inseparable from his veneration for his wife's family.

Richard's self-representation as one of the Three Kings was not simply a pious gesture; it was above all a political strategy to insert himself into his wife's pedigree. The Holy Roman Emperors were nominal heads (*Domherren*) of Cologne Cathedral, an important fact that would not have escaped the attention of the aspirant Richard.[10] As part of his bid to win the imperial throne, Charles IV had made every effort to demonstrate his descent from St. Wenceslas of Bohemia.[11] Charles's veneration for his maternal ancestor, whose own rule had been characterized by conciliation and compromise rather than violence and warfare, provided an appropriate model of peaceful governance as well as the necessary legitimization of his own divinely sanctioned rule. Charles wrote a Latin *vita* of Wenceslas in which the saint is represented as a gentle courtly knight. He also promoted the cult of Wenceslas's grandmother, the Bohemian protomartyr Ludmila, whom Charles mentions with great reverence in his autobiography.

Charles's identification with St. Wenceslas may have provided the inspiration for Richard's veneration of his own peace-loving ancestor Edward the Confessor. The cult of Edward the Confessor (canonized in 1161) had been revived by Henry III, who erected a shrine to him at

---

[9] See Dillian Gordon, *Making and Meaning: The Wilton Diptych* (London, 1997), 91–92.

[10] See Wilhelm Kisky, *Die Domkapitel der geistlichen Kurfürsten in ihrer persönlichen Zusammensetzung im vierzehnten und fünfzehnten Jahrhundert* (Weimar, 1906), 25–26.

[11] See Gábor Klaniczay, *The Uses of Supernatural Power. The Transformation of Popular Religion in Medieval and Early-Modern Europe*, trans. Susan Singerman and Karen Margolis (Princeton, 1990), 122.

Figure 5. Krumlov Madonna, 1400. Kunsthistorisches Museum, Vienna. Erich Lessing/Art Resource, New York.

Westminster Abbey; but it seems to have fallen into abeyance during the reigns of Edward I (an Arthurian enthusiast) and Edward III, who preferred the chivalric St. George. Richard departed from his predecessor's military policies by pursuing peace rather than war. In this respect he seems to have identified more closely with his Luxembourg father-in-law than with his own Plantagenet grandfather Edward III and his father Edward the Black Prince. In honoring his distant saintly ancestor rather than his martial grandfather and father, Richard was not simply privileging peace over war: he was consciously emulating Charles IV's identification with the family saints of the Přemyslid dynasty, Ludmila and Wenceslas.

From Troy to the Apocalypse:
Karlstein Castle and Westminster Hall

In the late fourteenth century the population of London was somewhat larger than that of Prague.[12] But unlike London, Prague was an imperial capital, its importance reflected in numerous architectural and artistic projects intended to enhance its prominence and prestige as the seat of future emperors. Many of the edifices commissioned by Richard II in London have a similar ideological function. An important area of affinity between Richard II and Charles IV is their use of architectural space and design to promote their pedigree and regality. As Paul Binski has observed, the artistic eclecticism of Westminster reflects the influence of Luxembourg Prague rather than Capetian Paris: the French-style interior of St. Vitus Cathedral and the mixture of Italian and Byzantine styles at Karlstein Castle near Prague.[13] Binski also points out that the integration of palace and church at Westminster in the name of a royal saint (Edward the Confessor) recalls the legitimating function of Charles's holy ancestor Wenceslas whose remains and relics were housed in the chapel of St. Wenceslas at St. Vitus Cathedral.

---

[12] Around 1400 London had a population of forty thousand while Prague had thirty-five thousand inhabitants. For London see Caroline M. Barron, *London in the Later Middle Ages. Government and People 1200–1500* (Oxford, 2004), 45. For Prague, see Thomas, *Anne's Bohemia*, 1–2.

[13] Paul Binski, *Westminster Abbey and the Plantagenets. Kingship and the Representation of Power 1200–1440* (New Haven, 1995), 51.

Whereas the cathedral space is in part dedicated to the secular glorification of the Luxembourg dynasty, Karlstein Castle combines the secular function of a family residence with the liturgical function of a church—in fact, three separate chapels—culminating in the Chapel of the Holy Cross at the top of the castle where the emperor's collection of relics and the imperial insignia were housed.

After he returned from his coronation as emperor in Rome in 1355, Charles commemorated the event by commissioning a series of wall paintings in the great hall of Karlstein Castle known as the *Luxembourg Genealogy*. Although these frescoes have not survived, it is possible to reconstruct them from copies in the sixteenth-century *Codex Heidelbergensis* (now in the National Gallery, Prague). The cycle depicted more than sixty of the emperor's alleged ancestors, beginning with Noah and culminating—through a panoply of biblical, classical, Merovingian, and Carolingian kings and other rulers—with Charles himself. These Luxembourg ancestors included Charlemagne and the heroes of the Trojan War. In his *Le Jugement du roy de Behaigne* Guillaume de Machaut informs us that he saw his master, King John of Bohemia, at his castle of Durbury,

> Seated in great joy upon a silken carpet,
> And a clerk, whom I cannot name,
> Was reading to him from the Battle of Troy.[14]

John's enthusiasm for the Trojan story suited his chivalrous temperament; but it also reflected his family's imperial ambitions. John's father, Henry IV of Luxembourg, was crowned Holy Roman Emperor, as Henry VII, at Rome on June 29, 1312.[15] Relative newcomers on the European dynastic stage, the Luxembourg rulers made every effort to use art and literature to bolster their pedigree and prestige in the eyes of their rivals and subjects. But they were not alone in these attempts at self-aggrandizement. The legend of Troy provided a mythic pedigree for many European rulers in the late and high Middle Ages and

---

[14] "En moult grant joye / Estoit assis sur .i. tapis de soye ; / S'i ot .i. clerc que nommer ne saroye / Qui li lisoit la bataille de Troie" (lines 1473–75). *Le Jugement du roy de Behaigne*, ed. James I. Wimsatt and William W. Kibler (Athens, 1988), 134–35.

[15] See William M. Bowsky, *Henry VII in Italy* (Lincoln, 1960).

frequently fueled their imperial fantasies.[16] Geoffrey of Monmouth, the author of the vastly influential *Historia Regum Britanniae* (written between 1130 and 1136), claimed Brutus, the grandson of the Trojan hero Aeneas, as the founder of Britain. Foundational myths such as these were important in providing a nation with the history it lacked. But they also helped to legitimize the ambitions of the nation's rulers. In order to justify his conquest of Scotland Edward I of England had appealed in a letter to the pope to his superior right as the descendant of Locrine, the eldest son of Brutus of Troy.[17]

The English interest in the matter of Troy was revived during the reign of Richard II, whose own political ambitions required him to emphasize England's imperial origins. Richard is known to have commissioned a history of the kings of England from Brutus to his own reign (Corpus Christi College, Cambridge, MS 251).[18] At a magnificent tournament held at Smithfield in 1390 Richard welcomed the participants to "la neuf Troie" ("New Troy") as London became known. Richard's investment in the Trojan myth can be partly understood in terms of his dynastic rivalry with his brother-in-law Wenceslas. According to the diplomat and chronicler Edmund de Dyntner (ca. 1375–1449), author of the *Chronica nobilissimorum ducum Lotharingiae, Brabantiae ac regum francorum* (1445), Wenceslas showed him the *genealogia* at Karlstein and boasted that he was descended from the Trojans and Charlemagne through his great-grandfather's marriage to the daughter of John of Brabant.[19] The inglorious story of Troy provided an apt foundational myth for those two unsuccessful rulers, the former deposed as king of the Romans and the latter as king of England at the same time.

Vernacular narratives about the fall of Troy were common in England and Bohemia at the end of the fourteenth and the beginning of the fifteenth century. James Simpson distinguishes between two traditions of the story of Troy during this period: the pro-imperialist tradition established by Geoffrey of Monmouth's *Historia Regum Britanniae*

---

[16] See Sylvia Federico, *New Troy. Fantasies of Empire in the Later Middle Ages*, Medieval Cultures at Minnesota, 36 (Minneapolis, 2003).
[17] Ibid., 68.
[18] Bennett, *Richard II and the Revolution of 1399*, 42.
[19] *Magister Theodoricus. Dvorní malíř císaře Karla IV*, ed. Jiří Fajt (Prague, 1997), 99.

and the anti-imperialist tradition, represented by the Laud *Troy Book*, John Lydgate's *Troy Book* (1412–20), and the alliterative *Destruction of Troy* by Master John Clerk of Whalley in Lancashire.[20] These last three versions were based on Guido delle Colonne's *Historia destructionis Troiae* (1287), itself a translation of the French *Roman de Troie* by Benoît de Sainte-Maure (ca. 1160/70). The popularity of Guido's version in Bohemia is reflected in two Czech translations of which six manuscripts survive. The anti-imperialist animus of Guido's *Historia* helps to explain the popularity of this "other Book of Troy" in early fifteenth-century Bohemia. At the end of the Strahov manuscript (1437) the scribe informs us that "these books were made on the order of the famous and brave knight Václav [Wenceslas] of Baštek, above all for the glory of God and the honor and profit of the knighthood of the Bohemian land...."[21] The knight in question was a Hussite supporter. His interest in the defense of the city of Troy reflects the values of the Hussite nobility which was engaged in a protracted defensive war against the imperial armies sent by Sigismund of Luxembourg to eradicate the Bohemian heresy. The later Czech version was commissioned by the Bohemian courtier Peter Zmrzlík of Svojšín, the master of the royal mint and supporter of Jan Hus.[22] Like Lydgate's *Troy Book* and unlike Chaucer's *Troilus and Criseyde*, this younger version retains more of the antifeminism of the original, reflecting the traditional tastes of the Bohemian gentry rather than the pro-feminism of the international court culture.

The absence of the imperialist tradition of the Troy legend in Czech literature reflected the long-established distrust of royal (and imperial) encroachments on the feudal prerogatives of the powerful Bohemian nobility. There was a similar distrust of Arthurian literature in the Czech Lands. According to Peter of Zittau, author of the fourteenth-century *Chronicon Aulae Regiae,* some young Bohemian noblemen requested John of Luxembourg to establish a Round Table, with jousts and festivities, so that his reputation and fame should spread abroad.

---

[20] See James Simpson, "The Other Book of Troy: Guido delle Colonne's *Historia destructionis Troiae* in Fourteenth- and Fifteenth-Century England," *Speculum* 73 (1998): 397–423.

[21] Quoted from afterword in *Kronika Trojánská,* ed. Jiří Daňhelka (Prague, 1951), 316.

[22] See the afterword to ibid., 315–16.

John duly invited princes and knights from all over Germany to come to Prague to attend a Round Table festivity in 1319. But no one responded to the invitation, prompting Peter of Zittau to reflect in characteristic clerical fashion on the folly of such enterprises.[23] The failure to attract interest in an Arthurian Round Table in Prague derives from an analogous ideological antipathy to a mythic ruler usually associated with military aggression.

If the power struggle between the Luxembourg dynasty and the indigenous nobility underpins the imperialist and anti-imperialist perspectives on the Troy legend in Bohemia, the same conflict between the king and his magnates can be seen as shaping narratives about Troy and King Arthur in England. However, the presence of Arthur in this narrative tradition makes the whole situation rather different from (and certainly more complicated than) that in Bohemia. As a symbol of royal and imperialist prerogative, King Arthur remains a marginal (and sometimes ridiculous) figure in medieval Bohemia, whereas in England he occupies a central and heroic role as the leader of the nation in its ancient conflict with France. However, in initiating a pro-French policy and by identifying with his Francophile Luxembourg relatives, Richard II may have tacitly encouraged an anti-Galfridian treatment of the Trojan and Arthurian material. Both Lydgate's *Troy Book* and the alliterative *Destruction of Troy* can be seen as texts which endorse this revisionism. If the latter was composed, as some scholars maintain, for the Stanley family of Lancashire with its strong affinity to the Ricardian court, its clerical distrust of imperial militarism would make a great deal of sense given the king's pacifist policy toward France and his conscious emulation of his Bohemian father-in-law's antipathy for warfare.

The Ricardian policy of peace would also explain a similarly dichotomous tradition of Arthurian texts in England in the second half of the fourteenth century. The continental mode of Arthurian romance, exemplified by *Sir Gawain and the Green Knight*, existed alongside the traditional epic treatment of Arthur as a great military figure as enshrined in Geoffrey's *Historia*. The alliterative *Morte Arthur* is an ex-

[23] Peter of Zittau, *Chronicon Aulae Regiae*, ed. J. Emler, *Fontes Rerum Bohemicarum* 4 (Prague, 1884), 252. For King Arthur's ideological function in Bohemia, see Thomas, "King Arthur and His Round Table in the Culture of Medieval Bohemia and in Medieval Czech Literature."

ample of the latter in presenting Arthur as a British king who vanquishes his imperial adversary Lucius and conquers Rome. This was the kind of narrative which would have appealed to the traditional regional gentry sympathetic to Edward III's military exploits in France, but it would certainly not have appealed to a king like Richard II. Although Richard had imperial ambitions, it is important to stress that these assumed a radically different form from the pro-war policy of his grandfather. Like Charles IV, Richard's imperial ethos was based on the peaceful principle of establishing dynastic ties through marriage rather than through war. It was precisely by virtue of his marriage to Anne of Bohemia that Richard's imperial claim derived its legitimacy.

Exemplary of the continental style of Arthurian romance, *Sir Gawain and the Green Knight* famously begins with the siege and destruction of the ancient city of Troy and the foundation of Britain by Brutus. Subsequently the foundation of Britain is linked with King Arthur (I, 25–26). It was Geoffrey of Monmouth who first linked the Trojan origins of Britain with Arthur. His purpose was to claim descent for Britain from Troy and also to create a great national hero in whom the nation would be symbolized, in the person of Arthur. Given the less than glorious fate of the Trojans, it is significant that the youthful Arthur depicted in *Sir Gawain and the Green Knight* is far from the standard model of military heroism. Arthur's knights are paralyzed by astonishment when the Green Knight runs riot through his court. Some scholars detect a parallel between the Richard who emerges from the works of the chroniclers (Walsingham, the Monk of Westminster, and the author of the *Vita Ricardi Secundi*) and the characterization of Arthur and his court at the beginning of the poem: the Green Knight's dismissal of Arthur's knights as beardless children finds an echo in Walsingham's famous reference to Richard's courtiers as knights of the bedchamber rather than the battlefield.[24] Like Arthur and Guinevere, Richard and Anne had no children, and contemporary audiences of the poem may have seen a veiled portrait of the king and queen in the glamorous young couple of the Round Table (figure 6).

It does not automatically follow, of course, that the author of *Sir Gawain and the Green Knight* is aligning himself with the criticism of the

---

[24] Ann W. Astell, *Political Allegory in Late Medieval England* (Ithaca, 1999), 119; Christine Chism, *Alliterative Revivals* (Philadelphia, 2002), 68–74.

Figure 6. Sir Gawain presents himself to King Arthur and Queen Guinevere. British Library/HIP/Art Resource, New York.

chroniclers. Rather, the poem dramatizes the ideological conflicts of the early 1380s between two divergent models of kingship: the traditional pro-war polity of Edward III—personified by the Green Knight and articulated by the anti-Ricardian chroniclers—and Richard II's policy of peace, which may have been as much strategic as moral. If Richard was serious about his imperial credentials—and all the evidence suggests that he was—he would have shared his Luxembourg relatives' distaste for a figure synonymous with military conquest. Furthermore, the traditional Arthur of the Round Table was poles apart from the Luxembourg and Ricardian policy of maintaining a distance between the ruler and his magnates by using "new men" drawn from the gentry and the merchant class (men like Chaucer) to conduct the everyday affairs of government. Charles IV staffed his chancery with clerics, leading him to be dubbed *rex clericorum* by his opponents in the Empire. This was not simply an act of piety; it was an astute attempt to reduce the power of the Bohemian nobility in the affairs of state after years of administrative neglect by his absentee father John of Luxembourg. As we have seen, some of these clerics, like his chancellor John of Středa, were prominent men of letters. Richard also drew upon clerics to staff his administration; and like Charles IV, he was particularly attached to Dominicans, perhaps on account of their doctrinal orthodoxy and great love of learning. The author of *Sir Gawain and the Green Knight* may have been one such member of this new clerical class at Richard's court. This would explain an aversion for traditional English militarism in *Sir Gawain and the Green Knight* as well as the representation of the youthful Arthur of the poem as a remote imperial figure rather than a primus inter pares at an egalitarian Round Table. Guinevere is even more remotely located on a high dais covered with a canopy of tapestries embroidered with gems in what may be an allusion to Anne of Bohemia's elevated status as the daughter of an emperor.

Whether *Sir Gawain and the Green Knight* was written for the regional gentry in the northwest Midlands or directly for the royal court in London (and the verdict is still out on this question) is less significant than the fact that the romance typifies the continental trends and cosmopolitan tastes of the Ricardian court. If the author of *Sir Gawain and the Green Knight* was active at a regional court in the northwest Midlands, it is difficult to explain how he could have had access to some of his more recherché continental sources. As Ad Putter has pointed out, Dante's *Commedia* or Boccaccio's *Olympia* (both possible sources for the poem *Pearl*, which is usually attributed to the same author as *Sir Gawain and the Green Knight*) may have been available to English poets through the community of Italian bankers and merchants living in London.[25] But as David Wallace has reminded us, it is equally likely that Queen Anne's Bohemian entourage provided a conduit through which the latest Italian culture could have reached court poets like Chaucer and the *Gawain*-poet.

If the eponymous hero of *Sir Gawain and the Green Knight* is a "clerical knight" in the tradition of Chrétien's romances rather than a military hero in the insular English tradition, he also exemplifies the new piety common to the Ricardian and Luxembourg courts. Characteristic of the international court culture is the espousal of intense religiosity rather than fervent militarism. The love of heroic exploits exhibited by John of Luxembourg and Edward III had clearly gone out of fashion (hence John's failure to establish an Arthurian Round Table in Prague). Richard II and Charles IV presided over courts in which clerical rather than knightly courtiers set the tone. The new heroes were men of deep personal piety and moral introspection. Motive becomes more significant than action. When Sir Gawain sets out on his journey through the frozen wastes of winter in search of the Green Knight, he undergoes an interior voyage of self-discovery which exposes the fault lines between his private and his public self.

If there is any residual chivalric glamour attached to the life of the court, it is manifested through the affect of fashion rather than the effect of heroism. In fitt II of *Sir Gawain and the Green Knight* the eponymous knight's armor and clothing reflect the latest haute couture of the international court culture. The cloth used to encase Sir Gawain's visor is patterned with parrots and popinjays, lovebirds and love-knots (II, 611–12). The motifs of parrots and love-knots are also attested in Bohemian court culture. In the relic scene triptych at Karlstein Castle Emperor Charles wears a white silk robe embroidered with green parrots facing each other. The knot was the device of Wenceslas IV, and blue love-knots appear prominently in the margins of his illuminated

---

[25] Ad Putter, *Sir Gawain and the Green Knight and the French Arthurian Tradition* (Oxford, 1995), 192.

Figure 7. Exterior view of Karlstein Castle, Czech Republic. Erich Lessing/Art Resource, New York.

German Bible. The fairytale castle of Hautdesert, which materializes miraculously before Sir Gawain, resembles Charles IV's private residence Karlstein Castle which is similarly surrounded by thick forests (II, 763–72) (figure 7).

Another important parallel between the court art at Karlstein and at Westminster is the extensive use of apocalyptic motifs and imagery. Like many an ambitious ruler before and after, Charles saw himself in chiliastic terms as the Emperor of the Last Days, a Christ-like figure who would bring unity and harmony before the end of the world. Apocalyptic motifs are often treated as strategies to subvert the power of popes, emperors, and kings by medieval popular movements such as the Hussites. But as the court art of Charles IV suggests, the Apocalypse can also serve the interests of powerful rulers in identifying their personal rule with the end of the world. Thus for Charles the deployment of apocalyptic imagery in the Lady Chapel at Karlstein served an ideological function in reinforcing his authority as the most powerful and influential ruler on earth. Like Charles, Richard saw himself as an *alter Christus* as illustrated by the frontal portrait of the king enthroned in the nave of Westminster Abbey (figure 8). The frame of this portrait, which is contemporary with the panel painting, displays the imperial eagle above the arms of England on both sides of the panel along with the initial "R" (Richard) and a sunburst along the top and bottom. Richard's robes are also patterned with his initial, a feature which may reveal the influence of the international court culture. In the margins of Wenceslas IV's Bible the king's initial "W" is everywhere in evidence. In some places the figure of the king is even intertwined with his initial.

It is a striking coincidence that scenes from the Apocalypse were executed during the 1390s at Westminster Abbey when the monks finally succeeded in ousting the House of Commons from the Chapter House and at the height of Richard's campaign to become emperor. Although there is no evidence that Richard played an active part in commissioning the paintings (the records make it clear that the patron was the monk John of Northampton), it is significant that the work was carried out prior to or around the year 1400 in which Wenceslas was deposed as king of the Romans. Paul Binski has commented on the fact that the Book of Revelation was becoming an important feature of European court art in the late fourteenth century:

> In the broader late fourteenth-century context, the Book of Revelation was proving to be a popular and versatile subject of monumental picture-making, whether at the court of Louis I d'Anjou (d. 1384), for whom the magnificent Angers tapestries of the Apocalypse were woven in Paris, or in Bohemia, where a series of Apocalypse wall paintings was undertaken at the behest of Charles IV in the Lady Chapel at the imperial castle at Karlstein. The east window of York Minster, glazed in 1405 to 1408 by John Thornton of Coventry, and the large late fourteenth-century altarpiece from the Hamburg workshop of Master Bertram depicting events from Revelation, indicate the comparatively widespread nature of this monumental renaissance of Apocalyptic material.[26]

[26] Binski, *Westminster Abbey*, 192.

Figure 8. Portrait of Richard II. Westminster Abbey, London. Copyright Dean and Chapter of Westminster.

With the exception of the Angers tapestries, all the examples of Apocalypse art cited by Binski are English or Bohemian-German. It is a striking coincidence that two of the most memorable late medieval literary depictions of the Apocalypse are found in *Pearl* and in the Czech *Life of Saint Catherine*. As we have seen, these works of literature were closely connected with the Ricardian and Luxembourg courts and reflected the interest of their rulers in the imagery of the Book of Revelation. Given the fact that the principal rivals for the title of Holy Roman Emperor were Richard II and Wenceslas IV, it is tempting to conclude that the deployment of apocalyptic motifs in their court art reflected these kings' political ambitions and ideological rivalry.

Shortly after the completion of the Karlstein frescoes Emperor Charles commissioned a series of sculpted busts of his ancestors to adorn the triforium of St. Vitus Cathedral in Prague (see figure 1, p. 23). As Paul Binksi has pointed out, this kind of ancestral display may have provided the instigation for Richard II to commission thirteen statues of his royal ancestors to decorate the Great Hall at Westminster.[27] The carving of these statues, which began with St. Edward the Confessor and ended with the young Richard himself, was carried out in 1385, when the king was still only eighteen years of age. By this time he had been married to Anne of Bohemia for three years, long enough for him to have learned a great deal about his father-in-law's artistic projects.

Relics of the Passion

In 1395 Richard II received a letter from the French diplomat Philippe de Mézières which made a plea for a lasting peace between England and France.[28] Philippe described the evils resulting from the wars between the two countries and the damage done by the schism in the West. The letter argued that a lasting peace, underlined by the marriage of Richard II to Isabel, daughter of Charles V of France, would lead to the reunification of Christian Europe and would make possible a crusade to the Holy Land under the banner of Philippe's proposed "Order of the Passion of Christ." In sending such a letter, Philippe was

[27] Ibid., 202.
[28] Philippe de Mézières, *Letter to King Richard II. A Plea Made in 1395 for Peace between England and France*, trans. G. W. Coopland (Liverpool, 1975).

most probably aware of the king's devotion to the Passion of Christ. This is borne out by the evidence provided by Ricardian court culture. A Crown of Thorns is visible between the crowns of England and France in the British Library manuscript Roy.20.B.VI, fol. 1v. In the Wilton Diptych the Christ Child is also Christ Crucified: His halo is stippled with the Crown of Thorns and contains the three nails of His Passion.

Richard was the recipient of a treatise on the Blood of Christ by William Sudbury, who was also the manager of the queen's manorial estates. This orthodox work contrasts starkly with a later treatise on the Blood of Christ, *De sanguine Christi*, by the Bohemian reformer Jan Hus. In addition to affirming the king's orthodox credentials, the dedication of Sudbury's treatise to Richard may have served an ideological function in demonstrating the king's affinity to Charles IV's devotion to the Passion and the relics associated with it. Richard's emulation of his father-in-law's cult of relics recalls Henry III's earlier attempts to rival Louis IX's relics at the Sainte-Chapelle in Paris with his own cult of the Holy Blood at Westminster.[29] Sudbury's connection with Queen Anne may also suggest that she inspired or encouraged the writing of the treatise. This would comport with the special devotion to the Body of Christ and His Passion displayed by Anne's ancestors. Her father, Emperor Charles, was a fervent collector of Passion relics, the most precious of which—two thorns from Christ's Crown of Thorns and a fragment of the True Cross—were gifts from his nephew Charles V of France. The donation of these gifts is recorded in the Lady Chapel in Karlstein Castle where the emperor is shown receiving the precious relic from the hands of the French king. In the second panel from the same cycle Charles receives a relic of the Holy Sponge (used to moisten Christ's lips with vinegar at His Crucifixion) from Pierre de Lusignan, King of Cyprus, whom the emperor had met at Cracow while the latter was conducting a tour of European courts to enlist support for a new crusade in the Holy Land.

Charles's passion for relics was probably influenced by his mother, Elizabeth Přemyslovna, who acquired a fragment of the Crown of Thorns from Charles IV of France in 1326. The following year Eliza-

---

[29] See Nicholas Vincent, *King Henry III and the Westminster Blood Relic* (Cambridge, 2001).

beth sent relics in a gem-encrusted gold reliquary to the pope in support of the canonization of her ancestor Agnes of Bohemia.[30] As we have seen in the previous chapter, female piety was highly developed in the Bohemian royal family; and this piety is especially apparent in devotion to Christ's Passion. Abbess Kunigunde's beautifully illuminated *Passional* focuses on Christ's suffering and the instruments of his Passion, while Bonne of Luxembourg displays a similar veneration for Christ's wounds in her famous book of hours (in the Cloisters, New York) with its startling image of the wound in Christ's side surrounded by the *arma Christi*.[31]

Evidently Richard II was greatly interested in relic collection. The chronicler Walsingham reports how Richard found the phial of holy oil given by the Virgin Mary to Thomas Becket while he was rummaging around in the chests stored in the Tower of London. Anecdotes such as this should not simply be read as evidence of Richard's antiquarian interest in English history but as a sign of the king's ideological commitment to enhancing the sacral nature of his kingship along the lines established by Charles IV for the crown of Bohemia. Like Charles, Richard regarded his regalia as an integral feature of his sacred role. He visited Westminster to witness these outward symbols of his kingship and commissioned William Sudbury to investigate their antiquity in the hope that they could be dated to the reign of Alfred the Great.[32] Charles named the royal crown of Bohemia for Wenceslas, patron saint of the Czech lands. Moreover, he had the procedure for the coronation of the Czech kings codified as the *Ordo ad coronandum regem Boemorum*. This document was commissioned in 1347, the year of Charles's coronation as king of Bohemia.

Books and Manuscripts

An important manuscript which sheds light on Richard's imperial designs is the *Liber Regalis* (London, Westminster Abbey, MS 38) (figure 9). This lavishly illustrated codex, which documents the procedure for

[30] Boehm, "Charles IV," 26.
[31] See Flora Lewis, "The Wound in Christ's Side and the Instruments of the Passion: Gendered Experience and Response," in *Women and the Book. Assessing the Visual Evidence*, ed. Jane H. M. Taylor and Lesley Smith (London, 1997), 204–29 at 206.
[32] Omrod, "Richard II's Sense of English History," 100.

Figure 9. Coronation of a king and queen. *Liber Regalis,* ca. 1382 or 1390s. Westminster Abbey, Ms. 38. Copyright Dean and Chapter of Westminster.

the coronation and the funeral of a king and queen, was probably commissioned by Richard either for his wife's coronation in 1382 or possibly as late as the 1390s. The 1390s represented a particularly complex and rich period of development for English art. This was a time when many foreign influences can be found in the workshops of London. In the words of Paul Binski: "the range of Lombard, central Italian, Netherlandish and German-influenced styles at Westminster and in London in the 1390s in fact presents a kind of mirror image to the fabulous internationalism of Luxembourg Prague."[33]

The elongated bodies and strange claw-like hands of the figures in the *Liber Regalis* resemble the stylistic features of contemporary Bohemian court art, especially the wall paintings of the *mulier amicta sole* in the Apocalypse cycle at Karlstein Castle (ca. 1360), the magnificent Bible of Wenceslas IV, and the Golden Bull of 1400, also commissioned by King Wenceslas (figure 10). If the manuscript was made as late as the 1390s, it may have been intended to circulate on the Continent as a coronation book designed to impress the electors and convince them of Richard's qualification for the title of Holy Roman Emperor. Having the manuscript illuminated in the Bohemian court style would have significantly strengthened the association between Richard and his Luxembourg relatives. The *Liber Regalis* may also have been intended as a counterpart to Charles IV's own coronation book, the *Ordo ad coronandum regem Boemorum*, made in 1347.

The later dating of the *Liber Regalis* (to the 1390s) would make it contemporary with Roger Dymmok's *Liber contra duodecim errores et hereses Lollardorum* (1395). This treatise was intended as a systematic refutation of the Twelve Conclusions of the Lollards affixed to the doors of Westminster Hall during the 1395 session of Parliament. Its author, Roger Dymmok, was a Dominican friar with a doctorate in theology from Oxford, and the eldest son of Sir John Dymmok, a retainer of John of Gaunt who served as Champion of England at Richard's coronation. The treatise is addressed to King Richard and a presentation copy (Trinity Hall MS 17) was given to the king in May 1395 after his return from Ireland. The book begins with a lengthy dedication to Richard which recalls Richard of Maidstone's earlier portrait of the

---

[33] Paul Binski, "The Liber Regalis: Its Date and European Context," in Gordon, *The Regal Image of Richard II*, 233–46 at 246.

Figure 10. Wenceslas IV, King of Bohemia (1361–1419) receiving gold and silver coins, ca. 1400. The Golden Bull of Wenceslas IV, Codex 338, fol. 22 recto. Österreichische Nationalbibiothek, Vienna. Bildarchiv Preussicher Kulturbesitz/Art Resource, New York.

king as a young Solomon in *Concordia facta inter regem Riccardum II et civitatem Londonie* (1993), a Latin poem in elegiac couplets commemorating the royal entry pageant held in London on August 21, 1392. Quoting from Proverbs 6:26, Dymmok refers to Richard as "a wise king" (*rex sapiens*).[34] In his reply to the corollaries to conclusion 10 and conclusion 12, Dymmok defends regal magnificence by reference to the wise example of King Solomon. As Fiona Somerset has pointed out, Dymmok's defense of heavy taxation and lavish spending in the interests of royal display would have appealed to Richard II.[35] But the identification of Richard with Solomon may also make sense in terms of the king's imperial ambitions. Wisdom was deemed a special attribute of the peace-loving emperor Charles IV, who was compared with Solomon by his Prague archbishop Arnošt of Pardubice.[36]

Dymmok was probably aware of Richard's campaign to be elected emperor and may have even supported it. The chivalric and heroic figures invoked to flatter the royal recipient of the text—Alexander the Great, Charlemagne, and Arthur—were intended to reinforce Richard's imperial pedigree and paralleled similar strategies of identification employed by the Luxembourg dynasty who boasted their descent from Charlemagne and Arthur. Both these figures were included in the *Luxembourg Genealogy*, the latter a spurious inclusion which reflected the emperor's readiness to invent his pedigree at the cost of historical truth. Dymmok's reference to Charlemagne is especially significant given Richard's geopolitical ambitions. Charles IV's former tutor at the court of the French kings, Pope Clement VI, encouraged the young Charles IV to emulate Charlemagne's generosity as a patron of the Church. Playing on the same theme, Charles's chancellor, John of Středa, referred to his master as the "living image" of Charlemagne. When Charles visited Paris in 1378, Charles V presented him with a gold goblet representing St. James directing Charlemagne's military expedition in Spain.[37] Charles himself claimed his namesake as his ancestor through his descent from the House of Brabant and identified

---

[34] Patricia J. Eberle, "Richard II and the Literary Arts," in *Richard II. The Art of Kingship*, ed. Anthony Goodman and James L. Gillespie (Oxford, 1999), 231–53 at 247.

[35] Fiona Somerset, *Clerical Discourse and Lay Audience in Late Medieval England* (Cambridge, 1998), 120.

[36] Jiří Fajt, "Charles IV: Toward a New Imperial Style," in *Prague, The Crown of Bohemia*, 3–21 at 6.

[37] Boehm, "Charles IV," 30.

closely with him, as the portraits of the holy rulers in the Chapel of the Holy Cross at Karlstein Castle attest.

Reinforcing the geopolitical implications of Dymmok's treatise are the paired images of Pope Sylvester and Emperor Constantine (fol. 13r), which, as the modern editor of the treatise has suggested, may reflect Richard's campaign to be elected emperor.[38] At a time when the papal claim of the Constantine Donation was coming under increasing criticism by Lollards in England—and a few years later by Hussites in Bohemia—these figures are significant in identifying Richard not only as a ruler with an impressive pedigree but also with immaculate orthodox credentials. Rumors of the English heresy must have reached the attention of the electors in Germany in the 1390s. It was crucial therefore that Richard should allay their fears by distancing himself from the Lollards—some of whose sympathizers included the king's chamber knights—and by emphasizing his total commitment to orthodoxy.

Dymmok's defense of the papal prerogative made him and his fellow Dominicans a predictable target for Lollard polemics, as we shall see in the next chapter. An important feature of the royal prerogative is Dymmok's defense of princely magnificence as a vindication of the Ricardian court.[39] If Richard was to be taken seriously as a candidate for the imperial throne, he needed to look and act the part. Dating from the same time as the *Liber contra duodecim errores*, the revised version of Smil Flaška's *New Council* includes a similar endorsement of princely magnificence. The allegorical figure of the Horse (representing the knightly class) admonishes the Lion King to dress in a manner appropriate to his regal status (lines 863–65). It is impossible to tell whether the counsel of the Horse dates from the first version of *The New Council* or from the later version when Wenceslas had lost the respect of many of the princes in the empire; but its satirical animus, in particular the sardonic description a joust, suggests that it was added or amplified in the 1390s and was intended to highlight the king's fail-

---

[38] Roger Dymmok, *Liber contra XII errores et hereses Lollardorum*, ed. H. S. Cronin (London, 1921). See also the brief discussion of Dymmok's treatise in Eberle, "Richard II and the Literary Arts," 246–48.

[39] See Patricia J. Eberle, "Politics of Courtly Style at the Court of Richard II," in *The Spirit of the Court: Selected Proceedings of the Fourth Congress of the International Courtly Literature Society* (Toronto, 1983), ed. Glynn S. Burgess and Robert A. Taylor (Woodbridge, 1985), 168–78.

ings at a time when it appeared increasingly unlikely that he would be crowned Holy Roman Emperor in Rome.

Another similarity between Richard and Wenceslas was their fascination for the arts of astrology and astronomy. Richard owned a magnificent encyclopedia of divination known as the *Libellus Geomancie* which described the sciences of astrology, physiognomy, the meaning of dreams, and geomancy (the interpretation of patterns in sand or small stones) (Bodley MS 581). In many ways the ownership of this book reflected Richard's troubled reign as he sought to find solace and certainty in the stars and their movements. But it probably also served an ideological purpose in reflecting the king's desire to divine his imperial future. Significantly, the text begins with an aphorism which recalls Dymmok's emphasis on the importance of kingly wisdom: "A wise man will grow wiser by listening."[40] But such books of divination were not limited to the ambitious Richard. The vast library of the French king Charles V at the Louvre in Paris included more than a hundred works on astrology and other forms of occult science. Charles V's cousin, Wenceslas IV, owned three beautifully illuminated treatises on astrology which are now in Madrid, Vienna, and Munich. The Madrid manuscript is a copy (ca. 1400) of the *Dragmaticon philosophiae* by William of Conches. The Munich text draws on three diverse traditions—Hebrew, Arabic, and Christian—and suggests a degree of cultural and intellectual tolerance which anticipates the ecumenicism of the Habsburg emperor Rudolf II in the early seventeenth century (hence the king's early support for Hus and his followers). Wenceslas' interest in astronomy is also apparent in Prague's famous astronomical clock, which was created by Master Johannes Šindel, royal physician and rector of the university, in collaboration with Nicholas of Kadaň.[41] The fact that all three kings shared an interest in astrology witnesses to its popularity at royal courts in the second half of the fourteenth century and the importance attached to its role in helping kings map the fortunes of their rule.

---

[40] Quoted from Mathew, *The Court of Richard II*, 40–41. For Richard II's and Charles V's books of astrology, see Peter Whitfield, *Astrology. A History* (New York, 2001), 131–32.

[41] Barbara Drake Boehm and Jiří Fajt, "Wenceslas IV," in Boehm and Fajt, *Prague. The Crown of Bohemia*, 91–103 at 99.

Figure 11. Tomb of Richard II and Anne of Bohemia, 1395. Chapel of Edward the Confessor, Westminster Abbey. Copyright Dean and Chapter of Westminster.

The Royal Tombs in Westminster Abbey

The most tangible evidence of Richard's imperial aspirations as well as his deep love for his wife is still evident today in the royal mausoleum at Westminster Abbey. In 1395, one year after Anne's death on June 7, 1394, Richard commissioned a double tomb for himself and his beloved consort (figure 11).[42] Unlike earlier regal monuments it was intended as a joint tomb for Anne and himself, a precedent possibly provided by German tomb production. On April 1 Richard contracted the London masons, Henry Yevele and Stephen Lote, to supply a "tomb of fine marble" ("une Toumbe, de fine Marbre"). On April 24 Richard commissioned two bronze effigies from the London coppersmiths, Nicholas

[42] For a detailed description of Richard and Anne's tomb, see Mark Duffy, *Royal Tombs of Medieval England* (Stroud, 2003), 164–73; and Binski, *Westminster Abbey*, 201–2.

Broker and Godfrey Prest. The contract specified that the figures were to be made as likenesses (*contrefait*), their hands clasped together, with their other hands holding scepters, with an orb placed between them. This sign of affection was unprecedented in royal tomb production and witnessed to the genuine love Richard felt for his deceased wife. References to Anne are apparent in the intricate chasework stamped all over the effigies themselves. The effigy plates are diapered with leopards, the two-headed imperial eagles, and the lion of Bohemia. The king's robes are powdered with the couples' initials, together with three badges: a chained and couched hart, broom plants, and a sunburst. The initials are repeated on Anne's surcoat and mantle, together with a crowned and collared ostrich and knots. Ostriches are found in the margins of the great Carmelite Missal which was probably completed in 1393. According to Gervase Mathew it is likely that the queen was one of its donors since the crowned and chained ostrich was her badge.[43]

Originating in Horace's *Ars Poetica*, the knot was a common feature of the international court culture. The pentangle on Sir Gawain's shield—the inside of which displays a painted image of the Virgin Mary—consists of an "endless knot," a figure of five points, each line linked and locked with the next for ever and ever. In addition to its amorous associations, the knot shares with precious jewels the symbolic function of memory. The five points of Sir Gawain's pentangle signify the five wounds of Christ and the five joys of the Blessed Virgin Mary. In the final prayer of *The Plowman* God's infinite love is imagined as a "tight knot that no one can untie."[44] In his *Testament of Love* Usk similarly plays on the significance of the knot as the mystical bond between God and man as well as between the writer and his beloved lady: "But for as moche as every herte that hath caught ful love is tyed with queynt knyttynges, thou shalt understande that love and thilke foresayed blisse toforne declared in this provynges shal hote the knot in the hert."[45]

The effigies at Westminster repose recumbent below a wooden tester depicting Christ in Glory and the Coronation of the Virgin, their childless marriage mirroring the chaste marriage of Mary and the

---

[43] Matthew, *The Court of Richard II*, 41–42.
[44] "Fester knode, den niemand aufbinden mag." *Der Ackerman*, 140.
[45] Thomas Usk, *Testament of Love*, ed. R. Allen Shoaf (Kalamazoo, 1998), 219.

Church.⁴⁶ As we saw in the previous chapter, this identification of Anne with Mary is consistent with an illustrious tradition of *imitatio Mariae* in the Bohemian royal family. In the dedicatory portrait on the title page of the *Passional* of Abbess Kunigunde, Anne's ancestor is seated on a throne as she receives a completed copy of the codex from the court theologian Kolda of Koldice. Above her two miniature angels are poised to place a heavenly crown on her head, a gesture which mimics the iconographic motif of the Coronation of the Virgin. It is known that Kunigunde played the role of the Virgin Mary in the Easter Passion play performed annually by the sisters of the St. George Convent at the Prague Castle.⁴⁷ Included in the codex is the "Parable of the Invincible Knight" (*De strenuo milite*), which draws a further parallel between Kunigunde's acceptance of the veil and the deliverance of the knight's beloved from the fiery chamber and her coronation by her lover (*coronacio sponse*) (fol. 3b).

Following the lead provided by Italian trecento and quattrocento art, Bohemian panel painting, stained glass, and book illuminations include many instances of the Coronation of the Virgin: an initial in the Breviary of Great Master Lev (fol. 44v) (ca. 1356), the stained glass from the Church of St. Bartholomew in Kolín nad Labem (ca. 1360), and the Clementine Almanach of Thomas of Štítné (1376). In the first and second examples, God and Mary are seated as equals on a shared throne or bench—as in the tester at Westminster Abbey—whereas in the third example the Virgin kneels before an enthroned Christ as He places a crown on her head.⁴⁸ Doubtless influenced by the contemporary visual arts, the Czech *Life of Saint Catherine* depicts the Coronation of the Virgin in Catherine's second vision where she sees God the Father and Mary, seated on separate thrones and each holding scepters, as in the funeral effigies of Richard and Anne: "She saw more beautiful wonders rejoicing in their beauty and beheld two thrones, placed side by side, next to the rising sun. On one sat God Almighty on His radiant throne; on the other, wearing a precious crown, sat Mary, His mother by the power of the Word, the Empress of the Archangels. Both held scepters in their hands."⁴⁹

---

⁴⁶ See Paul Binski, *Medieval Death. Ritual and Representation* (London, 1996), 105–6.
⁴⁷ See the catalog *Příběh Pražského Hradu* (Prague, 2003), 157.
⁴⁸ For these images, see the catalog *The Bride in the Enclosed Garden* (Prague), 108–13.
⁴⁹ *Medieval Hagiography. An Anthology*, ed. Thomas Head (New York, 2000), 774.

It is a tragic irony that Richard's vision of being elected emperor did not extend beyond the creation of a marvelous mausoleum for himself and his wife at Westminster. Following his wife's death in 1394 this vision seems to have become almost all-consuming and may have even undermined his political judgment, thus leading to his overthrow in 1399. The explanation for this misguided ambition was a combination of personal and political factors: it is important not to underestimate the king's opportunism which, according to Anne Curry, rivaled that of the ruthless Henry V.[50] Historians have tended to treat Richard as a ruler flawed by a narcissistic and insecure personality. This was probably true, but insecurity and ambition are not necessarily mutually exclusive personality traits. As Nigel Saul has pointed out, more images of Richard II survive than of any English king before Henry VIII.[51] But this was as much a political strategy of self-aggrandizement as an expression of an unstable personality. Charles IV, who could never have been accused of instability, commissioned numerous self-portraits, sixty of which survive throughout Bohemia and Europe.[52] The real difference between Richard II and Charles IV was the fact that the latter was a realist and the former was not. The ideological function of art and architecture was clearly not enough to turn an ambitious ruler into a successful one. Richard emulated Charles IV's deployment of art to advance his political agenda but he failed to learn crucial lessons of statecraft from his father-in-law. In this respect he shared the failings of his brother-in-law Wenceslas, who squandered almost all the achievements of his father. Rather it was Charles's daughter Anne instead of his son Wenceslas who seems to have inherited the emperor's gift for pragmatism. Ironically, it was her status as the daughter of an emperor that fueled Richard II's doomed quest for an imperial crown.

[50] Anne Curry, "Richard II and the War with France," in Dodd, *The Reign of Richard II*, 33–50 at 50.

[51] For Richard's personality, see Saul, *Richard II* (New Haven, 1997), 450.

[52] Iva Rosario, *Art and Propaganda: Charles IV of Bohemia, 1346–1378* (Woodbridge, 2000), xv.

Chapter 3

"Master Adversary"

Wyclif's Influence in Bohemia

Although, as we saw in chapter 1, Anne of Bohemia was thoroughly orthodox in her religious beliefs, her ability to read the New Testament in Czech, German, and Latin stimulated the Lollard demand that the Gospels be made available to the laity in their native tongue. Another important consequence of Anne's presence in England was the busy traffic of scholars between the universities of Oxford and Prague. In this chapter I shall trace the reception of the ideas of the Oxford theologian John Wyclif (1330?–84) in fifteenth-century Bohemia with special reference to the thought of John Hus and Peter Chelčický, the two most prolific and articulate spokesmen of the Bohemian reform movement, whose combined writings extend from the final, troubled years of the reign of Wenceslas IV (d. 1419), through the Hussite Wars, to the concordat between the Utraquists (moderate Hussites) and the Catholic Church. I shall examine how the localized religious, ethnic, and political circumstances of fifteenth-century Bohemia influenced both the perception and the reception of Wyclif's teachings in that country.

One of the difficulties in discussing Wyclif's reception in Bohemia is the blurred distinction between perception and reality. Hus in his own time was regarded as a disciple of Wyclif and was sent to his death at Constance as a Wycliffite heretic, although his writings were far more conservative than those of the Oxford heresiarch. If Hus and his Bohemian contemporaries were unable to distinguish between what Wyclif wrote and how they read him, so in a sense have historians been vulnerable to the subjective perspectives of their own time. In the nineteenth century the Austrian historian Josef Loserth advanced the thesis that Hus was a derivative thinker who copied large sections of Wyclif's works. In the interwar period this position was disputed by the Czech Hussitologist František Bartoš, who argued that Loserth's claims overlooked the late medieval understanding of originality and truth.[1] According to Bartoš, Hus' response to Wyclif was determined by the local circumstances of Bohemian politics and society. Hus' attachment to Wyclif's commitment to Church reform inspired the Bohemian preacher to return to the apostolic simplicity of the early Church. In addition to Hus' concern with the corruption of the church, Bartoš also stressed his antagonism to the German dominance in government, the Church, and the university. Just as Loserth's need to underestimate Hus' originality was an Austrian reaction to nineteenth-century Czech nationalism, so Bartoš's emphasis on Hus' nationalism may be said to reflect Czechoslovak anxieties about German military aggression in the early 1930s.

Although ethnic tensions between Germans and Czechs undoubtedly played a part in explaining the popularity of Wyclif's realism—as opposed to the prevailing nominalism favored by the German masters at the University of Prague—the linguistic split in the university is only one piece in the complex mosaic that created conditions favorable for a religious revolution. Perhaps most important of all was the utopian vision of a primitive or apostolic Church, a primordial myth of origins to which all the reformers of the day—Lollard as well as Hussite—were susceptible at a time of deep division and dissent within the Church.

Wyclif and Hus

Wyclif's works were not completely unknown at the University of Prague even in the late fourteenth century. Nicholas Biceps, a Prague

---

[1] František M. Bartoš, *Husitství a cizina* (Prague, 1931), 20–34.

professor, was arguing against Wyclif's eucharistic beliefs while the Englishman was still alive; and Matthew of Janov, a predecessor of Hus, displays a devotion to the Bible reminiscent of Wyclif's adherence to the principle of *sola scriptura*. But it was Wyclif's philosophical realism, rather than his theology, that first attracted attention in Bohemia.[2] Although realism represented a strong presence at the University of Prague, especially among the Czech masters and students, Wyclif's brand of ultrarealism was something quite new and audacious. Marginal comments from a Bohemian copy of Wyclif's *De Ideis* make this shocking effect quite clear: one warns the reader that the treatise should not be read by *non intelligentibus*, while another apostrophizes, with a mixture of admiration and apprehension: "O Wyclif, Wyclif, more than one head you will turn."[3]

Interest in Wyclif's philosophical ideas soon spread to the more contentious and dangerous realm of his theology. Access to such works was inevitably facilitated by the presence of Bohemians at the University of Oxford. One of these was Jerome of Prague who studied at Oxford from 1399 to 1401 and there copied Wyclif's *Dialogus* and *Trialogus* and perhaps also his *De Eucharistia*. He brought back these works to Prague where they were avidly read by Hus and other like-minded reformers.[4] A few years later (1407–8) two Bohemian students named Nicholas Faulfiš and George of Kněhnice were sent to England to establish contacts with Lollard communities. By this time the Lollards were suffering persecution following the inauguration of Archbishop Arundel's statute *De heretico comburendo* (1401). The Bohemians found Oxford purged of Wyclif's works and ideas. They traveled to Lollard centers at Kemerton (near Tewkesbury) and Braybrooke in Northamptonshire where they succeeded in acquiring a number of works by Wyclif and brought them back to Prague; they also brought a letter purporting to be an official recommendation by the University of Oxford bearing witness to Wyclif's orthodoxy. The letter was almost certainly fabricated and the seal appended by Peter Payne, an Oxford follower of Wyclif who later fled to Bohemia and became the chief spokesman of the Hussite party at the Council of Basel. The Bohemian

---

[2] Malcolm Lambert, *Medieval Heresy. Popular Movements from the Gregorian Reform to the Reformation* (Oxford, 1977), 294.
[3] Ibid., 295.
[4] Matthew Spinka, *John Hus. A Biography* (Princeton, 1968), 59.

students also visited Wyclif's grave at Lutterworth and brought back with them a fragment from his tomb, suggesting that even at this early stage Wyclif was beginning to achieve a saint-like status among the reform-minded Czechs.[5]

The arrival of Wyclif's theological works in Bohemia tended to polarize the situation at the University and in society at large. While his ideas gave a much-needed intellectual and philosophical impetus to the largely moral emphasis of the pre-Hussite reform movement, his ultrarealism drove a sharp wedge between the German nominalists and the Czech realists at the university. The ethnic split within the university thus made Wyclif's ideas at once appealing and deeply divisive. A frequently quoted example of this ethnic tension is the marginal comment in one Wyclif manuscript in which the Czech reader has written on finding a theological argument with which to beat the ethnic opposition: "Haha, Germans, haha."

This ethnic polarization was accelerated by an attack on the supporters of Wyclif by German masters, which began in 1403 with an appeal to the Prague diocesan authorities for action against Wyclif's works by John Hübner, a Silesian Dominican educated at the University of Prague. This was followed by an attack on the Czech Wycliffite and teacher of Hus, Stanislav of Znojmo, by John Stejna, an émigré from Prague, and then by an appeal to the Curia itself in 1408 by Ludolf Meistermann, a Saxon also educated at Prague. The situation was further exacerbated by King Wenceslas' indecisive policies. Withholding allegiance from the two rival popes in Rome and Avignon, he called upon the university masters to endorse his neutrality. The Czech masters supported the king but the German masters refused to relinquish obedience to the Roman pope. Early in 1409 Wenceslas summoned the university masters to Kutná Hora to discuss the papal issue. The king wished to weaken the German influence at the university so that his neutral policy would prevail. By royal decree he revised the statutes of the university so that the dominant vote in the university passed from the Germans to the Czechs. The controversy ended with a mass exodus of German masters and students from Prague to Leipzig, where they founded their own university.

[5] Ibid., 81–82. For Peter Payne, see František M. Bartoš, *Petr Payne diplomat husitské revoluce* (Prague, 1956); and William R. Cooke, "Peter Payne: Theologian and Diplomat of the Hussite Revolution" (Ph.D. diss., Cornell University, 1971).

The German attacks on the Czech Wycliffites culminated in the appointment of an archiepiscopal commission for the examination of Wyclif's works composed entirely of anti-Wycliffites. The result of the commission's findings was announced on June 16, 1410, at the palace of the Prague Archbishop Zbyněk of Hasenburk, who had been initially sympathetic to Hus and the Czech reformers. Fifteen of Wyclif's books were found to be heretical, whereupon the archbishop forbade the holding or teaching of any of the condemned tenets and ordered that all of Wyclif's books be surrendered to him. Hus countered this attack by composing a short treatise entitled *De libris hereticorum legendis* (June 21, 1410) in which he adduced the support of a number of Church Fathers for the proposition that heretical books should be read for the truth they contain and not be burned.[6] Hus further inflamed the situation by preaching a sermon at the Bethlehem Chapel in which he sought the support of the congregation for his opposition to the ban on the teaching and reading of Wyclif's works. The audience responded with the thunderous assertion that they would support Hus.

All this dissent proved too much for Archbishop Zbyněk, who on July 16, 1410, ordered two hundred books gathered in his courtyard to be burned. Fearing the reprisals of the mob, he fled to his castle at Roudnice, where, two days later, he excommunicated Hus and his fellow protesters. In defiance of this official ban on his priestly function, Hus continued to preach. Prague was now plunged into chaos as church services were disrupted and some priests threatened with death. The antipope John XXIII confirmed the archbishop's excommunication of Hus on August 25, 1410. Somewhat later Hus was cited to the Curia at Bologna; the citation reached Prague on September 20.

The case now reached the proportions of an international affair, with the king, queen, and court taking a position on behalf of Hus. Wenceslas wrote a letter of intercession to the pope in which he requested that Wyclif's works be spared. The burning of Wyclif's books and the citation against Hus prompted some English Lollards to send a supply of books to replace those which had been burned. The most prominent of these English sympathizers was the Lollard knight Sir John Oldcastle who sent a letter, dated September 8, 1410, from Cooling Castle (one of Oldcastle's holdings on the Thames estuary) to Hus'

---

[6] Spinka, *John Hus,* 109–11.

supporter, the courtier Voksa of Valdštejn, exhorting him to steadfastness in the faith and praising King Wenceslas for his support of the reformers. On the same day (the Feast of the Nativity of the Virgin) another Lollard named Richard Wyche sent a letter from London to Hus in Prague. Wyche was a priest of the Hereford diocese who had been active as a heretic in Northumberland in 1401–2. While preaching there (probably in Newcastle) in 1402, he was summoned to appear before Bishop Walter Skirlaw of Durham. On December 7, 1402, he was interviewed by Skirlaw at Bishop Auckland and, failing to provide satisfactory answers, was excommunicated and consigned to the bishop's prison in his castle there. From December 1402 to about March 1403 Wyche was incarcerated and periodically examined before the bishop or his council. At this time Wyche composed a long letter to a lay friend in Newcastle in which he describes the proceedings against him and the authorities' attempts to make him recant. Wyche was indeed brought to recant sometime between late 1404 and early 1406. But his heretical activity continued until his eventual execution at Smithfield in 1440.[7]

Wyche was presumably known in Bohemian reformist circles even before he sent his letter to Hus in September 1410, since an earlier letter he composed for his Lollard brethren while in the prison was smuggled out in 1403 and eventually turned up in a Bohemian manuscript. It is clear that Oldcastle and Wyche, whose letters were sent on the same day, were acting in concert, probably to make use of a messenger's imminent departure for Bohemia. There were several opportunities for the transmission of these letters to Bohemia. Bartoš claims that a Czech student in Oxford named Simon brought the letters back to Prague via the circuitous route of Hungary, which would explain their late arrival on March 8, 1411.

Wyche's letter strikes a tone of consolation and encouragement at a time of uncertainty for the Bohemian reform movement and only two years before Hus was exiled from Prague. But whereas Lollardy had gone underground because of the English authorities' ruthless crackdown on religious dissent, in Bohemia the Church and the secular

---

[7] For Wyche's career, see Rita Copeland, *Pedagogy, Intellectuals, and Dissent in the Later Middle Ages. Lollardy and Ideas of Learning* (Cambridge, 2001), 151–90. For an account of the fate of Wyche's letter in a Bohemian manuscript, see Anne Hudson, "William Taylor's 1406 Sermon: A Postscript," in *Medium Aevum* 64 (1995): 100–106.

power were clearly unable to prevent Hus and his associates from preaching their message to large crowds of enthusiastic listeners. Although Wyche's letter was intended to offer comfort to and solidarity with his persecuted brethren in Bohemia, its introspective and fatalistic tone actually reflects the Lollards' far greater problems in England. Whereas Hus' letter to Wyche places emphasis on the public and communal expression of dissent, Wyche's epistle clearly reflects the isolation and alienation of the Lollards. Instead of dwelling on the future, its focus is fixed on the past and the martyrs of the early Church: "Let us consider the holy fellowship of our fathers that have gone before us. Let us consider the saints of the Old and New Testaments. Did they not all pass through this sea of tribulation and persecution? Were not some of them cut in pieces, others stoned, and others slain with the sword?"[8] As Anne Hudson points out, Wyche's letters here and elsewhere "echo in their biblical language the salutations of many Pauline epistles."[9] Wyche's identification with apostolical persecution contrasts with Hus' exuberant and even ecstatic reply (dated March 1411). Hus informed the Englishman that he had read his letter aloud during a sermon attended by ten thousand people, a figure which was almost certainly exaggerated. If Wyche is identifying with Pauline persecution, Hus goes one step further back into the history of the early Church by identifying with Christ preaching the Sermon on the Mount:

> I said in a large assembly of people, numbering, I suppose, nearly ten thousand, as I was preaching in public, "See, my beloved brothers, what a care for your salvation is shown by the faithful preachers of Christ in other countries; they yearn to pour out their whole soul, if only they can keep us in the gospel of Christ, even the Lord." And I added, "Why, our dear brother Richard, partner of Master John Wyclif in the toils of the gospel, hath written you a letter of so much cheer, that if I possessed no other writing, I should feel bound by it to offer myself for the gospel of Christ, even unto death. Yea, and this I will do, with the help of our Lord Jesus Christ." Christ's faithful ones were fired

---

[8] *The Letters of Jan Hus,* trans. Herbert B. Workman and R. Martin Pope (London, 1904), 33.

[9] Anne Hudson, *The Premature Reformation. Wycliffite Texts and Lollard History* (Oxford, 1988), 222.

with such ardour by the letter that they begged me to translate it into our mother tongue.[10]

Hus' ostensibly personal letter to Wyche reads like a public endorsement of their shared beliefs. Ironically, it is Hus who offers Wyche encouragement, rather than the other way round. For both men, the other's homeland becomes synonymous with the utopian ideals of the early Church. At the close of his letter Wyche solicits from Hus the very comfort he was supposed to be sending to Bohemia: "I would desire also to see letters of yours written back to us, for know that they shall comfort us not a little." Conversely, Hus looks to England as the source of Bohemia's good fortunes: "I am thankful that Bohemia has under the power of Jesus Christ received so much good from the blessed land of England through your labours."[11]

After the exchange of letters with Hus, Wyche disappears from public records until October 1417 when he was required to appear at Westminster to make disclosures about money that had belonged to Sir John Oldcastle and had been forfeited to the king following Oldcastle's uprising. In 1419 Wyche was summoned under suspicion of heresy once again. He was imprisoned and released in 1420. Thereafter he occupied several livings in Kent and Middlesex from the early 1420 through the 1430s, but was eventually arrested and burned as an obdurate heretic at Smithfield in 1440.

Why were Wyclif's works so deeply contested in early fifteenth-century Bohemia? The main attraction for Hus and his fellow reformers was less Wyclif's theological and eucharistic polemics than his social critique of the corruption within the Church. This corruption, a remedy for which was sought and found in *De Civili Dominio,* seemed especially topical and relevant at the time of the Schism when two rival popes contended for power and Christian Europe was split in its allegiance. Wyclif's work may also have been of special interest and urgency to the reform-minded students at the University of Prague, a

---

[10] Workman and Pope, *The Letters of Jan Hus,* 35. For the letters between Wyche and Hus, see Konstantin Höfler, *Geschichtsschreiber der Hussitischen Bewegung in Böhmen,* Fontes rerum Austriacarum 6 (Vienna, 1865), 210–14. The letter from Oldcastle to Valdštejn is edited in Josef Loserth, "Über die Beziehungen zwischen englischen und böhmischen Wiclifisten," *Mittheilungen des Instituts für österreichische Geschichtsforschung* 12 (1891): 254–69.

[11] Workman and Pope, *The Letters of Jan Hus,* 34, 36.

city in which the gap between the rich, privileged Church and the poor had been growing for several decades.

Wyclif's great work on the theme of civil dominion addresses the vexed question of the Catholic Church's vast wealth and property. Essential to Wyclif's argument is the basic belief that since God alone holds dominion over the earth and its immense bounty, the rightful possession of such bounty depends upon one's possession of God's grace. If one is in a state of mortal sin, Wyclif argues, one automatically relinquishes the right to remain in possession of property, be this ecclesiastical or secular. If the Catholic Church was in a state of mortal sin—as Wyclif propounded—it too relinquished its moral right to own property. Wyclif's solution to the practical problem of realizing such a program of reform was to call upon the secular branch of society—that is, the king and his magnates—to administer the transferal of goods and lands from the ecclesiastical to the secular sphere. This was one reason why his teachings were early on so well received by many members of English nobility, in particular, by John of Gaunt, the king's uncle, who invited him to deliver a series of sermons on the subject.

It was this Wycliffian proposition that Hus accepted and promoted more fervently than any other. In his own writings—most notably, *On Simony* and *On the Church*—Hus applied Wyclif's general ideas to the specific circumstances of the Bohemian Church. Since the time of Charles IV (as we have seen, a loyal and orthodox son of the Church) the Bohemian ecclesiastical hierarchy had become ever wealthier and more corrupt. Simony and nepotism were common features of church conduct. Hus argued that ecclesiastical simony should be promptly punished and that sinful clerics should be deprived of their goods. Like Wyclif, Hus looked to the secular branch (the king) to carry out the necessary reform of the Church. In this quest he was making progress until his exile from Prague in 1412, by which time he had lost the support of Wenceslas.

The Wycliffian proposition that sinful clergy should be punished was later to be incorporated into the manifesto of the Hussite revolution known as the Four Articles of Prague. A second Wycliffian proposition that was to be drafted into the Four Articles was the idea that the civil authorities had the right—and indeed the duty—to reform the abuses of the church, by force if necessary. But Hus fell short of Wyclif's assumption that the king was supreme in all temporal matters, including the punishment of the clergy for public sins, for the simple reason that his experience taught him that he could not trust the secular authorities to act in strict accordance with moral law. Although King Wenceslas was initially sympathetic to the reform party and—under the influence of his consort Sophie—even appointed Hus as rector of the University of Prague, the increasing political instability of the country caused the king to reverse his policies. Under pressure from the archbishop of Prague, Wenceslas exiled Hus from the city in 1412. Hus could trust even less the younger brother and heir of Wenceslas, Sigismund, king of Hungary and emperor-elect, who was orthodox in his religious beliefs and made no secret of his hostility toward the Hussites. When Hus took Sigismund at his word and accepted his promise of a guarantee of safe conduct to the Council of Constance, he paid for it with his life.

Although Hus accepted and promoted Wyclif's ideas on such political matters as simony and civil dominion, he was less enthusiastic about the Englishman's doctrinal beliefs, in particular his denial of the real presence in the Eucharist and his refusal to accept the sacramental authority of the priesthood. In these matters Hus was more conservative than Wyclif. Although the right to communicate in both kinds (*sub utraque specie*) would eventually be enshrined as the first of the Four Articles of Prague, and the chalice would become the symbol of the reformers in their twenty-year military struggles against invading imperial and papal-sponsored armies, Hus himself never made the case that the laity should have the right to partake of the bread and the wine. This was the innovation of his followers, in particular, Jakoubek of Stříbro.

Wyclif and Chelčický

Hus' follower of the next generation, Peter Chelčický, also entertained a complex and ambiguous attitude toward Wyclif's ideas. If Hus' response to Wyclif was largely conservative, Chelčický was more radical than both men, especially in his pacifism and his insistence on the total separation of Church and state. In both cases, the reception of Wyclif's writings was shaped by the specific circumstances of time and place. As we have seen, Hus was neither an original nor a revolutionary thinker; and much of the moral emphasis of his work was formed by the Bohemian reformers who preceded him. Chelčický, by contrast, was writing a generation later in a very different community where the vision of an uncorrupted primitive Church was felt to be realizable. Chelčický reacted vehemently to many of Wyclif's precepts—in particular the latter's traditional model of a tripartite society—because the Englishman's vision of the ideal society contrasted so glaringly with reality.

Peter Chelčický was born around 1390 near the small town of Chelčice in southern Bohemia and spent most of his life in the area with rare visits to Prague. He was not educated at the Prague University and probably did not read and write Latin with any fluency. His learning was made possible by the many translations of the Bible and theological works into Czech as well as the powerful oral culture of preaching and discussion. Wyclif was a major source of influence on Chelčický. He especially admired Wyclif's insistence on the Bible as the sole source of authority. Although Wyclif and Peter interpreted the Scriptures in differing ways, they both rejected all ecclesiastical writings that did not derive their authority directly from the Bible. Ironically, it was Peter's strict adherence to the principle of *sola scriptura* that later led him to take issue with Wyclif's social and political interpretation of theology. Peter found no scriptural evidence to support Wyclif's belief that the civil authorities should act as guardians of the faith. On the contrary, for him, the doctrine of civil dominion had no precedent in the Gospels and therefore no rightful place in the Christian life. By analogy, Peter also rejected as unbiblical Wyclif's acceptance of the use of force in the defense of Christian truth. He derived his justification for rejecting violence by relying exclusively on the New Testament and Christ's message of love as enshrined within it. In rejecting the authority of the Old Testament, Peter not only parted company with Wyclif, whom he increasingly referred to as "Mistr Protiva" ("Master Adversary"), but also with fellow Hussites like Jakoubek of Stříbro, who invoked the authority of the Hebrew prophets to justify their violent resistance to the imperial armies entrusted by the Papacy with the task of crushing the Bohemian heresy.

During a visit to Prague in 1420, Peter disputed on two separate occasions with the Utraquist theologian Jakoubek on the issue of the use of violence to resist violence. Master Jakoubek accepted Wyclif's principle of the just war. Peter asked Jakoubek to justify his position from Scripture. Jakoubek conceded that "only the saints say it is so," a reference to St. Augustine's doctrine of the justified war. Jakoubek was forced to fall back on the Old Testament as the only authority for a Christian defense of a secular society. In spite of the hospitality and honor shown to him by Jakoubek, Peter refused to accept the Augustinian and Wycliffian principle of the just war. This was a truly radical position to assume, not least since at the time of Peter's first meeting with Jakoubek in Prague in the spring of 1420, an imperial army was advancing toward the city. Peter's adamant refusal to accept that violence was sometimes justified—even in the face of a hostile foe determined to root out heresy—constitutes the most controversial and original aspect of his thought and his principal area of dissent from Wyclif's writings.

Whereas Wyclif saw the resolution to the problem of a sinful church in its subordination to secular authority—if necessary by violent means—Peter saw the salvation of Christ's true church in its total separation from the secular power of the state and its complete espousal of pacifism. The reason for this separatist view has provoked a great deal of scholarly discussion. One explanation was the pervasive influence of Waldensian thought in southern Bohemia and Austria, but this theory has been largely refuted in recent years. A more plausible explanation for Peter's departure from the ideas of Wyclif and Jakoubek is the difference between their status as university-trained clerics and his status as a layman. Wyclif and Jakoubek spent most of their lives in or near major centers of learning, Oxford and Prague, respectively. Furthermore, Wyclif was writing at a time and in a society where his ideas may have had a theoretical appeal but could not be put into practice. By contrast, Peter was living at a time and in a place where reformist ideas had already been implemented, so that he was in a privileged position to judge their practical implications. As a layman living beyond the confines of academe, he experienced the actual consequences of Wyclif's ideas on civil dominion and the justified war. To his dismay he discovered that these beliefs did not necessarily improve the welfare of ordinary people such as the small townsfolk and the peasantry. On the contrary, Peter suggests that life on the land during the Hussite theocracy was worse than ever before.

After his return from Prague, Peter witnessed the transformation of the primitive Christian pacifism of the radical Hussites—the Taborites of southern Bohemia—into militant revolution. This about-turn was caused by the very real military threat to their survival by the imperial armies of Sigismund. Abandoning their original commitment to pacifism, the Taborites, under the leadership of John Žižka, became a much-feared fighting force and successfully repelled and defeated wave after wave of imperial onslaughts. Peter's aggrieved response to the Taborite espousal of millenarian force was a treatise entitled *On Spiritual Warfare*, which took as its point of departure a pericope from St. Paul's epistle to the Ephesians (6:10–20). In his epistle Paul urges the Christians of Ephesus to prepare for spiritual warfare by putting on the "whole armor of God that you may be able to stand against the wiles of the devil." Peter's deployment of Paul's martial metaphor to designate a spiritual, nonviolent resistance to evil was deliberately intended as a rebuke to the Taborites for abandoning their initial pacifist posture. Peter provocatively aligned the newly militarized Taborites with the devil against whom they were supposed to be fighting; and given his citation from St. Paul, he was implicitly associating the Taborite militants with the pagan oppressors of the early Church.

A major consequence of the Taborite reversal of policy was their abandonment of their original program of economic and land reform. They had initially announced the end of serfdom and feudal rents and had even established a common treasury into which all incomes and proceeds were to be deposited. With their espousal of militarism, this practice of equal distribution of wealth was abandoned and abolished. Peasant rents and dues were restored by the Taborite oligarchy, prompting Peter to attack their revised society as unchristian. The object of his criticism was both the Taborite clergy and the nobility with which it was in alliance: "Proud, greedy, carnal, and blind men who do not fear God and care nothing for the people since they do not look after the people as a shepherd cares for his flock, but the people exist only for them to serve their bellies and elevate their pride."[12]

Peter's next important tract, *On the Triple Division of Society*, was conceived and written as a further attack on the revisionism of the Taborite oligarchy and especially their deployment of Wyclif's defense of the traditional estates of Christendom to justify their reinstatement of the

---

[12] Petr Chelčický, *Drobné spisy*, ed. Eduard Petrů (Prague, 1966), 28–98.

feudal order. Peter was familiar with Wyclif's arguments from his *Dialogus*, which he had read in Jakoubek's translation.[13] His theological radicalism notwithstanding, Wyclif was rather conservative in his defense of the triple division of feudal society into clergy, the nobility, and the peasantry (those who pray, those who fight, and those who plow). The medieval feudal ideal of the tripartite society was traditionally envisioned in terms of the parts of the human body.[14] According to this corporeal metaphor, the upper parts (the head and shoulders) were equated with the clergy and nobility and the lower parts with the peasantry. Just as the head is the organ of reason, so is the Church divinely mandated to articulate and justify its supremacy through dogma and prayer. Correspondingly, the upper limbs or arms denote the nobility who fight on behalf of Holy Church, while the lower limbs designate the manual activity of the peasantry. If the medieval ideal presented this societal body as totally integrated and healthy, the various limbs cooperating for the harmonious welfare of the whole, Peter saw it as a monstrously deformed organism in which the limbs were in conflict with each other.

Peter reserves his particular animosity for the nobility who oppress the peasants in their charge: "The crooked limbs that hold the sword oppress the other, lesser limbs, afflicting them, beating them, putting them into prison, weighing them down with forced labor, rents, and other contrivances, so they go about wan and pale."[15] Far from honoring the peasants for their hard work, the nobility abuses them in vile language, referring to them as "peasant blister" ("*opar sedlský*"), "screech owl" ("*výr*"), and "churl" ("*chlap*"). The tract also singles out priests who collude with the nobility and neglect their spiritual duties for easy profit and gain. The clerical class is universally identified with the Antichrist, the monstrous offspring of the papacy, the Roman Whore of Babylon, "To whom the whore who sits on the Roman throne has given birth, freely and without pain, sitting on silken cushions, and whose lives she has established in soft effeminacy."[16] Such virulently

---

[13] Murray Wagner, *Peter Chelčický. A Radical Separatist from Hussite Bohemia* (Pennsylvania, 1983), 94–95.

[14] See Giles Constable, *Three Studies in Medieval Religious and Social Thought. The Interpretation of Mary and Martha; The Ideal of the Imitation of Christ; The Orders of Society* (Cambridge, 1995), 324.

[15] Chelčický, *Drobné spisy*, 124.

[16] Ibid., 118.

anticlerical imagery recalls later visual representations of the Antichrist in the Jena Codex (ca. 1500), where the corrupt and luxurious Papacy is contrasted with the simplicity of Christ and closely aligned both with the Antichrist and with the apocalyptic Whore of Babylon.

Peter's condemnation of the traditional tripartite vision of Christian society comports with his later, more developed assault on the Constantinian alliance of Church and state in his magnum opus *The Net of Faith* (ca. 1440–41). The main object of Peter's criticism was the so-called Donation of Constantine, a document forged in the papal chancery in the eighth century purporting to be a grant in which Constantine conceded supreme authority in the Church and unrivalled control in Italy to Pope Sylvester I (314–35). In Peter's view the enrichment of the Church had transformed her into "the Great Whore who sits on the Roman throne," the Pope no longer the Vicar of Christ but the "vicar of proud Lucifer, which will not humble itself before God and man."[17]

As usual, Peter derives his justification for this all-out assault on what he understood to be Constantinian Christianity with close reference to the New Testament. Since the time of St. Augustine, Romans 13, in which St. Paul urges his followers to submit to the authorities in power, had been used to validate the medieval partnership of Church and state. While recognizing the Pauline authenticity of this pericope, Peter sought to relativize the traditional interpretation of it by appealing to the historical and social context in which it arose. According to Peter, St. Paul wrote to advise his fellow Christians on how to deal with the secular power of the Roman Empire and did not direct his remarks to the civil authorities in order to justify their Christian dominion. His concern was to provide the Christians living under Roman rule a modus vivendi which would allow them to obey the secular power while remaining true to their private consciences. Peter's point was that such a compromise was no longer necessary if a society was a true expression of the *corpus christianum*, since there should be no distinction between pagan and Christian. Peter insisted, however, that this was precisely the dichotomy that still obtained in fifteenth-century society.

In his next treatise, *Reply to Bishop Rokycana*, Peter veers away from

---

[17] Quoted from Wagner, *Peter Chelčický*, 96–97.

the questions of secular dominion expressed in his previous work in order to address the purely theological and dogmatic issue of the Hussite right to communicate in both kinds. In fact, for late medieval people, such a distinction between the secular and the theological spheres was wholly artificial since Christ's sacred body, made manifest in the miracle of the Mass, provided the theological paradigm for the secular ordering of society. In this sense, Peter's treatise on the chalice was consistent with his previous thoughts on the triple division of society. Inevitably, Peter's reflections on the chalice go back to Wyclif's doctrine of remanence, which claimed that the bread and wine of the Mass are not annihilated but remain, supplemented rather than replaced by Christ's body and blood. Despite the charges leveled against him at Constance, Hus never subscribed to Wyclif's heresy on the sacrament of Holy Communion and upheld the orthodox view that in the Eucharist, Christ's body and blood replaced the annihilated elements and became substantially present in the Host. The principal follower of Hus after his death and the leader of the moderate Utraquist party that advocated the use of the lay chalice was Jakoubek. Not only did Jakoubek popularize the ordinance of the lay chalice throughout Bohemia, he also deviated from Hus' orthodox position on the Eucharist by promoting the doctrine of consubstantiation, the belief that Christ's body and the bread continued to coexist in the host. Jakoubek believed this theory to be wholly consistent with Wyclif's less than precise analysis of the sacrament of Holy Communion.

The more radical Taborites, led by Bishop Rokycana, appeared to reject the real presence of Christ altogether. In fact, Rokycana's position on the real presence was vague in that it could mean either figurative presence or physical presence, depending on one's point of view.[18] This relativist position was a conscious and deliberate response to political exigency since Tábor was wedged between the moderate Utraquists of Prague and the true radicals of Peter's own rural community and had to exist harmoniously alongside both. Typically, Peter was unhappy with Wyclif's doctrine of remanence, Jakoubek's consubstantialist interpretation of it, and Bishop Rokycana's relativist accommodation of all possible points of view. Peter rightly saw that the Utraquist espousal of consubstantialism and Rokycana's deliberately

[18] Ibid., 104.

vague response to it provided a theological pretext and justification for the partnership between the secular and spiritual powers. Just as the Host consists of Christ's Body and the bread, so does Christian society combine spiritual and secular agency. These conflicted ideas about the Eucharist reflected the manifold divisions within fifteenth-century Bohemian society itself. From the moderate Utraquists to the revolutionary Adamites (a breakaway sect of Taborites who went naked and treated the Eucharist as the pretext for a love feast), the interpretation of Holy Communion lay at the heart of the social and political vision of the medieval body politic. Peter was appalled by the perceived excesses of the Adamites, in particular their espousal of sexual primitivism. At the same time he deplored what he considered to be the pagan secularism of the militant Taborites. Thus his quest for a viable understanding of the Eucharist was synonymous with his attempt to define a truly Christian society dedicated to the New Testament principles of love and peace. If Peter's position lacks theological precision and amounts to what Murray Wagner has termed the dissolution into moralistic fuzziness of Wyclif's scholastic attempt to reconcile realism with universalism, such an inability to find the perfect solution to the doctrine of the Eucharist reflects his ongoing struggle to produce a blueprint of a unified and harmonious Christian society.

All these secular and theological questions combined in Peter's greatest and longest work, *The Net of Faith.* The title of this work again invokes the early Church in deriving from the Gospel of St. Luke 5: 1–11, where Christ commands his disciples to cast their net into the deep with the result that they win a great catch of fish. For Peter, the net of faith is the law of God and the catch of fish God's elect. But the net of faith has been ripped through by two enormous fish, the pope and the emperor. The poison introduced into the early Church by Constantine's acceptance of Christianity as the official faith of the empire has, according to Peter, infected every limb of the *corpus christianum.* Every social class, especially the clergy and the nobility, has succumbed to this poison and has been corrupted by secular wealth and power. Drawing upon Wyclif's *De Civili Dominio,* Peter locates the origin of this corruption in the postlapsarian myth of Cain's murder of his brother Abel. According to Wyclif, the fratricide Cain built the first city as a place to hide from God's anger and vengeance. Peter elaborated this image of the city as the site of primordial evil, citing it as the place where Cain's offspring still pursues a life of greed and violence. Cain's race invented a system of weights and measures to disguise their devious profiteering and drew boundary lines to demarcate the extent of their property and their possession of material things. Cities developed high walls to provide protection for the murderers and swindlers within.

Although Peter's antiurban animus takes its cue from Wyclif's *De Civili Dominio*, it also belongs to a long-standing tradition in medieval Czech writing of antagonism toward the city, for example, the scene at the end of the verse *Legend of Saint Prokop* where the German monks are driven back to Prague by the avenging ghost of the deceased saint. In this legend the Czech saint embodies the ideal of rural simplicity in contrast to the pride and corruption of the city represented by Prague. Peter's virulent attack on the city also anticipates *The Labyrinth of the World and the Paradise of the Heart* (1623) by the last bishop of the Bohemian Brethren, John Amos Comenius, in which the classical motif of the world as a labyrinth is conflated with the medieval image of the city as a den of vice and the home of the Antichrist.[19]

Peter's absolute rejection of violence even to resist the Catholic foe set him apart from all his co-religionists in Bohemia and led to his decision to establish his own community of followers in his home region of southern Bohemia. Peter's philosophy of nonviolence and radical separatism was accepted by his followers and became one of the fundamental doctrines of the Bohemian Brethren, a movement founded on his ideas which flourished in the fifteenth and sixteenth centuries.[20] Although the separatist ideals of the Bohemian Brethren would not survive the catastrophe of 1620 and the triumph of the Counter-Reformation, they remained alive in the diaspora and would later provide the basis of the strict separation of Church and state in the Protestant New World. If America may be said to have inherited Peter's principle of the separation of Church and state, the subordination of the former to the power of the latter enacted by the English Reformation of the sixteenth century equally looked back to Wyclif's original doctrine

---

[19] John Amos Comenius, *The Labyrinth of the World and the Paradise of the Heart*, trans. Howard Louthan and Andrea Sterk with a preface by Jan Milič Lochmann (New York, 1998).

[20] Peter Brock, *The Political and Social Doctrines of the Unity of Czech Brethren in the Fifteenth and Sixteenth Centuries* (The Hague, 1957).

of civil dominion. As Stephen Justice has recently observed: "Henry VIII's break with Rome and the Protestant agitation that followed realized many of Wyclif's ambitions. Wyclif himself was remembered less as a controversial teacher than as an exemplary figure of the past, both by the reformers who hailed him and their opponents who blamed him."[21]

It would be no exaggeration to claim that the divergent beliefs of the English theologian Wyclif and his Czech follower Chelčický formed the basis of the fundamental difference between the British and American conceptions of the relationship between Church and state. More importantly, Wyclif's influence in Bohemia has to be measured less in terms of what the English reformer actually wrote and more in terms of how his ideas affected ideals that were already present in the Bohemian tradition of reform. In many ways the vision of apostolic simplicity modeled on the example of Christ's earthly mission and the early Church had been formed well before Wyclif's works were known in Bohemia. When the Bohemian reformers read the Englishman's writings, they tended to do so from their own particular moral perspective. In Hus' case, this meant diluting Wyclif's radicalism, while in the case of Chelčický, Wyclif's teachings became the instigation for a radical separatism that the Englishman himself neither envisaged nor advocated.

Conclusion: Lollardy and Hussitism

The modification of Wyclif's radicalism in Bohemia to fit local needs may go some way to explaining the success of Hussitism. But it does not explain the whole story. It has been suggested that King Wenceslas' support for Hus was a major factor behind Hussite success, a situation that did not exist in England where Lollardy was fervently opposed by the Lancastrian regime.[22] But we should be careful not to attach too much significance to royal support for Hus and his reforms. Wenceslas was a notorious vacillator, and his active support for Hus did not continue beyond 1412. Far more significant in attempting to

---

[21] Steven Justice, "Lollardy," in *The Cambridge History of Medieval English Literature*, ed. David Wallace (Cambridge, 1999), 687.

[22] See Hudson, *The Premature Reformation*, 513.

understand why the Hussites succeeded while the Lollards failed is the fact that the Bohemian nobility had long since enjoyed far greater political autonomy than their English counterparts. The nobility had been the key player in Bohemian politics for at least a hundred years before the Hussite revolution. The first Czech-language account of Bohemian history, the *Dalimil Chronicle* (ca. 1314), was probably written by a member of the gentry or one of its sympathizers. At the end of the chronicle the anonymous author makes it clear that the newly elected king, John of Luxembourg, should comply with the policies of the lower nobility (*zemané*) or leave the realm in peace. John did not abandon his kingdom entirely but he spent a great deal of his reign abroad as an absentee landlord, leaving the affairs of state to the nobility.

In England the situation was very different. The Lancastrian kings Henry IV and Henry V were highly effective in stamping out the Lollard heresy. In Bohemia it was not simply Wenceslas' initial sympathy for the Hussite cause that allowed the movement to flourish; it was the success of Hus and his followers in harnessing the political support of the Czech gentry and nobility.[23] Following Hus' death at Constance in 1414, the nobility was mobilized to oppose the Council abroad and the king at home. The result of their activism was a twenty-year interregnum during which the state was governed by an alliance of clerics and members of the noble class; the most famous example of the latter was the military leader John Žižka of Trocnov.

Ethnicity and language also played an important role in the success of the Hussite cause. Hus adroitly exploited ethnic tensions between German and Czech speakers within and beyond the University of Prague by aligning the reformers with the Czech language. In his homilies he expresses concern for the purity of the Czech language, insisting that a Czech who has a German wife should educate his children to speak Czech and not mix the two languages. He lists certain German household terms which threaten to oust the native Slavic words, such as *haustuch* (napkin), *šorc* (apron), *knedlík* (dumpling); *trepky* (stairs), *mantlík* (coat) and so on.[24] He founded the Bethlehem Chapel

[23] See John Klassen, *The Nobility and the Making of the Hussite Revolution* (Boulder, 1978).

[24] *Výbor z české literatury doby husitské*, ed. Bohuslav Havránek et al., vol. 1 (Prague, 1963), 147. For a discussion of Hus' linguistic reforms, see Alfred Thomas, "Czech-German Relations as Reflected in Old Czech Literature," in *Medieval Frontier Societies*, ed. Robert Bartlett and Angus Mackay (Oxford, 1989), 199–215 at 214.

in the Old Town of Prague for the specific purpose of preaching in the Czech language.

Hus created what Benedict Anderson has called an "imagined community" based on linguistic and ethnic differences between the German and Czech communities.[25] Since most members of the Bohemian gentry spoke Czech rather than German, Hus encouraged them to identify their native language with the language of reform. Hus' letter to Wyche (1411) discussed earlier bears out this notion of an "imagined community." Writing to the persecuted and isolated Lollard, the Bohemian reformer paints a rosy picture of thousands of adherents clamoring for a Czech translation of Wyche's Latin epistle.

The linguistic situation in England was quite different. French was still the principal language of the English nobility, although French was gradually replaced by English as the fifteenth century progressed. Although the Lollards advocated the translation of the Bible into English, most of them were members of the middle and mercantile class. In England it was not the reformers who capitalized on the ideological potential of the vernacular: it was the authorities who used it to reinforce orthodoxy. Henry V propagated the English language for patriotic purposes to drive an ideological wedge between English and French national identities. But it was a top-down formation, whereas in Bohemia the notion of a collective based on linguistic and ethnic difference was created lower down the social ladder by an alliance of clerics and gentry. In his letter to Voksa of Valdštejn, Sir John Oldcastle praised Wenceslas as an "exemplum and mirror" in supporting the Hussite reformers. Here he was reproducing English rather than Bohemian conditions in imagining that the king was the key player in the affairs of state.[26] This misconception has also characterized some historians' perspectives on the Hussite reformation. To understand why Hussitism succeeded it is necessary to examine many interrelated factors: class, ethnicity, and language as well as the relations between the king and the church.

---

[25] Benedict Anderson, *Imagined Communities: Reflections on the Origin and Spread of Nationalism*, 2nd ed. (London, 1991).

[26] Loserth, "Über die Beziehungen," 238.

Chapter 4

"The Wycliffite Woman"

Reading Women in Fifteenth-Century Bohemia

One of the most difficult problems to be faced in reconstructing the historical role of women in the Hussite movement—and for that matter in English Lollardy—is the antifeminine and antiheretical bias of most of the sources. Not only is there relatively little extant evidence of Bohemian women assuming an active and dynamic part in the reform movement; even in those documents that have survived it becomes difficult—at times impossible—to distinguish between traditional anticlerical attitudes to women, orthodox fears of heresy in general, and the social role played by real women. Paradigmatic of this tension between representation and reality is the Czech anti-Hussite satire known as "Viklefice" ("The Wycliffite Woman"), the unique copy of which survives in an early fifteenth-century manuscript in the Třeboň Library (MS A 7, fol. 155).[1] Both the form "Viklefice" and its variant "Viklefka," which occurs several times in the same text, are derived from the proper name of John Wyclif whose works were widely disseminated in and around the University of Prague.[2] In fact, several

---

[1] *Staročeská lyrika*, ed. Jan Vilikovský (Prague, 1940), 120–22.
[2] For Wyclif's life and times, see K. B. McFarlane, *John Wyclif and the Beginnings of Nonconformity* (London, 1952).

important Wycliffite manuscripts are extant only in Prague, having been copied by Czech students at Oxford and brought back to Bohemia. By the early fifteenth century some of these works had been translated or adapted into Czech, for example, Jakoubek of Stříbro's version of the *Dialogus,* the *Trialogus,* and *De Civili Dominio,* which were translated at much the same time.[3]

Referring to another misogynistic Czech satire, "The Beguines," the editor of the text, Jan Vilikovský, states: "This (satire) is directed specifically against a certain group of women, namely those women who were trying to live a more zealous and true religious life and whose numbers increased from the time of Milíč's activities."[4] The Dominican preacher Jan Milíč of Kroměříž, mentioned here, was famous not only for his fiery sermons but also for his pastoral work among the prostitutes of the Prague Old Town. Milíč transformed one of these brothels into a religious house for women known as "Jerusalem."

In reading such texts as "The Wycliffite Woman" and "The Beguines" we must be careful not to assume that they reflect directly the social experience of real women, especially since in the latter Middle Ages the misogynistic representation of women as sinful and promiscuous becomes inseparable not only from the standard clerical antifeminine discourse of the schools but also from topical fears of heresy and heterodox discourse. So to what extent is the role played by gender in these texts simply a way for the author to talk about heresy? Why do gender and heresy become inextricably intertwined categories of representation?

In this sense, the poem "The Wycliffite Woman" can serve as a paradigm of the difficulty not only of "reading" medieval women—that is to say, of differentiating clearly between women as objects of male writing and as reading subjects in their own right—but also the prob-

---

[3] See Maurice Keen, "The Influence of Wyclif," in *Wyclif in His Times,* ed. Anthony Kenny (Oxford 1985), 127–45 (140). See also František Šmahel, "Doctor Evangelicus super omnes evangelistas: Wyclif's Fortunes in Hussite Bohemia," *Bulletin of the Institute for Historical Research* 43 (1970): 16–34 at 21.

[4] *Staročeská lyrika,* 191. For more up-to-date scholarship, see Božena Kopičková, *Historické prameny k studiu postavení ženy v české a moravské středověké společnosti* (Prague, 1991); also John Klassen, "Women and Religious Reform in Late Medieval Bohemia," *Renaissance and Reformation* 5, 4 (1981): 203–21; Jana Nechutová, "Ženy v Husově okolí. K protiženským satirám husitské doby," in *Jan Hus. Mezi epochami, národy a konfesemi,* ed. Jan Blahoslav Lášek (Prague, 1995), 68–73.

"The Wycliffite Woman" 121

lem we face in trying to distinguish between heresy and gender. It was also, I suggest, a problem for the anonymous medieval author himself: his difficulty in drawing a clear line between orthodox and heterodox discourses about women reflects his own struggle as an orthodox vernacular writer to distance himself from the growing identification of the Hussite reformers with the Czech language. Although writing in Czech had served the interests of the Church and the court for a century or more, by the early fifteenth century the vernacular had become a powerful tool in the hands of the reformers to make the Bible accessible to the ordinary laity and to propagate heterodox ideas and beliefs to a larger heterogeneous audience.

All the available Bohemian sources concerning female literacy involve men writing specifically for a female audience (such as John Hus or Thomas of Štítné) or second-hand accounts of women as readers and writers such as *Knížky* (*Little Books*), a work purportedly written in Czech by an anonymous woman defending Hus against the Antichrist.[5] Even the Latin epistles addressed to the antipope John XXIII protesting against the prohibition of Wycliffite books, traditionally ascribed to Queen Sophie, wife of Wenceslas IV, have recently been shown to be the later work of men rather than unmediated products of a female authorship.[6]

In chapter 1 we saw how royal women like Anne of Bohemia were often highly literate and had access to devotional books (including the Bible) in Latin and in the vernacular. If this traditional female literacy had a "trickle-down" effect to include female members of the nobility and the gentry, it does not necessarily follow that all these women were sympathetic to Hussitism. As we shall see, some of them, including Queen Sophie, supported Hus and his teachings. But given the evident success with which the Dominicans had used the vernacular to instill strict notions of orthodoxy into their female audience—and Anne of

---

[5] For more details of these second-hand claims, see Alfred Thomas, *Anne's Bohemia. Czech Literature and Society, 1310–1420.* Medieval Cultures at Minnesota, vol. 13. Minneapolis, 1998, 46–47.

[6] See Božena Kopičková and Anežka Vidmanová, *Listy na Husovu obranu z let 1410–1412. Konec jedné legendy?* (Prague, 1999). See also John Klassen, *Warring Maidens, Captive Wives, and Hussite Maidens. Women and Men at War and at Peace in Fifteenth-Century Bohemia* (Boulder, 1999), 260 n. 24. For a detailed discussion of Sophie's letters, see ibid., 232–33. For the Latin documents in question, see *Documenta Mag. Joannis Hus,* ed. František Palacký (Prague, 1869), 411–12, 413, 423, 424–25.

Bohemia, by all accounts was scrupulously orthodox—we must be careful not to assume that female access to vernacular texts immediately implicated all women in the reform movement. As we shall see in our close reading of "The Wycliffite Woman," authorial anxieties about women reading the Bible without proper supervision may actually reflect the Dominican practice of using the vernacular to steer lay women from the temptation of heresy just as much as the Hussite practice of "seducing" women in the name of reform.

The widespread assumption that Bohemian women were innately drawn to Hussite teachings is supported less by contemporary sources than by modern assumptions about the Hussite movement. One can trace it from the nineteenth-century writings of František Palacký through T. G. Masaryk's influential view that the true meaning of Czech history has been its unchanging commitment to the humanist values of truth, tolerance, and democracy. Typical of this approach is Anna Císařová–Kolářová's pioneering study *Woman in the Hussite Movement* (1915). Most recently, John Klassen has argued that medieval Czech women identified in their words and deeds with the mythic models provided by the ancient legends of Libuše, Vlasta, and the Bohemian Maidens.[7] If Císařová–Kolářová's study reflects the late nineteenth- and early twentieth-century Czech nationalist movement— and especially women's perceived role within it—Klassen's view of Czech medieval women as self-assertive seems to me to be redolent of North American 1970s feminism, which places an emphasis on women's neglected and positive experiences. My own approach does not claim to assume an ideologically neutral position but proceeds from a later model of feminism, one which acknowledges that women's frequent lack of cultural participation represents as significant and legitimate a subject of scholarly enquiry as their positive contribution to human culture.

I shall be arguing, therefore, that a close attention to the medieval sources suggests that the situation of women in medieval Bohemia was altogether more complicated than we have often assumed and that it is not so easy to generalize about women's role as autonomous readers of "unofficial" literature. For one thing, what did "literacy" actu-

---

[7] Anna Císařová–Kolářová, *Žena v hustiském hnutí* (Prague, 1915); Klassen, *Warring Maidens*.

ally amount to in a premodern culture in which private reading was far less common than group listening, and group listening less common than "visual literacy"? As in England at about the same time, it seems that the majority of Bohemian women were ignorant of Latin, largely accustomed to listening (whether in large or small groups) rather than reading alone, and were strongly attracted to the traditional veneration of holy images, an orthodox practice that Hus himself approved of and advocated for those who could not read.[8] Moreover, the Hussites certainly did not possess a monopoly on writing and preaching for the female laity. The Bohemian Dominicans, historically linked with the *studium generale* even before the official foundation of the University of Prague in 1347, had been writing specifically for women (whether as nuns or as the laity, in Latin and the vernacular) since the thirteenth century and continued to do so until the Hussite wars put an end to their activities.

Before addressing such questions in detail, I provide a literal translation of "The Wycliffite Woman" with a rhymed version in the appendix.

"The Wycliffite Woman": Text

It happened once upon a time,
Perhaps on such a holiday as this,
That a Wycliffite Woman
Invited a young lad to her house,
Wishing to teach him the true faith.   5
She said: "For Jesus' sake,
Come to me very quietly!
I wish to teach you the faith,
And if you want to listen,
I will reveal the Scriptures to you.   10

---

[8] Jan Hus, *Expositio decalogi,* in *Spisy M. Jana Husa,* ed. Václav Flajšhans (Prague, 1903), 110. It is worth citing the account (albeit mediated through satirical male writing) of peasant women dropping to their knees and kissing the holy images of the cleric in *The Dispute between the Groom and the Scholar* (ca. 1380), in *Staročeské satiry Hradeckého rukopisu a Smilovy školy,* ed. Josef Hrabák (Prague, 1962), 122 (lines 255–62). See also Thomas, *Anne's Bohemia,* 146. For the importance of nonscriptural religion to lower-class woman in England, see Shannon McSheffrey, *Gender and Heresy: Women and Men in Lollard Communities, 1420–1530* (Philadelphia, 1995), 138. For the problem of defining "reading" in the later Middle Ages, see Joyce Coleman, *Public Reading and the Reading Public in Late Medieval England and France* (Cambridge, 1996).

The lad answered the Wycliffite Woman
And looked at her lovingly,
Saying: "I am glad to do all
If you wish to teach me
And join your order.   15
The Wycliffite said: "Look at me,
My young lad, come to me
When all is still,
When no one is about and
I'll reveal the Holy Scriptures.   20
Without delay the lad
Did as she commanded.
After dinner on Sunday,
When the time was right,
He came to her quietly.   25
Eagerly the woman said:
"Welcome, my dear guest,
Whom I have so long desired,
For whom my soul has yearned!
Please come in,   30
And sit with me for a while.
I wish to expostulate on the Scriptures,
And also the reading of the Bible.
You will find plenty
To keep you busy."   35
Here the hag laid out
Two chapters of the Bible,
Pretty and very round;
They were like pears
And also very white.   40
The lad said without fear:
"Give them here, my dear.
He began to examine the Bible
And interpret the chapters
From evening till dawn.   45
And when it began to grow light,
The lad was about to leave.
But the Wycliffite grabbed him

And said: "you must stay
And perform matins with me."   50
They began to sing a Te Deum
As befits that court.
. . . .
and started to descant.   55
When they had finished the morning mass,
They embraced each other nicely
In God's love and grace.
There was no anger
That I could detect.   60
Well, you young lads,
And you fair pages,
Who wish to join the order,
You must ask the Beguines
And learn from them.   65
They are versed in the Gospels,
The Book of Kings and Solomon,
And the Psalms of David
More than most priests.
You should serve them gladly.   70
They have sweet expositions,
Complete, and without fault.
Whoever lets himself be used by them
Will be very happy.
God grant them success!   75

"The Wycliffite Woman": Context

"The Wycliffite Woman" was composed in a society in which orthodoxy was increasingly on the defensive and heresy in the ascendancy. In distinction to the early years of Lancastrian rule in England, the situation in Bohemia was highly unstable. After the king's death in 1419, churches were sacked and razed to the ground, and monasteries plundered, while clerics—both secular and monastic—lost their livelihoods and sometimes even their lives. A Czech poem titled "Lamenting to Heaven," extant in a manuscript from the Rajhrad Monastery, expresses this situation very forcibly and eloquently.[9] Written from the standpoint of a dispossessed cleric (perhaps a monk of the Rajhrad Monastery itself), this text utilizes the genre of complaint literature to show how Catholics had become outsiders, their parishes robbed and burnt down by "Wycliffites" ("*Viklefuov*") (line 5). The anonymous author reserves special censure for those women who have led men to adopt such heretical ideas in the first place (45–46) and likens their seduction to Eve's temptation of Adam in the Garden of Eden (49–50).

"The Wycliffite Woman" belongs to the same tradition of blaming women for a bad political situation. However, it is more ingenious and witty than "Lamenting to Heaven" in assuming the form of a mock-courtly *alba* (dawn poem) in which a female follower of the English reformer lures a young squire to her house under cover of darkness in order to seduce him with vernacular readings from the Scriptures. Cleverly subverting the *loci communes* of the *alba* in which the lover secretly visits his lady at sunset and leaves her shortly before dawn, the satire consists of a series of skilful double-entendres which equate lay learning with female promiscuity and illicit scriptural readings with casual sex. The anonymous author is here conflating and popularizing two genres which were especially prominent in fourteenth- and early fifteenth-century Latin and vernacular rhymed verse: the antifeminine satire, exemplified by the poem "Beguines," and the *alba* such as the Czech "Dear Radiant Day."[10] Our anonymous author's familiarity with the conventions of the *alba* is evident from formulaic lines such as "you should serve them gladly" (line 70) as well as its dialogic alternation between a woman and a student which parodies the Bohemian-Latin lyric "Filia, si vox tua" and its Czech variant "Dear Student" in which a virgin (*virgo*) and a cleric (*clericus*) express their illicit love for each other.[11]

In the course of the poem, the female follower of Wyclif assumes the false role of preacher and priest, displaying her lovely breasts in a gesture reminiscent of the sacerdotal ritual of revealing the open Gospels or raising the host to the congregation during the celebration of the

---

[9] Jan Vilikovský, *Staročeská lyrika* (Prague, 1940), 123–24.
[10] Ibid., 118–19, 58–60.
[11] Ibid., 68–69 (for the text of the poem) and 83–84 (for information about the manuscript and the Latin source).

Mass. To all intents and purposes, then, the poem would appear to be an antifeminine satire on the audacious desire of religious women to usurp the roles of preacher and priest. These functions had been denied them by St. Paul himself, and the denial had been given elaborate doctrinal justification in Catholic writings dating back to Peter Lombard's *Libri Sententiarum*, which around 1223–27 had been established as the dominant textbook in the Parisian faculty of theology and soon attained a canonical status at other universities, including the University of Prague.[12] Like those writings, our satire draws upon an equally long-standing association of erroneous teachings with the sinful snares of the female body and of female preaching with prostitution, which culminated in orthodox polemics against the Waldensian heresy of the twelfth and thirteenth centuries.[13]

The connection between women and heresy became particularly acute in late fourteenth- and early fifteenth-century Bohemia and England, where women were frequently associated by the authorities with the desire to preach and even to usurp the role of the Church hierarchy, as the official deposition of the Lollard Walter Brut in October 1393 and Margery Kempe's trial and detention at Leicester on charges of heresy in 1417 make clear.[14] The traditional association between

---

[12] See A. J. Minnis, "De impedimento sexus: Women's Bodies and Medieval Impediments to Sexual Ordination," in *Medieval Theology and the Natural Body*, ed. Peter Biller and A. J. Minnis, York Studies in Medieval Theology, 1 (York, 1997), 109–39 at 110ff.

[13] See Beverly Mayne Kienze, "The Prostitute-Preacher: Patterns of Polemic against Medieval Waldensian Women Preachers," in *Women Preachers and Prophets through Two Millennia of Christianity*, ed. Beverly Mayne Kienzle and Pamela J. Walker (Berkeley, 1998), 99–113.

[14] For Brut's ideas on women, see Fiona Somerset, "*Eciam mulier:* Women in Lollardy and the Problem of Sources," in *Voices in Dialogue. Reading Women in the Middle Ages*, ed. Linda Olson and Kathryn Kerby-Fulton (Notre Dame, 2005), 245–60, and Alastair Minnis, "'Respondet Walterus Bryth . . .': Walter Brut in Debate on Women Priests," in *Text and Controversy from Wyclif to Bale. Essays in Honour of Anne Hudson*, ed. Helen Barr and Ann M. Hutchinson, Medieval Church Studies, 4 (Turnhout, 2005), 229–49. For Brut's other ideas, see David Aers, "Walter Brut's Theology of the Sacrament of the Altar," in *Lollards and Their Influence in Late Medieval England*, ed. Fiona Somerset, Jill C. Havens, and Derrick G. Pitard (Woodbridge, 2003), 115–26. For accusations of Lollardy against Margery Kempe, see *The Book of Margery Kempe*, ed. Barry Windeatt (Harlow, 2000), 23–24. For Brut's deposition, see Margaret Aston, *Lollards and Reformers: Literacy and Imagery in Late Medieval England* (London, 1984), 52, and *Woman Defamed and Woman Defended. An Anthology of Medieval Texts*, ed. Alcuin Blamires (Oxford, 1992), 250–60.

women and heresy has its origins in the biblical myth of the Garden of Eden in which Eve attracts Adam with the forbidden fruit of the Tree of Knowledge, a detail that finds an explicit parallel in the pear-like breasts which the Wycliffite Woman offers to the young lad. Complicating this assessment of the Czech poem as a standard antifeminine and antiheretical tract tout court is the deployment of the love lyric as the vehicle of the satirical humor. If the Wycliffite Woman's active agency as a seducer of men and as a reader of the Bible is a parodic reversal of normative gender behavior, it equally inverts the passive status of the lady expecting the arrival of her lover in the dawn poem. Although she awaits the young man at home, it is made clear at the opening of the poem that the Wycliffite Woman instigates the visit. Reinforcing the visitor's naiveté is the frequent attestation of the term *panic* (young unmarried lord) to describe him. The same word is used by the female speaker in the Czech religious lyric "A Bundle of Myrrh"—a paraphrase of chapter 3 of the Song of Songs—to refer to the beloved whom she seeks at midnight (line 27). Here the female speaker of the poem is identified with the Soul in quest of the Bridegroom Christ:

> Arising I will go and seek him,
> I will ask for him for whom my heart faints,
> Saying: beloved,
> My love,
> Show me your face, little falcon.[15]

Another source of parody are eucharistic or elevation prayers welcoming Christ's immanence in the Host, for example, the Czech "Prayer of Kunigunde":

> Welcome, almighty king,
> In all places all-seeing
> All penitents loving,
> Eternal life giving![16]

---

[15] Vilikovský, *Staročeská lyrika*, 144.
[16] *Nejstarší česká duchovní lyrika*, ed. Antonín Škarka (Prague, 1949), 76.

This formulaic invocation is clearly parodied when the Wycliffite Woman welcomes her guest to her home:

> Welcome, my dear guest,
> whom I have so long desired,
> For whom my soul has yearned!

The popularity of religious parody in fifteenth-century Bohemia was not restricted to vernacular writings. The list of names enumerating Christ's descent from King David at the beginning of the Gospel of St. Matthew is parodied in an anti-Hussite Latin satire from the early fifteenth century known as *The Wycliffite Mass* which was actually performed in church and begins with the words "Liber maledictionis omnium haereticorum, filiorum diaboli, filiorum Wiklef" and continues: "Wiklef autem genuit Joannem Hus in Bohemia, Joannes Hus genuit Corandam, Coranda genuit Capkonem."[17] The list goes on to name the most prominent academic followers of the Hussite heresy in Bohemia and concludes with regret that the errors have now spread from the literati (those with a knowledge of Latin) to the laity and with the hope that their eyes will be illuminated with the truth.[18]

Although religious parody was meant to generate a humorous reaction, it also signals considerable anxiety about the dangerous proximity of orthodoxy to heresy in early fifteenth-century Bohemia. As we shall see, by the end of the fourteenth century orthodox writers both in England and Bohemia had become so attentive to the spiritual needs of the laity by providing vernacular translations of sacred texts (albeit carefully glossed by the doctors) that they risked losing control of their audience altogether. In this sense, the relationship between orthodox and heterodox discourses become increasingly hard to differentiate, especially in Bohemia where, before Hus' condemnation and execution at Constance, the reform movement was far less radical than it subsequently became. The real threat posed by Hus and his followers to the ecclesiastical authorities was his skill in appropriating official

---

[17] For the Latin text of the so-called Younger Wycliffite Mass, see František Palacký, *Urkundliche Beiträge zur Geschichte des Hussitenkrieges*, vol. 2 (Prague, 1873), 521–22. For secondary literature, see Zdeněk Nejedlý, *Dějiny husitského zpěvu*, 2d. ed., vol. 3 (Prague, 1955), 369–74.

[18] Palacký, *Urkundliche Beiträge*, 522.

discourses and practices in the service of a dissenting, vernacular-reading laity. It is this anxiety which animates "The Wycliffite Woman" and other misogynistic satires of the day. Such fears of the laity usurping the authority of the Church are personified by the Wycliffite Woman assuming the active role of the priest in the Mass, and, by implication, the authority of Christ himself. This suggestion is reinforced by the fact that the "service" she performs takes place on a Sunday.

It is because she appears to usurp the authority of Christ and his Church in this way that the Wycliffite Woman is synonymous with the name of Wyclif, which had become a byword in Bohemia for heretical teachings on a whole range of doctrinal issues from the sacramental problem of the Eucharist to the disputed authority of the pope and his bishops. The poem's conflation of Wyclif's reputation for heretical teachings and the conventional association of wayward women with sexual promiscuity is, of course, part of its satirical *pointe* in equating old ideas about gender with new ideas about heresy. By the early fifteenth century Wycliffism and Hussitism had become more or less synonymous in Bohemia. Moreover, Hus seems to have taken a special interest in the spiritual welfare of his female congregation. While in exile from Prague in 1412 he actually wrote a work in Czech specifically for his female followers at the Bethlehem Chapel, Dcerka (*The Daughter*), so named since each of its ten chapters begins with the words of the bridal passage from Psalm 44:11 "Audi filia" ("Listen, my daughter"): "Listen, my daughter, hear my words: forget your own people and your father's house; / And, when the king desires your beauty, remember that he is your lord."[19] The wording of the psalm is significant here in inviting the female addressee to forget her family and prepare herself for her impending marriage. In the same way, Hus' tract addresses the daughters of the Bohemian gentry and aristocracy who had left their fathers' households and chosen to live together in the service of their celestial husband, Christ.

The reference in the psalm to the king desiring the daughter's beauty inevitably recalls the erotic content of "The Wycliffite Woman," thus reinforcing its topicality as an antiheretical satire. More significant

---

[19] *Biblia Sacra Vulgata*, ed. Robert Weber (Stuttgart, 1969), 825. For the Czech text of *The Daughter*, see Jan Hus, *Sebrané spisy české*, ed. Karel Jaromír Erben, vol. 3 (Prague, 1868), 104–30.

still is the fact that Hus' invocation of Psalm 44 was not original at all but derived from orthodox discourse. The biblical verses with which he begins his treatise were familiar from the liturgy for the Assumption of the Blessed Virgin Mary and also evoked the Presentation of the Virgin in the Temple, the archetypal scene of monastic enclosure for women. A good visual example of the latter is the *Buch der Ersetzung* by the fifteenth-century German Dominican Johannes Meyer, which was transcribed and illustrated by nuns at the Dominican Katharinenkloster in Nuremberg shortly after 1455.[20] The full-page drawing of the friar high in his pulpit and the enclosed sisters in miniature below him in many ways parallels the familiar image from the Jena Codex of Hus preaching to the laity at the Bethlehem Chapel, a manuscript compiled about fifty years later than the *Buch der Ersetzung*. The important point here is that Hus' use of the verses from the "Audi filia" does not offer a unique or unprecedented case of writing for women but partakes of a long-standing orthodox tradition. The language of initiation into monastic enclosure has simply been appropriated for the needs of the laity. This would explain the ironic reference in "The Wycliffite Woman" to the young man's desire to join the lady's "order" (*zákon*) (line 19).[21]

Although the Hussite appropriation of monastic and liturgical discourse in the interest of reform is being mocked in "The Wycliffite Woman," the proximity between monastic and lay experience it presupposes must have caused considerable alarm for the Church authorities, since the heretics were seen to be stealing the initiative in appealing to the laity with the language of traditional devotion. This was a particular concern for the Dominicans, one of whose principal aims since the foundation of their order was to wrest female members of the urban laity from the clutches of heretical preaching and bring them back into the orthodox fold. Particularly after the Decree of Kutná Hora (1409), when the *nacio bohemica* achieved a majority vote in the administration of the University of Prague and most German masters and students left the city, the Czech nominalists who remained

---

[20] See Jeffrey F. Hamburger, *The Visual and the Visionary: Art and Female Spirituality in Late Medieval Germany* (New York, 1998), 19–21.

[21] Compare also the use of same word in connection with women in line 46 of "Lamenting to Heaven."

would have felt highly vulnerable and isolated among their Wycliffite opponents.[22]

In Bohemia Wyclif was perceived as an advocate of the use of the vernacular, probably because of the so-called Wycliffite Bible. As Anne Hudson reminds us, it was Hus who made the claim that Wyclif translated the whole Bible into English (*per Anglicos dicitur*), although the assertion was rarely made by Wyclif's own countrymen.[23] The irony inherent in this perception was that Wyclif and his Lollard followers had identified the use of the vernacular with Queen Anne's Bohemia. The anonymous poet of "The Wycliffite Woman" was probably equating the name of Wyclif not only with dangerous heretical ideas but also with the reading of the vernacular Bible. Having enticed the squire to her house, the Wycliffite Lady refers specifically to reading the Bible in line 33.

To what extent was this fear of women reading and disputing Holy Scripture an imaginary anxiety on the part of men in authority and to what extent was it rooted in social practice? As we have seen, anxieties about female readership are virtually inseparable from orthodox attempts to control lay knowledge of the Bible. By the end of the fourteenth century, lay access to the Bible and other religious works was no longer limited to a small minority of noble initiates, although royal patronage may have set the reformist wheels in motion. In his *De Triplici Vinculo Amoris,* Wyclif cites the example of Anne of Bohemia, who allegedly owned copies of the New Testament in Latin, German, and Czech, to justify a translation of the Vulgate into English for the benefit of the English laity.[24] French Dominicans translated the greater part of the Old Testament for King John the Good in 1384 and in 1390 a new German Bible was prepared for Anne's brother, King Wenceslas of Bohemia.[25]

---

[22] The standard study of this event is Ferdinand Seibt, "Johannes Hus und der Abzug der deutschen Studenten aus Prag 1409," in *Hussitenstudien. Personen, Ereignisse, Ideen einer frühen Revolution,* Veröffentlichungen des Collegium Carolinum, 60 (Munich 1987), 1–15.

[23] Anne Hudson, "Wyclif and the English Language," in Kenny, *Wyclif in His Times*, 85–103 at 87.

[24] For relevant bibliographical data on Wyclif's claim, see Anne Hudson, *The Premature Reformation: Wycliffite Texts and Lollard History* (Oxford, 1988), 30 and n. 127. For its exploitation by Lollard propagandists, see ibid., 248–49.

[25] Margaret Deanesly, *A History of the Medieval Church 590–1500* (London, 1994), 225.

It is a peculiar irony that it was those quintessential guardians of orthodoxy, the Dominicans, who were so active in translating the Bible into the vernacular in late medieval France and Bohemia for the benefit of a lay readership, even though this audience was highly circumscribed and limited to royal circles. The inevitable consequence of John the Good of France and Wenceslas and Anne of Bohemia having access to the Holy Scriptures in French, German, and Czech was a clamor for vernacular translations of the Bible to be made available to the laity regardless of royal birth. This is, of course, precisely what happened in England when Lollard propagandists claimed the otherwise orthodox Anne of Bohemia as a major precedent for their own desire for an English Bible.

In Bohemia this aspiration became a reality with more far-reaching consequences for societal transformation. Whereas in England the Wycliffite Bible went underground after the prohibition of English translations of the Scriptures, in Bohemia the Czech Bible was read openly and by all classes of society. Many of these lay people were aristocratic ladies such as Agnes, daughter of the prolific lay writer and nobleman Thomas of Štítné, who translated devotional works from Latin for the benefit of his family and his immediate circle in the south of Bohemia. In 1401 Agnes left her provincial home and went to live in Prague where she became a frequent visitor to the Bethlehem Chapel, founded in 1393 for the purpose of preaching in the Czech language. Other female adherents of the Bethlehem Chapel were Eliška Kravař, the wife of Jindřich of Rožmberk; Anna of Mochov, wife of Jan of Kamenice the Younger; Anna of Frimburk, the wife of the royal Master of the Mint, Peter Zmrzlík of Svojšín; and the wives of Jindřich Škopek of Dubá, Jan of Chlum, and Jindřich Lefl of Lazaň.[26]

That these noblewomen were as bold and as forthright as the Wycliffite Woman is doubtful. Certainly, there is little evidence to support the claim in either England or Bohemia that women were instrumental in the religious instruction of men. It is more likely that Bohemian and English women—whether orthodox or reform-minded, aristocratic like Agnes of Štítné or middle-class like Margery Kempe—

---

[26] See Alfred Thomas, "Women Readers and Writers in Medieval and Early Modern Bohemia," in *A History of Central European Women's Writing*, ed. Celia Hawkesworth (London, 2001), 7–13 at 10.

played a largely passive role in Hussite and Lollard circles. Even though Margery Kempe was illiterate and had to be read to by her orthodox confessors, her ostentatious and assertive piety was enough to arouse the suspicion of the laity and churchmen alike. The situation for women in Hussite Bohemia was not so very different. As in so much else, Hus himself was conservative in his view of women. Before leaving for Constance he wrote a letter to Martin of Volyně to be opened only in the event of the master's death. In it he exhorts Martin to avoid consorting with women and to be cautious while hearing the confession of women lest he be beguiled by their hypocrisy. Claiming to cite St. Augustine, but in fact quoting from a letter from Pope Alexander III to the Archbishop of Canterbury, Hus affirms of women's piety: "Do not believe female devotion; for the more devout, the more lascivious it is, and under the pretext of piety it conceals the birdlime of concupiscence."[27]

These alleged female attributes—lasciviousness, hypocrisy, false piety—are precisely the negative characteristics attributed to the Wycliffite Woman. Hus' view of women is here indistinguishable from the orthodox picture presented by the author of the pro-Catholic satire. The same antifeminine sentiment is found in the literature favored by many of Hus' aristocratic followers. As mentioned in chapter 2, the Hussite courtier Peter Zmrzlík of Svojšín commissioned a Czech translation of Guido de Colonne's Trojan chronicle which reproduces all of the Latin author's aphorisms on the evil of women. Such antifeminine literature contrasts with courtly works such as the Czech *Life of Saint Catherine,* which emphasizes women's high intelligence, erudition, and holiness. There seems to be a correlation here between the intensification of antifeminine discourse in the Hussite period and the polarization of religious discord in the society at large. The same is true of Lancastrian England compared with the preceding Ricardian period. In contrast to Chaucer's pro-feminine *Troilus and Criseyde* and *Legend of Good Women,* which arose in the context of a court presided over by Richard and Anne, John Lydgate's *Troy Book* not only returns to the antifeminine animus of pre-Ricardian culture; it also coincides with a new climate marked by hostility to all forms of religious dissent.

[27] Matthew Spinka, *John Hus at the Council of Constance* (New York, 1965), 95.

Another way in which gender is inseparable from questions of faith in the later Middle Ages is the deployment of the myth of Pope Joan on both sides of the religious divide. Hus follows Wyclif in using this myth to turn the tables on the Catholic Church by equating Joan's deception with the deceit of the established Church. At his trial Hus invokes the example of Joan (or Agnes as he calls her) to defend his treatise *De Ecclesia*. Hus was accused of claiming in chapter 13 of this work that the pope was simply the head of a particular, rather than the universal, church unless his supremacy was predestined by God. Hus confirmed his position with the following argument: "This is clear because otherwise the Christian faith would be perverted and a Christian would have to believe a lie. For the Church was deceived in the case of Agnes."[28] In spite of the equation of Joan with the established Church, Hus paradoxically aligns himself with the misogynist discourse of orthodox teaching.

That Hus' female supporters played a less active role than their orthodox contemporaries (and modern scholars) have attributed to them tells us as much about traditional views of women on both sides of the religious divide as it does about the actual status of female Hussites. After all, the association of preaching with prostitution, as personified by Mary Magdalene who allegedly preached of Christ's resurrection to his disciples, was itself a product of traditional Catholic teaching.[29] Ironically, it was the most fervently antiheretical spokesmen of this tradition, the Dominican friars, who idealized the Magdalene as the *apostolorum apostola* in one breath and excoriated women preachers in the next. And it is worth remembering that the pre-Hussite preacher Milíč, who was so involved with the spiritual welfare of prostitutes in the Prague Old Town, was also a member of the Dominican Order.

In his *De eruditione praedicatorum*, the Dominican sermon-writer Humbert of Romans (d. 1277) provides four reasons why women should not preach, one of them being that, in doing so, they provoke lust. Seen in this light, the scene of seduction played out between the male virgin and the Wycliffite Woman may be regarded as a fantasy originating in the male clerical imagination. Since many Czech texts of

---

[28] Quoted from Alain Boureau, *The Myth of Pope Joan*, trans. Lydia G. Cochrane (Chicago, 2001), 157–58.

[29] See Katherine Ludwig Jansen, "Maria Magdalena: Apostolorum Apostola," in Kienzle and Walker, *Women Preachers and Prophets*, 57–96.

orthodox devotion had been written by Dominicans in the fourteenth century—including the parable of Christ-as-Knight (*De strenuo milite*) by the court theologian Kolda of Koldice—it is possible that "The Wycliffite Woman" is also the work of a friar-preacher concerned to reach a broader lay audience by writing in the vernacular.

By the late fourteenth and early fifteenth centuries, as Anne Hudson has shown with respect to English at this period, writing in the vernacular was becoming the most effective way for the Church to attract the support of the laity in the struggle against the heretical ideas of the Lollards.[30] Among such devotional works are Nicholas Love's *Mirror of the Blessed Jesus Christ*, a loose adaptation of the pseudo-Bonaventuran *Meditationes Vitae Christi*, which was officially endorsed by Archbishop Arundel for use against the Lollard movement; and the Middle English Pseudo-Augustinian *Soliloquies* (dated between 1365 and 1425) which has an anti-Wycliffite commentary attached to it.[31]

Yet even orthodox works that purport to ignore Wycliffite ideas altogether sometimes seem to blur the distinction between orthodox and heterodox discourses. One such example is the late fourteenth-century Middle English *Book to a Mother*, which, in the words of Anne Clark Bartlett and Thomas Bestul, "weaves together strands of virulent clerical antifeminism against a generous, even remarkable validation of the female intellect."[32] It is at such moments that this scrupulously orthodox text begins to read like an apology for women's right to read the Bible: "And you can better learn Holy Writ than can any Master of Divinity who loves God less than you do; for whoever loves God best understands Holy Writ best."[33] When the Wycliffite Woman lures the young lord to her house, it is precisely this privileged female access to the ultimate understanding of Holy Writ that she repeatedly invokes in lines 10, 20, and 31. By giving voice to these aspirations in the vernacular, the satire risks undermining its own orthodox project by implanting the very heterodox ideas it wishes to eradicate.

---

[30] Anne Hudson, "*Laicus litteratus:* the Paradox of Lollardy," in *Heresy and Literacy, 1000–1530,* ed. Peter Biller and Anne Hudson, Cambridge Studies in Medieval Literature, 23 (Cambridge, 1994), 222–36 at 234–35.

[31] For a commentary on and English translation of this text, see *Cultures of Piety. Medieval English Devotional Literature in Translation,* ed. Anne Clark Bartlett and Thomas H. Bestul (Ithaca, 1999), 41–63.

[32] Ibid., 8.

[33] *Book to a Mother,* ed. Adrian James McCarthy, Studies in the Middle English Mystics, vol. 1 (Salzburg, 1981), 39.

Another way in which orthodox and heterodox discourses become dangerously indistinguishable in "The Wycliffite Woman" is the setting of the lady's home as a secret place to hold illicit services and as a house of ill repute. By 1415 there were at least eighteen lay houses in Prague where Beguines gathered together for a life of prayer and good works.[34] My concern here is less heterodox practice than heterodox discourse: what interests me is not so much where women practiced their beliefs as where and how they were perceived to do so in the writings of the time. As the Czech satire "The Beguines" makes clear, such women were held in great suspicion by orthodox writers and were believed to be readers of the vernacular Bible, an association that dates back to the early fourteenth century when the Beghards and Beguines of Languedoc and Catalonia were exposed to works written in the local languages of those regions.[35] The author of this satire makes the point that these women are argumentative and gossipy, and have no Latin.

Suspicion of such lay gatherings to discuss religious texts is also characteristic of official writing in England. Rita Copeland cites the example of the register of Henry Wakefield, bishop of Worcester (1375–95), which lists the case of the Norwich Lollard Margery Baxter who allegedly invited her neighbor Joan Cliffland and Joan's maidservant to come "secretly and by night into the chamber of the said Margery" where her husband would read the law of Christ under the safe cover of darkness.[36] As with "The Wycliffite Woman," it is difficult to state where actual Lollard practice ends and orthodox fantasies about such practices begin.

The equation of heretical women with secret meetings reminds us of "The Wycliffite Woman" when the host insists that the lord come to her house "very quietly" (line 7) and after dark when no one is around (lines 16–18). Here there is a convergence not only between female gossip and secretive heretics but also between these categories and the orthodox practice of priests hearing confession. Ironically, the Wycliffite Woman's secretive invitation to the young lord bears an uncomfort-

---

[34] See John Klassen, "Women and Religious Reform in Late Medieval Bohemia," *Renaissance and Reformation* 5/4 (1981): 203–21 at 205.

[35] Robert E. Lerner, "Writing and Resistance among Beguins of Languedoc and Catalonia," in Biller and Hudson eds., *Heresy and Literacy*, 186–204.

[36] See Rita Copeland, *Pedagogy, Intellectuals, and Dissent in the Later Middle Ages. Lollardy and Ideas of Learning* (Cambridge, 2001), 12.

able resemblance to the sinner going to church to make confession. As Karma Lochrie states, "Confession and gossip are closer in nature than the medieval church would have liked, in spite of the elaborate system of regulations it devised for the sacrament following the Fourth Lateran Council."[37]

When Agnes of Štítné moved to Prague in the fall of 1401, she also established a household next to the Bethlehem Chapel for herself and other unmarried young ladies. However, the idea of worshiping and reading religious texts in a private domestic space was hardly initiated by such women. In early fifteenth-century Bohemia there was no need for the reformers to conceal their beliefs at night behind closed doors, as the frequent attendance of Agnes of Štítné and her lay sisters at the Bethlehem Chapel demonstrates. In fact, the idea of worshiping in secret has its origins in Christ's injunction in the Sermon on the Mount (Matthew 6:6): "But when you pray, go into a room by yourself, shut the door, and pray to your Father who is there in the secret place; and your Father who sees what is secret will reward you."[38] This scriptural precedent became a convention of the most orthodox saints' lives. For example, the fourteenth-century Czech *Life of Saint Catherine*, a text scrupulously orthodox in tone and content, depicts the virgin-martyr locking herself into her private chamber and praying before an image of the Virgin Mary and the Christ child at the instigation of her hermit-counselor: "This is a painting of the young Lord, whom I told you about with His mother. Take the picture and go home with your mother. When you are in your room lock yourself in and kneel humbly before this picture, raise your eyes to heaven and earnestly request this dear lovely, most radiant and gracious virgin to reveal her son to you."[39] Having complied with the hermit's advice, Catherine weeps copiously before the image in her chamber and eventually falls asleep, whereupon she has a vision of her celestial Bridegroom, Jesus, who is described as a "beautiful" courtly lover and who sings to her "in an appealing, sweet, precious voice":[40] "Welcome, my most precious one! Welcome, my lovely bride! Come here to me, little face that I have cho-

---

[37] See Karma Lochrie, *Covert Operations. The Medieval Uses of Secrecy* (Philadelphia, 1999), 56.
[38] *Biblia Sacra Vulgata*, 1533.
[39] Thomas Head, *Medieval Hagiography. An Anthology* (New York, 2000), 773.
[40] Ibid., 775.

sen, my dear little dove."[41] This feminized description of Jesus and his sung epithalamium (with its obvious echo of the Song of Songs) recalls the portrayal and greeting of the Wycliffite Woman. In this sense, the entire poem can be seen as a parodic inversion of the traditional monastic ritual of enclosure, with the Wycliffite Woman playing the part of the celestial Bridegroom and her young visitor cast in the role of the *sponsa Christi*.

Another way in which "The Wycliffite Woman" expresses clerical anxiety is the spectral threat of the "priest's wife," the repressed tradition of the early Church of allowing priests to marry. Significant in this connection is the fact that the term *Viklefka* (used twice, in lines 11 and 16) can be translated not only as the "Wycliffite Woman" but also as "Wyclif's wife." Dyan Elliott has discussed how the desire of the Church during the eleventh century to broaden the gap between the clergy and the laity resulted in the "erasure of the female," a process whereby sacerdotal wives were banished to the margins of society.[42] Elliott goes on to show how subsequent *vitae* of married saints struggled to discredit their spouses. In some cases, priests' wives were elided altogether, a good example being the fourteenth-century Czech prose *Life of Saint Prokop*, the work of an anonymous Dominican friar writing at the behest of Emperor Charles IV. The historical Prokop, founder and abbot of the Monastery of St. John and the Virgin Mary on the Sázava River, had been a married nobleman with a son. All of these aspects are excluded in the prose account of his life with the saint emerging as a poor celibate preacher, an ideal role model for the mendicant orders. However, the prereformist verse life of the same saint, written around the middle of the fourteenth century, includes a direct reference to the abbot's son and thus tacitly alludes to his marital status.

In early fifteenth-century Bohemia and England there was increasing clamor in reformist circles for the reinstatement of married clergy. The Wycliffite Woman can be seen as an embodiment of this clamor as well as a reincarnation of ancient ecclesiastical fears for the preservation of the priest's unique authority over—and superiority to—the laity. As Dyan Elliott has persuasively argued, the repressed motif of

[41] Ibid.
[42] See Dyan Elliott, *Fallen Bodies. Pollution, Sexuality, and Demonology in the Middle Ages* (Philadelphia, 1999), 80–85.

the "priest's wife" returned to haunt the late medieval Church in the Freudian "splitting" of women into good and bad polarities.[43] The good imago was personified as the Virgin Mary while the bad imago became increasingly identified with the female desecrator or thief of the Host, a denigrated role that was often conflated with the misconduct of witches and Jews.

We see a crucial example of this female splitting in the representation of the Wycliffite Woman. When she offers her bare breasts to her young visitor, her gesture echoes the Marian function of lactation as well as the sinful invitation to commit fornication: the roles of the intercessor Mary and the seductress Eve are skillfully conflated in the same gesture. As suggested earlier, the proffering of the round white breasts to the young lad can also be seen as a mock-sacerdotal gesture of elevating the Host at the Mass. The anxiety about women usurping the priestly function was related to orthodox concerns about Wyclif's denial of the real presence in the Eucharist as well as fears of Jews desecrating the eucharistic wafer. One way to explain this conflation of women with heretics and Jews is in the Freudian terms of projective inversion: orthodox doubts about the truth of transubstantiation are repressed by being attributed to the Other.

An eloquent example of the use of parodic inversion to vilify Jews is the *Passio judaeorum secundum Johannes rusticus quadratus* (*The Passion of the Jews According to John the Stocky Peasant*), which concerns an alleged Host desecration in Prague in 1389 during the reign of Wenceslas IV.[44] The *passio* is a narrative in scriptural language evoking Christ's Passion. In the *Passio judaeorum* the genre is parodied, with the Jewish children of Prague cast as monstrous Christ killers and their elders as Pharisees: a Jewish boy throws a stone at a monstrance as it is being carried by a priest though the streets near the Jewish Quarter. This alleged incident provided the instigation for the wholesale persecution of Prague Jews, many of whom were murdered and/or lost their properties and livelihood in the ensuing disturbances.[45] The trope of

---

[43] Ibid., 114. See also Peter Dinzelbacher, *Heilige oder Hexen? Schicksale auffälliger Frauen in Mittelalter und Frühneuzeit* (Munich, 1995).

[44] For the Prague pogrom of 1389, see Miri Rubin, *Gentile Tales. The Narrative Assault on Late Medieval Jews* (New Haven, 1999), 135–40.

[45] The *passio* reflected the anger of the Church hierarchy against King Wenceslas, who was embroiled in a bitter feud with his archbishop, John of Jenštejn, over the Schism and other ecclesiastical matters. This feud would culminate in the king's po-

parodic inversion shared by the *Passio judaeorum* and "The Wycliffite Woman" recalls the vilification of women, Jews, and Germans in the Latin-Czech play *Unguentarius* (ca. 1320–40s).[46] If this exemplum and other official texts cited so far deploy parodic inversion as the principal trope in their attack against women, Jews and heretics, this surely tells us a great deal about the Church's fear of relinquishing primacy in a world in which sexual, ethnic and religious difference represents a permanent threat to the religious and political status quo.

If "The Wycliffite Woman" may be said to articulate such fears, it may also be said to mark a diachronic transition from high- and late-medieval connections between female sexuality and heresy to early-modern associations of witchcraft with demonology. According to Dyan Elliot in her discussion of pollution, sexuality, and demonology in the Middle Ages, "woman's reproductive capacity rendered her additionally ripe for uncanny insemination."[47] In the widely disseminated clerical stories of demonic offspring, women become the bodily agents of diabolical reproduction (the "demon seed") which usually takes place at night while the female victim is dreaming. An interesting variant on this theme is Marie de France's well-known courtly lai *Yonec* about a beautiful young woman trapped in a sterile marriage. Elliott delineates this supernatural tale in the following way: "In her loneliness, she (the lady) fantasises about the perfect lover, whereupon a huge bird flies through her window and promptly transforms itself into a handsome knight (lines 91–115)."[48] Although Marie's *lai* is subversive of clerical misogyny in presenting the fantasy in valorized terms, it resembles "The Wycliffite Woman" in conflating a clerical exemplum about the "demon seed" with a courtly narrative of illicit love and reveals the extent to which such master-plots could be recycled to serve the ideological interests of the author.

---

litical murder of the vicar-general of Prague, John of Nepomuk, in 1393. In his traditional role as the protector of Bohemian Jews, Wenceslas was accused of being a "Jew-lover." The resentment of Jewish influence suggested by this epithet clearly articulates the insecurity felt by the Church authorities during the reign of Wenceslas. Although anti-Jewish invective was nothing new in medieval Bohemia—earlier examples can be found in texts as disparate as the *Passional* of Abbess Kunigunde and the Latin-Czech liturgical play *Unguentarius*—it seems to have escalated in the years following the death of Emperor Charles in 1378, the fateful year in which the Schism also occurred.

[46] See Thomas, *Anne's Bohemia*, chapter 4.
[47] Elliott, *Fallen Bodies*, 56.
[48] Ibid., 59.

In the case of "The Wycliffite Woman," the clerical motif of the "demon seed" is made explicit in the mock-aspiration in the final line of the poem that God should make female heretics fruitful. The point about this tongue-in-cheek conclusion is that it betrays deep-rooted clerical fears and fantasies of sinful women giving birth to monstrous offspring, fears that also animate the aforementioned Wycliffite Mass in which Wyclif is the progenitor of a long succession of Bohemian heretics. If this parodic inversion of Christ's descent from King David equates Wyclif with Antichrist, it also associates the English heresiarch's teachings with out-of-control female sexuality and procreation.

These misogynistic examples should suffice to make it clear that heretical practices with which women were frequently identified did not necessarily derive from social reality but more often than not originated in orthodox discourse itself. In spite of the fact that Margery Kempe's orthodox piety was modeled closely on that of St. Bridget of Sweden, who had been recently canonized by the Catholic Church, the very characteristics of such piety—her independent behavior, her knowledge of scripture and her readiness to moralize in public—made her suspect in the eyes of many people, most notably, the Mayor of Leicester. Discussing the literalism that the authorities condemned in the Lollard Margery Baxter, Rita Copeland makes a similar point with respect to anti-Wycliffite writings in England: "But the literalism that marks her hermeneutic as heretical is in essence the same literalism that the late medieval church encouraged in the form of affective devotion to images of Christ's life."[49] The same irony accrues in relation to the image of the Wycliffite Woman who bares her breasts to her male visitor. As Copeland points out with reference to anti-Lollard discourse in England, the author of the Czech satire manages to have it both ways at once in enjoining women to espouse literal devotion to images (rather than texts) and condemning them for their ignorance of Latin learning.

Exposing the slippage in the text between orthodox and heretical discourse begs the question why our anonymous author chooses the courtly form of the dawn poem as the vehicle of his satire. Why is a

---

[49] Rita Copeland, "Why Women Can't Read: Medieval Hermeneutics, Statutory Law, and the Lollard Heresy Trials," in *Representing Women. Law, Literature, and Feminism*, ed. Susan Sage Heinzelman and Zipporah Batshaw Wiseman (Durham, North Carolina, 1994), 253–86 (278).

genre which traditionally celebrates illicit love and which exalts the lady as the sublime object of desire deployed to denounce illicit religious practice and perpetuate antifeminist sentiments? What does the deployment of the dawn poem in the ideological battle against heresy tell us about social relations between the Church, the university and the court in the early fifteenth-century Bohemia? There is no absolute opposition, of course, between courtly forms such as the *alba* and clerical forms of antifeminist writing. Although it ostensibly exalts the love between a lady and her knight, the secretive context of the *alba* sometimes implies a ludic critique of both parties. Sometimes, as in the *pastorela* "Exiit diluculo" from the *Carmina Burana*, it is the girl who seduces the student:

> She espied a scholar
> Sitting on a sod:
> "What are you doing here, master?
> Come and play with me!" (90, stanza 3)[50]

Clerical writers had long since been adept at composing love songs like those contained in the *Carmina Burana*. Conversely, courtly writers such as Chaucer often inscribe antifeminist discourse within genres ostensibly intended to praise women's virtues as in *The Legend of Good Women*. This is also true of the continental vernacular tradition as exemplified by the prose dispute *The Weaver*, which was probably intended for a courtly audience such as the Queen's regional court at Hradec Králové. Wenceslas IV's consort Sophie was evidently an enthusiastic reader of literature: among her posthumous effects were discovered one book in German and ten in Czech, including a psalter, a copy of the satirical *Decalogue*, and a romance of the life of Alexander the Great.[51]

Queen Sophie was a supporter of Hus and the reform movement in general. It is possible, therefore, that the deployment of a courtly lyric in the interests of antifeminine discourse in "The Wycliffite Woman" reflects the anonymous writer's antagonistic relation to Queen So-

---

[50] "Conspexit in cespite / Scolarem sedere: / "Quid to facis, domine? / Veni mecum ludere." *Carmina Burana. Die Gedichte des Codex Buranus. Lateinisch und Deutsch*, ed. Carl Fischer. Zurich, 1974, 302.
[51] Thomas, *Anne's Bohemia*, 46.

phie's influence. Certainly, the Wycliffite Woman's dominance of the young lord in the satire resembles Sophie's alleged influence over her weak-willed husband Wenceslas. And the sexually predatory quality of the Wycliffite Woman recalls the image of Queen Sophie dressed as a scantily clad bath maid in the margins of her husband's illuminated German Bible.

The possibility that the satire was aimed at reformist elements at the royal court would explain the ironic apostrophe at the beginning of the thirteenth strophe to "fair pages" (*"nádobné panoše"*). The poem's anti-courtly animus would also shed light on the ironic reference to the "court" (*"dvór"*) in connection with the Wycliffite Woman's sexual farewell to her lover. Such jokes at the expense of the court reinforce the possibility that the figures of the Wycliffite Woman and her lover were intended to parody Queen Sophie and her husband, King Wenceslas. Certainly, the Luxembourg court's reputation for *luxuria* would comport with the sexual content of the satire. Yet even here it is difficult to distinguish precisely between reality and representation. Medieval Czech literature in general is characterized by an antipathy toward courtly mores. The Czech love lyric was largely limited to an elite court audience familiar with French, German, and Italian models. The Czech courtly romances are untypical of the genre as it is known in France and Germany and deviate in spirit from their German sources, evincing at times a skeptical, even hostile, attitude toward the courtly life.[52] Such skepticism was shared by writers of other genres as well. Smil Flaška of Pardubice, author of *The New Council*, displays profound ambivalence toward the values of the court. The mocking description of the joust in the Council of the Horse, for example, combines an established clerical tradition of attacking tournaments with a personal satire aimed against the luxurious court of Wenceslas IV.[53] The kind of criticism leveled by Smil against Wenceslas, who is allegorized as the Lion King—his love of luxury and his laziness—are formulaic and recall contemporary English criticism of Richard II and his court.

In late fourteenth- and fifteenth-century Bohemia the literary gen-

---

[52] See Thomas, *The Czech Chivalric Romances Vévoda Arnošt and Lavryn in their Literary Context*. Göppinger Arbeiten zur Germanistik 504 (Göppingen, 1989).
[53] See Thomas, *Anne's Bohemia*, 130.

res preferred by writers and audiences alike were epic rather than romantic, heroic rather than courtly, reflecting the pious values of the gentry rather than the hedonism of the royal court. "The Wycliffite Woman" should be seen in this Bohemian context of anticourtly writing. Ironically, its anticourtly animus is one shared by the Hussite audience it seeks to mock. But the satire also partakes of an established clerical tradition that attacks the excesses of court life, including courtly dress. Knights were frequently condemned for dressing in too feminine a fashion, while ladies were mocked for following suit. As E. Jane Burns points out with regard to the attack on female courtly fashion by the French Dominican Gilles of Orleans in a sermon he delivered in 1273, clerical opprobrium could result in the absurd conclusion that women were simultaneously "too knightly and too seductive."[54] Gilles of Orleans's condemnation of courtly dress highlights a further anxiety about gender and heresy in our text: just as courtly attire blurs the difference between male and female bodies, so too have the corrupt values of the court made it impossible to distinguish between orthodox and heretical practices and beliefs.

"It Takes One to Know One": Hussites and the Friars

In her response to Fiona Somerset's essay *"Eciam Mulier:* Women in Lollardy and the Problem of Sources," Kathryn Kerby-Fulton argues that Lollardy was a peripheral concern for the English Church as it battled with the issue of women preachers, and that in order to understand the *Frauenfrage* in late medieval Europe it is necessary to see England in a larger continental context of religious turmoil.[55] According to Kerby-Fulton, the claims for female leadership in the Church were being made within the ranks of orthodoxy, especially in the continental movement known as the *Devotio Moderna*. Discussing the contribution of the Dominicans to the vexed question of women's role in the Church, she shows how the frequent anti-Dominican accusation

---

[54] See E. Jane Burns, "Refashioning Courtly Love: Lancelot as Ladies' Man or Lady/Man?" in *Constructing Medieval Sexuality,* ed. Karmie Lochrie et al. (Minneapolis, 1997), 111–34 at 128.

[55] Olson and Kerby-Fulton, *Voices in Dialogue,* 261–78.

that the order seduced unlearned women with their arguments is gleefully reversed by the English Dominicans to attack the Lollards on the same grounds that they lead ignorant women into error.

Carolyn Dinshaw detects the same trope of inversion in the "reverse accusation" of sodomy leveled by Lollards at the mendicant friars.[56] Wyclif himself had accused the friars of sodomy in book 1 of his *De Antichristo*. His followers attached a short poem to the Twelve Conclusions of which they posted on the doors of Westminster Hall during the 1395 session of Parliament. Later the accusation of sodomy was reversed and directed back at the Lollards by Roger Dymmok in his systematic refutation of the Conclusions. Sodomy in itself seems to have been less the issue here than other transgressions such as simony. Hus himself had linked these crimes in his infamous characterization of the deposed antipope John XXIII as "a base murderer, a sodomite, a simoniac, and a heretic."[57] Like the sodomite, the Wycliffite Woman becomes the vehicle of a larger religious struggle between supporters of orthodoxy and heterodoxy. I have argued elsewhere that women and homosexuals were yoked together as deviant Other in the Czech-Latin play *Unguentarius* which predates the rise of Hussitism by several decades.[58] The same conflation can be detected in the English and Czech manifestations of orthodoxy and reform.

The conflict between the Lollards and the friars in England corresponded to the antagonisms between the Hussites and the mendicant orders in Bohemia. The reason for this parallel is not far to seek: in many ways these groups resembled each other. The friars had long been active promoting orthodoxy among the urban laity just as the reformers proselytized among the town dwellers of Bohemia and England. The similarities which underlay and belied the surface oppositions meant that both groups eyed each other with particular suspicion and hostility. The anti-Hussite Czech satire "You will recognize the wolf by its coat" ("Vlka poznáš po srsti") is typical of this paradoxical situation. The satire attacks those monks who become secular priests of the Hussite persuasion. The author maintains that such renegades are nonetheless recognizable:

---

[56] Carolyn Dinshaw, *Getting Medieval. Sexualities and Communities, Pre- and Postmodern* (Durham, N.C., 1999), 55–99.
[57] Quoted ibid., 63.
[58] See Thomas, *Anne's Bohemia*, 63–76.

You will recognize the wolf by its coat
And the monk by his cunning.
When he throws off his cloak
And takes on a secular robe
He thinks that the devil will not recognize him
And that he will gain access to God. (1–6)[59]

The irony here is that the former monk is not so easily recognizable as the opening line suggests. Moreover, the facility with which he makes the transition from the religious house to the secular priesthood constitutes a source of anxiety for the author: how can one tell friend from foe, self from other? The anxiety which animates "The Wycliffite Woman"—the slipperiness between orthodoxy and reform—is also true of this satire.

Given the onslaught directed by the friars at reformers both in England and Bohemia, and their deployment of gender and sexuality to assert their case, it is likely that "The Wycliffite Woman" was written by someone familiar with these antimendicant polemics involving women, or possibly by a friar himself. Ironically, the antifeminine animus of the poem may reflect not just the Hussite practice of seducing women away from orthodox circles but also the Dominican tradition of advocating greater female participation within them. Recent scholarship has begun to demonstrate the degree to which women played a more active role within the bounds of orthodoxy than previously thought. This reform within the ranks of orthodoxy was especially pronounced in the Low Countries and in Germany.[60]

Dyan Elliott has detected an element of despair in the Czech poem; but we might speak, rather, of frustration that the Hussites were stealing the reformist thunder of the Dominicans: the Czech satire may be confronting less the despairing prospect of a world in which the Hussites have assumed a dominant role in society than the realization that they have successfully appropriated the orthodox discourse of female empowerment.[61] Thus the Wycliffite Woman cannot simply be re-

---

[59] *Veršované skladby doby husitské*, ed. František Svejkovský (Prague, 1963), 99–101 at 99.
[60] See Anne Winston-Allen, *Convent Chronicles. Women's Writing about Women and Reform in the Late Middle Ages* (University Park, 2004).
[61] See Dyan Elliott, "Response to Alfred Thomas's '*The Wycliffite Woman:* Reading

duced to an antifeminine metaphor for the words and deeds of male heretics: she is an all too real creation of a reforming animus that began within the orthodox world of the friars but has spread with unstoppable force beyond their reach into society as a whole. Thus the Wycliffite Woman symbolizes less the specter of heresy tout court than the prominent role in it played by lay women like Queen Sophie and Agnes of Štítné. In his "Remonstrance against Sir John Oldcastle," Thomas Hoccleve also sees women as susceptible to heretical activities such as reading and disputing about Holy Writ. But these women are humble artisans, not influential queens and ladies of the court:

> Somme women eek, thogh hir wit be thynne,
> Wole arguments make in holy writ.
> Lewed calates, sittith down and spynne
> And kakeles of sumwhat elles, for your wit
> Is al to feeble to despute of it. (145–49)[62]

Class, then, is one of the main differences between Lollardy and Hussitism. With the exception of Sir John Oldcastle and the so-called Lollard Knights, most of the Lollards came from the middle ranks of society, whereas in Bohemia the Hussites had successfully infiltrated the royal court and the nobility. The Czech poet presents this topsy-turvy world in terms of a perverse reversal of gender roles in which a woman dominates a man. If this is a standard misogynistic metaphor which the author uses to attack heresy, it is also an indirect reflection of social reality: a few women like Queen Sophie did support the reform movement and were active within it. At the same time, the Czech poem seems to be haunted by its own orthodox ghosts, for it was, as we have seen, the Dominicans who encouraged lay women to take a more active part within the life of the church. In attributing the monstrous phenomenon of the Wycliffite Woman to the Hussite opposition, the author appears to be replicating what the Dominicans were doing in England: accusing the Lollards of the selfsame vice which had traditionally been blamed on the friars. If the Wycliffite Woman represents a threat to orthodoxy, it is because she is a creature of their own making.

Women in Fifteenth-Century Bohemia,'" in Olson and Kerby-Fulton, *Voices in Dialogue*, 302–5.

[62] *Selections from Hoccleve*, ed. M. C. Seymour (Oxford, 1981), 64.

Chapter 5

Peregrinus et alter Ulysses

Leo of Rožmitál's Mission to England (1466)

A beautifully illuminated Bohemian manuscript of *The Travels of Sir John Mandeville* (now in the British Library) depicts the eponymous English knight setting out on his voyage for the Holy Land. The bucolic coastline along which his ship sails represents an idealized version of England as seen through the eyes of the anonymous Czech artist. Turning reassuringly to his companions behind him, Sir John points in the opposite direction toward the east. This simultaneous perspective—looking backward to one's home or point of origin while gesturing in the direction of one's destination—defines the tension at the heart of all medieval travelogues. However exotic and distant the destination, it is always home that provides the fixity to which the narrative is tethered. As Geraldine Heng states in her analysis of the *Travels:* "Everywhere the traveler passes, the secrets, curiosities, and adventures of the world are gathered and brought back to one's ultimate destination, home."[1] Like all medieval accounts of foreign parts, the *Travels* combine fact and fiction, established knowledge of alien lands and fanciful embellishments based on lore and learning acquired in libraries,

---

[1] Geraldine Heng, *Empire of Magic. Medieval Romance and the Politics of Cultural Fantasy* (New York, 2003), 247.

revealing as much about the traveler's own culture as they do about those of the peoples encountered. The movement they define is internal as well as external, spiritual as well as physical. In the words of Donald R. Howard, "travels are fictions to the extent that the traveler sees what he wants or expects to see, which is often what he has read."[2]

In the British Library manuscript of the *Travels* the exotic and the familiar mingle effortlessly: Constantinople with the Cathedral of St. Sophia and the statue of Emperor Justinian is imagined as a typical central European town with arcaded buildings arranged around a square. Only on closer observation does one notice the insertion of microcosmic localized details into the larger picture of an idealized and fanciful world. This subtle mode of acculturation—making the Other conform to the expectations and values of the viewer as well as satisfying his fantasies—is also typical of late medieval "translations" of foreign romances. The Burgundian adaptation of Chrétien's Arthurian romances or the Czech versions of Germanic minstrel epics involve a subtle merging of the familiar and the exotic. At first glance the adaptations seem to be uninspired wholesale translations of the original into the native idiom; but on closer analysis it becomes clear that the adaptor has actually transformed the exotic material into a mental landscape familiar and acceptable to his audience.

I would like to explore this mode of acculturation, as well as the interplay between art and life, in two written accounts of a Bohemian diplomatic mission undertaken to the courts of Europe in the years 1465 to 1467.[3] Just as Sir John's fashionable attire and the elegant walled city in the distance depicted by the artist of the *Travels* mirror the sophistication of the Prague court of Wenceslas IV, so too the Bohemians' account of England reflects the familiar mental landscape of central Europe. Like the adaptations of romances from a foreign into a

---

[2] Donald R. Howard, *Writers and Pilgrims. Medieval Pilgrimage Narratives and Their Posterity* (Los Angeles, 1980), 10.

[3] For the Latin and German texts, see *Des böhmischen Herrn Leo's von Rozmital Ritter-, Hof- und Pilger-reise durch die Abendlande 1465–67. Beschrieben von zweien seiner Begleiter*, ed. Franz Pfeiffer (Stuttgart, 1844). For an English translation of both versions, see *The Travels of Leo of Rožmitál through Germany, Flanders, England, France, Spain, Portugal and Italy 1465–1467*, ed. Malcolm Letts (Cambridge, 1957). For an early study of the travelogues, see Mrs Henry Cust, *Gentlemen Errant. Being the Travels and Adventures of Four Noblemen in Europe in the Fifteenth and Sixteenth Centuries* (London, 1909). For the life and times of George of Poděbrady, see Otakar Odložilík, *The Hussite King. Bohemia in European Affairs 1440–1471* (New Brunswick, N.J., 1965).

native idiom, the travelogue reproduces the perceptions, values, and beliefs of the writers and their audience.

The Bohemian Mission

The Bohemian mission was by led by Baron Leo of Rožmitál and Blatná on behalf of his brother-in-law, King George of Poděbrady, who had been excommunicated the year before (in 1465) and hoped to exert diplomatic pressure on the papacy to relax its censure through the benevolent mediation of the rulers of Germany, Burgundy, England, France, Castile, Aragon, Portugal, and Italy. George's choice of ambassador was judicious: Rožmitál was a devout Catholic as well as the king's own kinsman. Who better than this Catholic magnate to reassure the rulers of Europe that Bohemia was no longer the home of heresy?

Described by the seventeenth-century antiquarian and Jesuit Bohuslav Balbín as "peregrinus at alter Ulysses," Rožmitál was born in 1426 at the height of the Hussite Wars. The ancestral castle of the family dominated the town of Rožmitál in the south Bohemian district of Blatná. He died in 1480 and was buried in St. Vitus Cathedral in Prague. Initially, Rožmitál was an implacable enemy of George of Poděbrady, but when his sister married the latter in 1450, he made his peace with his erstwhile foe and threw in his political lot with him. Before discussing the accounts of the mission in detail, it would be helpful to place it in context by sketching out the political background to the whole enterprise and how fifteenth-century Englishmen and Catholic Europe in general regarded the heretical kingdom of Bohemia.

English Responses to Hussite Bohemia

As we have seen, the early years of the fifteenth century witnessed the outbreak of heresy in both England and Bohemia. But unlike the vacillating Wenceslas IV, Henry V of England (1413–22) was determined to confront the rising tide of heresy, especially when it assumed the form of a rebellion against the royal power. After the defeat of Sir John Oldcastle at the skirmish of Fickett's Field near London on January 9, 1414, the Lollard threat was removed indefinitely. It was Henry's decisive policies and his consistent support for the Church that made the situation in England very different from Bohemia. Like Henry and unlike Wenceslas, the latter's half-brother Sigismund of Luxembourg (elected Holy Roman Emperor in 1410) was a fervent upholder of Catholic orthodoxy and a sworn enemy of heresy. He was instrumental in convening the Council of Constance which lasted from 1414 to 1418 and whose purpose was to end the Schism, elect a new pope, and eradicate heresy in Bohemia.

In the spring of 1414 the emperor visited England to strengthen diplomatic ties with Henry V and broker a peace between England and France. After a rather cool reception by the French court, he left Paris and traveled to Calais, where he was welcomed by Richard Beauchamp, earl of Warwick, and embarked for Dover on May 1. On landing, he was greeted by the king's youngest brother, Humphrey, duke of Gloucester, Constable of Dover and Warden of the Cinque Ports. Accompanied by a thousand men on horseback, Sigismund traveled to London through Canterbury, Rochester, and Blackheath before reaching the capital, where King Henry rode out to meet him as he approached and accompanied him into the city. The guest was lodged in Henry's own palace at Westminster while the king moved over the river Thames to stay at the Archbishop of Canterbury's residence at Lambeth. On May 24 Sigismund was taken to Windsor for the St. George's Day service of the Order of the Garter to which he was admitted as knight. The emperor gave Henry a special gift—the heart of St. George, to whom the English king had a special devotion.[4] The imperial visit to England lasted for four months and reflected the importance of the Anglo-German alliance. For Sigismund the alliance was mainly intended to unify Christianity and facilitate the work of the Council of Constance, while King Henry's alliance with the emperor was part of his strategy to surround and isolate his enemy France.

In 1436 Sigismund was finally recognized as king of Bohemia by the moderate wing of the Hussite nobility. In return, the reformers obtained considerable concessions in religious matters, including the right to communicate in both kinds, which were formulated in the so-called Compacts of Basel. Sigismund died one year later in 1437 and was succeeded by his son-in-law, Albert of Austria, who died in 1439.

---

[4] Christopher Allmand, *Henry V* (New Haven, 1992), 104–6.

The latter's son, Ladislav the Posthumous, was still a child when he succeeded to the throne. He died in 1457 at the age of seventeen. A year later the Hussite nobleman George of Poděbrady, who had served as governor of the kingdom during Ladislav's minority, was elected king by the Bohemian nobility. The new king had to contend with domestic unrest as well as with the suspicion of the papacy. In an attempt to make peace with the Catholic Church, he sent an embassy to Rome in 1452. For several years a climate of relative tolerance toward the moderate Hussites (also known as Utraquists from their insistence on the use of the chalice) was maintained, thanks largely to the judicious and tolerant Pius II, who, as Aeneas Sylvius, had written a book about the troubled history of the Church in Bohemia. But following Pius' death the situation deteriorated. The new pope, Paul II, was not as well informed about Bohemia as his predecessor, knew far less about the Hussite Church, and was certainly less tolerant of it. In 1465 he excommunicated King George and religious war broke out again in Bohemia.

Distrust of heretical Bohemia typified English public opinion in the fifteenth century. One of the most prominent English delegates to the Council of Constance was King Henry's half-brother Henry Beaufort, bishop of Winchester and Lincoln and Lord Chancellor of England. He was among Hus' most virulent opponents at his trial, an antagonism that defined English attitudes toward Bohemia for more than a century. Some years after the Council of Constance Bishop Reginald Pecock lamented the Hussites' destruction of Bohemia and its famous university at Prague in his *The Repressor of Over Much Blaming of the Clergy* (1449). Pecock opines that the Bohemians have learnt their bitter lesson and are now keen to return to the Catholic fold:

> Certis in this wise and in this now seid maner and bi this now seid cause bifille the rewful and wepable destruccioun of the worthi citee and universite of Prage, and of the hoole rewme of Beeme, as y have had ther of enformacioun ynough. And now, aftir the destruccioun of the rewme, the peple ben glad for to resorte and turne agen into the catholik and general feith and loore of the chirche, and in her poverte bidith up agen what was brent and throwun doun, and noon of her holdingis can thrive.[5]

---

[5] Reginald Pecock, *The Repressor of Over Much Blaming of the Clergy*, ed. Churchill Babington, 2 vols. (London, 1860), vol. 1, 86.

Writing in a similar vein, Sir John Fortescue, tutor to Edward, prince of Wales, son of Henry VI, regarded Bohemia as symptomatic of class chaos and religious anarchy. Chiming in on the same theme, Henry VI wrote a letter to Pope Eugenius IV (dated May 18, 1440) in which he denounced the English heretic and defector to Bohemia, Peter Payne, as that "cruel and monstrous beast, and dangerous enemy who has, forsooth, intoxicated many nations and peoples innumerable with his pestilential and poisonous doctrines, and has impiously burned, overthrown, destroyed, and profaned hundreds of monasteries, churches, altars, and religious places in all directions."[6] Right up to the eve of the Reformation most Englishmen saw Bohemia in negative terms. Alexander Barclay, the English translator of Sebastian Brant's *Narrenschiff* (*Ship of Fools*) (1509), wrote of the diabolical school of Prague and "they of Boeme" as treacherous and deceitful.[7] In his satirical poem "Collyn Clout" John Skelton, tutor to Henry duke of York (the future Henry VIII), links the pernicious teachings of Wyclif and Hus with the heresies of Arius (d. 336) and Pelagius (d. 420):

> And some of them barke,
> Clatter and carpe
> Of that heresy arte
> Called Wytclifista,
> The devylyshe dagmatista.
> And some be Hussians,
> And some be Arryans,
> And some be Pollegyans,
> And make moche varyans
> Bytwene the clergye
> And the temporalyte. (546–56)[8]

The Bohemian mission to the courts of Catholic Europe was conceived by King George as a diplomatic rebuttal to such accusations of inveterate national heresy. The orthodox piety displayed by Rožmitál

---

[6] Quoted in Alfred B. Emden, *An Oxford Hall in Medieval Times* (Oxford, 1927), 159–60.
[7] See Josef Polišenský, *Anglie a Bílá Hora* (Prague, 1949), 37–38.
[8] John Skelton, *The Complete English Poems*, ed. John Scattergood (New Haven, 1983), 260.

and his entourage, and especially their devotion to the saints, may have been intended to convince their hosts that Bohemia was not synonymous with heresy. But there may also have been a penitential motive in the decision to visit the shrines of Thomas of Canterbury and James of Compostela. In this sense the Bohemians were reacting against the Hussite condemnation of pilgrimages and veneration of saints and were keen to be seen doing the opposite of heretical practice.

The Travelers Set Forth

The travelers left Prague on November 26, 1465. The retinue consisted of about forty people, noblemen, attendants, jesters, and even a lute-player. At Nuremburg Rožmitál enlisted the services of a local burgher named Gabriel Tetzel as his official chronicler. Tetzel has left us a detailed account of the tour written in German, which is now preserved at the Bavarian State Library in Munich. The other account was written in Czech by Rožmitál's squire and arms-bearer, Václav Šašek of Bířkov. Unfortunately this version is lost. However, it was translated into Latin and printed at Olomouc in 1577.[9] Although both German and Latin texts correspond in several particulars, they also differ in reflecting the writers' divergent interests, temperaments, and cultural backgrounds.

One of the fundamental differences between the accounts is their authors' social standing. Tetzel was a former mayor of Nuremburg and a successful merchant. As the official chronicler, he is more concerned with the diplomatic and formal aspects of the trip than his Czech counterpart. His evident fascination with the glittering world of the fifteenth-century court may also reflect his bourgeois background. As Johan Huizinga famously points out in *The Autumn of the Middle Ages*, class in the later Middle Ages was rigidly hierarchical and clearly differentiated: "Every estate, order, and craft could be recognized by its dress. The notables, never appearing without the ostentatious display of their weapons and liveried servants, inspired awe and envy."[10]

---

[9] Letts, *Travels of Leo of Rožmitál*, vii.
[10] Johan Huizinga, *The Autumn of the Middle Ages*, trans. Rodney J. Payton and Ulrich Mammitzsch (Chicago, 1996), 1.

As a member of the Bohemian gentry, Šašek is less impressed by the world of the court and reveals a preference for the everyday aspects of life such as folk customs, local religious practices, and topographical details. In some ways this quotidian focus reflects Šašek's temperament, but it is also typical of the medieval travel genre as a whole such as Oderic of Pordenone's *Itinerarius* and Mandeville's *Travels*. As is frequently the case with travel narratives, it is often difficult to determine where subjective experience ends and literary convention takes over.

The voyage to England began inauspiciously. The Bohemian party had to wait several days for a favorable wind at Calais before embarking for Sandwich, the English port of entry. When they finally set sail, a large hole appeared in the hull of the ship and submerged the horses up to their bellies in water. The entire company was forced to return to the French coast. The second attempt was more successful. Finally the foreigners caught their first glimpse of England. Tetzel omits to mention the English coast and launches into a detailed description of Canterbury Cathedral with its famous shrine of St. Thomas Becket. But Šašek was clearly fascinated by the English coastal landscape. The ship sailed toward the port of Sandwich, passing by Dover Castle and the famous white cliffs. Šašek notices that the white cliffs looked from a distance like walls of snow and asserts that the strongly fortified castle was built by demons, a remark presumably based on an anecdote heard during his stay in England. It should not surprise us that real-life observation mingles with anecdotal detail, since the anecdote is the basic structural principle of all medieval travel narratives. According to Geraldine Heng, Mandeville's *Travels* "are organized like a self-interrupting network of nodules made up of anecdotes and vignettes—brief stories rumored or vouched for—profusely interspersed with digressions, observations, flashes of memory or insight."[11]

Šašek's description of Sandwich reveals his fascination with the trappings of a seafaring land. It includes a detailed list of the different types of ships docked in the harbor. He also relates the charming custom that the townsfolk of Sandwich were given to walking through the streets at night while playing stringed instruments and sounding trumpets as a warning to seafarers that the direction of the wind had changed. This custom seems to have been shared by other towns in fif-

---

[11] Heng, *Empire of Magic*, 241.

teenth-century England: "All the commons shared in supporting the minstrels and players of the borough. The 'waits' (so called from the French word *guet*) were originally and still partly remained watchmen of the town, but it was in their character of minstrels, 'who go every morning about the town piping,' that they were paid by pence collected by the ward-men from every house."[12]

The next stop on the journey to London was Canterbury, which was one of most important religious shrines in Europe and an obvious place for the foreign visitors to interrupt their journey. Archbishop Thomas Becket had been murdered in his own cathedral by four knights of Henry II on December 30, 1170, and canonized three years later. His shrine, made of gold and studded with numerous precious gems, was one of the most spectacular in Christendom and was an international site of pilgrimage throughout the medieval period. Tetzel provides a detailed account of the marvels of the cathedral, in particular the magnificent shrine of St. Thomas. Relying on information that must have been given to him by local guides, he narrates an extensive anecdote about King Louis VII of France who came to the shrine in 1179. Louis wanted to thank St. Thomas for the recovery of his son and heir, Philip Augustus, who had almost died from exposure after having been lost in a forest. The king was wearing a valuable ring with a precious stone in it that the incumbent archbishop begged the king to give to the shrine. The king was reluctant to part with his precious ring, which he regarded as a good-luck charm. Instead of the ring he agreed to give a hundred thousand florins for the further embellishment of the shrine. No sooner had the king made his promise than the stone sprang from the ring and embedded itself in the shrine as if placed there by a goldsmith. Having witnessed this miracle, Louis prayed for forgiveness and gave the money and the stone to the cathedral. This precious stone (a ruby) was known as the Great Regale.[13] After the Reformation and the destruction of the shrine it was worn in a ring by Henry VIII and later in a necklace by his daughter Mary Tudor. The story of King

---

[12] A. S. Green, *Town Life in the Fifteenth Century*, vol. 1 (London, 1894), 145. For her information Green draws on William Boys, *Collection for an History of Sandwich in Kent* (Canterbury, 1792), 673, 676, 684.

[13] See Diane Webb, *Pilgrimage in Medieval England* (London, 2000), 50; Ben Nilson, *The Cathedral Shrines of Medieval England* (Woodbridge, 1998), 188; William Urry, *Thomas Becket. His Last Days*, ed. Peter A. Rowe (Stroud, 1999), 171.

Louis is recorded in the thirteenth-century stained-glass "miracle" windows in the Trinity Chapel of Canterbury Cathedral which can still be seen today.

Tetzel also mentions that a coarse hair shirt—worn by the saint although it was infested with lice to punish himself for temptations of the flesh—was displayed above the shrine. The presence of this relic is confirmed by other pilgrimage accounts and reveals the extent to which legend and fact become inextricably mingled in medieval travel narratives. Tetzel also refers to a spring located to the left of the shrine where St. Thomas himself used to drink. Tetzel adds that during the saint's lifetime the water from the spring changed five times into milk and blood. In honor of the saint, Lord Rožmitál and his servants all drank from this spring.

Whereas Tetzel's interest in the shrine of St. Thomas is largely anecdotal, Šašek is concerned with the social and political implications of the saint's cult. He notes St. Thomas's popularity among ordinary people, a claim confirmed by the worn steps leading to the shrine still visible today. He asserts that St. Thomas strenuously opposed "the unjust laws which King Henry had decreed against the rights of the Catholic Church."[14] In addition to revealing some knowledge of English history Šašek evinces a distrust of monarchical power characteristic of the Bohemian nobility. Many works of medieval Czech literature reflect noble resistance to the royal encroachment on their feudal privileges. The Czech life of Alexander the Great (*Alexandreida*), the *Dalimil Chronicle*, and *The New Council* all address the rights of the knightly class and the need for the king to respect these rights.

After leaving Canterbury the Bohemian party spent the night at Rochester before proceeding to the capital. Even in London Šašek continues to dwell on St. Thomas, mentioning the church where he was christened and the tombs of his mother and sister in the same church. Tetzel omits these details in his eagerness to describe the Bohemians' munificent reception by the English king and his court. Tetzel's account of the English court is of great historical interest, but it provides no political insights into the dynastic Wars of the Roses which formed the turbulent background to the visit. It is striking, in fact, that neither Tetzel nor Šašek refers to the circumstances which had brought the

---

[14] Pfeiffer, *Des böhmischen Herrn*, 37.

young duke of York to the throne as Edward IV. It is true that the Bohemian mission arrived during a temporary lull in the violence. Yet it is odd that there is no mention of the political situation. Foreign visitors, especially ambassadors, often provided detailed and perceptive insights into the political intrigues of the English royal court, although they sometimes confused the titles of the key players.

One explanation for the Bohemians' strange silence is the fact that the political situation in England was uncomfortably close to that at home. Both kingdoms had recently experienced a bloody civil war and the kings of both Bohemia and England had a weak claim to the crown. Although George of Poděbrady had come to throne with the overall support of the Bohemian nobility, he was not—unlike Edward IV—of the blood royal. Edward of York had usurped the crown after years of political instability and weak rule by Henry VI. If Tetzel had alluded to Edward's usurpation, he would have run the risk of reminding King George that his title was also suspect.

In failing to mention the Wars of the Roses, the foreign visitors were not necessarily ignorant of what was happening in England. The members of the English court remain nameless and even the king is not mentioned by name. The Bohemians' evocation of the English court is not intended to reflect social reality but to present an idealized mirror image of Bohemia itself. As Stephen Greenblatt has pointed out, the imagining of foreign parts is to some extent a reflection of the real conditions which prevail at home: "This is the utopian moment of travel: when you realize that what seems most unattainably marvelous, most desirable, is what you almost have, what you could have—if you could only strip away the banality and corruption of the everyday—at home."[15]

In the perception of the Bohemians England was a peaceful and prosperous land. As we know, fifteenth-century England was in fact far from a peaceful place, although it was prosperous. Henry VI's reign had been characterized by ineffectual and corrupt government. Responding to malcontent in the realm, especially among the commons, Richard, duke of York, the king's kinsman, claimed his own right to the throne but soon afterwards was killed in battle. His successor, Edward,

---

[15] Stephen Greenblatt, *Marvelous Possessions. The Wonder of the New World* (Chicago, 1991), 25.

earl of March, followed his father's example by claiming the crown of England. Following his rout of the Lancastrian army at the Battle of Towton on Easter Sunday in 1461, Edward imprisoned Henry VI in the Tower of London and was immediately crowned king in Westminster Abbey.

In the five years between the momentous victory at Towton and the Bohemian mission to England, Edward was kept busy putting down rebellions and consolidating his rule. His most important and powerful supporter in this ongoing effort was Richard Neville, earl of Warwick, known to history as "the King Maker."[16] By the time of the Bohemians' arrival in England, relations between the king and his greatest magnate were beginning to sour. Warwick had been offended by the king's secret marriage to a commoner, Elizabeth Woodville, in 1461. Another area of tension between the two men was the king's desire to establish an alliance with Burgundy while Warwick was in favor of détente with France. The splendid reception received by the Bohemian party makes a great deal of diplomatic sense in terms of Edward's anti-French policies, since the Empire was the main rival of France for the political dominance of Europe. Warwick felt increasingly frustrated by the king's diplomatic initiatives and, two years after the Bohemians left England, withdrew from the court at London to his vast estates in Yorkshire.

Already strained by the king's advancement of his wife's parvenu relatives and his refusal to allow his younger brother, George, duke of Clarence, to marry Warwick's older daughter and heiress, Anne Neville, the relationship between the two men broke down completely in 1468 and Warwick defected to the Lancastrian camp. After many reversals of fortunes, which included the temporary restoration of Henry VI as Warwick's puppet and Edward's brief exile in Burgundy, Edward finally prevailed. After defeating Warwick at the Battle of Barnet in 1471, Edward entered the capital in triumph. On the same day Henry VI was murdered in the Tower of London, almost certainly at Edward's instigation.

Largely a dynastic war fought between rival camps of magnates, the Wars of the Roses did not radically affect everyday life in fifteenth-cen-

---

[16] Paul Murray Kendall, *Warwick the Kingmaker and the Wars of the Roses* (Aylesbury, 1973).

tury England. Our popular perception of Yorkist England as violent and unstable has been shaped by Tudor propagandists (such as Shakespeare) and perpetuated by the historians of the nineteenth century. Only in recent years has the Tudor myth been subjected to critical scrutiny.[17]

At all events, the Bohemians received a warm welcome from Edward IV. This was partly a manifestation of the young king's amiable and extrovert temperament, but it was also an astute diplomatic gesture on his part. Edward was far from secure in his rule and needed all the foreign support he could get. As the richest and strategically most powerful part of the Holy Roman Empire, Bohemia was of great political importance in the fifteenth century. Edward would have regarded the Bohemian mission as a major endorsement of his insecure regime. In this sense the mission was mutually advantageous to both King George of Bohemia and King Edward of England.

His recent marriage to Elizabeth Woodville and the birth of their first child gave Edward the opportunity to enhance his regal status by displaying her magnificence as a consort and mother. This motivation would explain the prominence attached to Queen Elizabeth in the scenes described by Tetzel. The first mention of the queen is her public churching following the birth of her daughter, Elizabeth of York, on February 11, 1466. Tetzel relates how King Edward summoned Rožmitál to witness the queen's formal procession from childbed to church. The queen, covered by a canopy, was preceded by clerics, singing choirboys and ladies-in-waiting. She was escorted by two unnamed dukes, probably King Edward's younger brothers, George of Clarence and Richard of Gloucester (later Richard III). Although Warwick is not mentioned at this point, he must have been present since he stood as godfather to the newborn infant. He is almost certainly the "powerful earl" who hosts the subsequent banquet in honor of Lord Rožmitál.

The Bohemians were allowed to stand in an alcove where they could secretly watch the queen dine: "The queen sat alone at a table on a costly golden chair. The queen's mother and the king's sister had to stand some distance away. And when the queen spoke with her mother

---

[17] For a discussion of the historical tradition of the Wars of the Roses, see Charles Ross, *The Wars of the Roses. A Concise History* (London, 1986), 7–15.

or the king's sister, they kneeled down before her until she had drunk water."[18] Neither Tetzel nor Šašek mentions the queen or any member of the royal household by name. This may reflect a lack of curiosity or simple ignorance of the English court. But it is more likely that their observation of the court is influenced by the conventions of the chivalric romance in which characters are often presented as two-dimensional types rather than real people. The scene of the Bohemians observing the queen from the hidden alcove also recalls the voyeuristic perspective of romance.[19] In the German minstrel epic *Herzog Ernst* (*Duke Ernest*) and its fourteenth-century Czech adaptation *Vévoda Arnošt*, the young duke of Bavaria and his faithful companions voyage to the east where they encounter the exotic land of Grippia populated by a race of bird-headed men. The latter have captured a beautiful Indian princess; and the king of Grippia is trying to make love to her by kissing her on the cheek with his sharp beak. With a mixture of horrified fascination and helplessness, Ernst and his men watch from a hidden vantage point just as Tetzel and his companions observe the English queen at dinner. When they discover the interlopers, whom they assume to be the princess's Indian kinsmen come to rescue her, the Grippians take vengeance by stabbing her to death with their beaks, prompting the hero and his companion Wetzel to intervene and kill the assailants.[20]

Tetzel's romantic account of Queen Elizabeth dining alone and in silence for three hours may equally reflect court protocol which was frequently modeled on the conventions of courtly romance. This blurring of art and life is suggested by minor discrepancies in Tetzel's account. He asserts that "not a word was spoken" during the meal but he also refers to the queen speaking with her mother and the king's sister, so he was perhaps exaggerating the formality of the meal to reflect his larger-than-life expectations. At the same time the segregation of the queen and her ladies from the rest of the court was part of the standard

---

[18] "Also setzt sich die kunigin in einen kostlichen guldenen stuol allein uber ein tafel. Der kunigin muoter und des kunigs schwester muosten weit herab sten. Und wenn die kunigin mit ir muoter oder mit des kunigs schwester redet, so kniet sie all mal so lang bis die kunigin wasser nam." Pfeiffer, *Des böhmischen Herrn*, 156–57. My translation.

[19] For voyeurism in medieval literature, see A. C. Spearing, *The Medieval Poet as Voyeur. Looking and Listening in Medieval Love-Narratives* (Cambridge, 1993).

[20] *Herzog Ernst. Ein mittelalterliches Abenteuerbuch,* ed. Bernhard Sowinski (Stuttgart, 2003).

procedure of late medieval birthing and churching, which required the mother to retire from court life about a month prior to the anticipated birth of the child.[21]

Tetzel's account also provides us with some fascinating insights into the political situation at the Yorkist court. Although Queen Elizabeth was probably conforming to queenly tradition, her regal isolation at dinner and the subordinate status of the king's sister who attended upon her must have caused resentment in the royal family. Allegations of Elizabeth Woodville's hauteur have been exaggerated by some historians. But the fact that a woman of nonroyal origin behaved in such a regal way may help to explain Richard of Gloucester's draconian decision to bastardize her sons and usurp the throne after his brother's death in 1483.

Following the banquet, the segregation of the queen and her ladies came to an end and the ladies and gentlemen of the court began to dance together. Among these were the king's sister and two dukes—presumably his brothers Clarence and Gloucester—neither of whom is identified by name. After dinner Rožmitál was admitted to the king's private chapel where Tetzel was impressed by the choir's beautiful singing. Following the service, the nameless earl (probably Warwick) invited the Bohemian entourage to a meal consisting of sixty courses. This munificent hospitality is consistent with what we know of the earl of Warwick's preference for lavish display. Perhaps it was intended to impress his fellow Englishmen as much as the Bohemian visitors. Rožmitál reciprocated by inviting several English lords to his dwelling where Bohemian dishes were served to the great surprise and delight of the English guests.

Whereas Tetzel shows a preference for describing formal diplomatic events, Šašek is more interested in the everyday sights of London life. His account of the city corresponds in many ways with historians' reconstruction of fifteenth-century London. He mentions, for example, that there are two castles situated at each end of the city and the stone bridge across the river Thames with many houses built upon it. He also refers to the large number of kites in the city and adds that it is a capital offence to harm them, a fact that is borne out by an Italian visitor in 1500.

---

[21] J. L. Laynesmith, *The Last Medieval Queens. English Queenship 1445–1503* (Oxford, 2004), 113.

Šašek frequently notes topographical differences between the English and Bohemian landscapes such as the absence of black fir trees, and points out English habits and practices that are for him peculiar or outlandish. When the Bohemians approach their inn in London, the hostess comes out with her entire family and greets the visitors with a kiss instead of proffering her right hand in the Bohemian manner. One of his most amusing observations is the uproar caused by the sight of the Bohemians' long hair. Šašek mentions that many people gathered around the visitors to stare at the foreigners and maintained that their long hair was artificially attached to their heads with tar ("*bitumine adglutinatos*"). This observation comports with what we know of contemporary Bohemian fashion. In the personal breviary of Ladislav the Posthumous, the boy king is depicted at his devotions with blond hair flowing over his shoulders, while English royal portraits of the same period—such as those of Henry VI and Edward IV in the National Portrait Gallery in London—show their sitters sporting collar-length hair.

After leaving the capital, the Bohemian entourage spent the first night at Windsor Castle where they were shown the heart of St. George, brought to England in 1414 by Emperor Sigismund. St. George was one of Bohemia's most important saints and patron of the famous Benedictine Convent of St. George at the Prague Castle where a lovely equestrian statue of the saint by the fourteenth-century sculptor Henry Parler is still to be seen today. The gift of this precious relic was a token of the importance of the Anglo-German alliance and Sigismund's admiration for Henry V. Šašek is characteristically brief in his description of these diplomatic details and turns to the subject of the fallow deer in the park at Windsor. The next stage of the journey was Reading (sixteen miles from Windsor), the site of England's third-largest and most wealthy abbey. Šašek praises the incomparable beauty of the image of the Virgin in the abbey church.

The final stop on the English leg of the journey was Salisbury, which Tetzel typically fails to name. More important for him is the golden shrine of St. Osmund, whose name he Germanizes as Sigmund. St. Osmund, bishop of Salisbury (d. 1099), had been canonized only nine years previously by Pope Calixtus III in 1457.[22] His cult and shrine would have been of great topical interest to the Bohemian visitors. By

---

[22] Webb, *Pilgrimage in Medieval England*, 63.

identifying the English saint as Sigmund, Tetzel's account is characteristic of medieval travel writing in its tendency toward microcosmic acculturation. In distinction to Renaissance travelogues, which are usually concerned to colonize the Other, medieval perspectives seek to familiarize what they encounter so that it can be "gathered and brought back to one's ultimate destination—home."[23]

Tetzel also mentions mechanical figures of the Three Magi bringing gifts to the baby Jesus with Mary and Joseph bowing in gratitude as well as of angels opening the tomb from which Christ arises with a banner in his hand. These figures were probably part of a clock that was built at the order of Ralph Erghum, bishop of Salisbury, in 1388.[24] The same mechanical figures are also mentioned by Šašek in his description of Salisbury, and he and Tetzel provide the only records of the figures, which were probably destroyed at the Reformation. These figures would not have struck the visitors as strange or exotic since they were a typical feature of European Catholic culture. A remarkable set of mechanical figures of Christ and the apostles can still be seen as part of the astronomical clock in the Old Town Hall in Prague.

The Bohemian party spent Palm Sunday in Salisbury and witnessed a splendid procession reenacting Christ's entry into Jerusalem. Rožmitál was welcomed by the duke of Clarence, who invited his guest to walk beside him in the procession. This event was followed by a three-hour banquet hosted by Clarence. Easter Day (April 6) was spent at Poole, the port of departure for France. When the Bohemians had taken ship for the Continent, they were blown off course by a storm and attacked by two English pirate vessels. Only when they showed their imperial credentials were they released and allowed to continue their voyage to the island of Guernsey.

Šašek mentions Salisbury by name and describes the castle park, with its rich stock of deer, rabbits, and hares, in great detail. He also refers to the well-known legend that England was unable to support wolves, a topic of perennial interest to Europeans well into the sixteenth century, as Sir Philip Sidney was to discover during his sojourn on the Continent. Alluding in passing to Clarence, Šašek dwells upon

[23] Heng, *Empire of Magic*, 247. Stephen Greenblatt states that "Sir John Mandeville is the knight of non-possession" (*Marvelous Possessions*, 28), whereas Heng sees the *Travels* as seeking to acquire or possess what is encountered for domestic consumption.
[24] Letts, *Travels of Leo of Rožmitál*, 57 n. 2.

the religious practices of the town, in particular, the Easter celebrations and the royal custom of washing the feet of twelve paupers on Maundy Thursday in imitation of Christ washing the feet of His disciples at the Last Supper.

Šašek concludes his travel account of England with the assertion that the English are "infidi et astute" ("treacherous and cunning"), a somewhat surprising remark considering the munificence and hospitality shown to the Bohemians—not to mention the ladies' kisses. Here too received opinion may be as significant as real-life experience. Negative stereotypes about the English were common in the late medieval and early modern period, especially following the Reformation. In 1444 Jean Juvenal des Ursins, archbishop of Rheims, spoke of "the habit of the English of evilly killing their kings."[25] This statement was clearly exaggerated and formed part of a larger prejudice that the English were innately perfidious. Following the English Reformation the Spanish maintained that all Englishmen were "un gente barbara e muy heretica" ("a barbarian and highly heretical people"), who executed monks and had no fear of God or His saints.[26] Šašek's anti-English sentiments are wholly consistent with contemporary Continental opinion in reflecting the values of the writer as much as those of the people described.

As we have seen, real-life experience is often difficult to distinguish from subjective observations derived from private reading and folklore. On the whole the Bohemian visitors give an impression of an economically prosperous, politically stable, and religiously unified England. We know that this was not entirely the case, but more significant than historical fact is the foreign perception of England as stable and harmonious. In this sense their England becomes an idealized reverse mirror-image of a troubled and internecine Bohemia.

---

[25] Nigel Saul, *The Three Richards. Richard I, Richard II and Richard III* (London, 2005), 215–16.

[26] David Loades, *Mary Tudor: A Life* (Cambridge, Mass., 1989), 230–31.

Chapter 6

Shakespeare's Bohemia

English Men and Women in Renaissance Prague

"Thou art perfect, then, our ship hath touched upon / The deserts of Bohemia?" These famous lines, spoken by the Sicilian lord Antigonus at the beginning of act 2, scene 3 of *The Winter's Tale*, have led to endless speculation concerning William Shakespeare's intentions in endowing the landlocked kingdom of Bohemia with a coastline. Was it evidence of the playwright's ignorance of European geography, as Ben Jonson claimed in 1618? Or was the nonexistent shore an oxymoronic joke analogous to the Swiss Navy or Wigan Pier, as Stephen Orgel has suggested? Or was it, as Tony Tanner has argued, simply a dramatic device allowing Shakespeare to introduce a coast on which to wash up the shipwrecked Antigonus and the infant Perdita?[1]

Shakespeare did not invent the seashore of Bohemia but inherited it from his principal source, Robert Greene's prose romance *Pandosto. The Triumph of Time* (1588). Greene also gave Bohemia a sea coast, even though Bohemia played the opposite part in his plot to what it played in Shakespeare's plot. Shakespeare switched Greene's settings to make

---

[1] See the introduction to William Shakespeare, *The Winter's Tale*, ed. Stephen Orgel (Oxford, 1996), 38, and Tony Tanner's introduction to William Shakespeare, *Romances* (New York, 1996), xciv.

Bohemia—rather than Sicilia—a safe haven for King Leontes' abandoned daughter Perdita. Given the association of Perdita with Properpina, it makes sense that the play begins in Sicily where the original classical legend is set. Shakespeare also changed the names of his protagonists. Greene's Pandosto of Bohemia becomes Leontes of Sicilia and Egistus of Sicilia changes into Polixenes of Bohemia.

Shakespeare's decision to invert Greene's settings was not prompted by the exigencies of dramatic plot alone but reflected the playwright's keen interest in—and awareness of—European politics. By fusing the image of Bohemia on the sea with the idea of Bohemia as a refuge, Shakespeare implicated the imaginary world of Greek romance in the real world of religious politics. Sixteenth-century and early seventeenth-century Bohemia was one of the most tolerant places in Europe, so tolerant in fact that many English Catholics sought refuge there. Much has been written on the New World allusions in a play like *The Tempest*; rather less attention has been paid to the role played by the European continent—and especially east-central Europe—in shaping Shakespeare's vision of utopia.

The references to Bohemia in Greene and Shakespeare were far from incidental in English literature of the time. George Chapman's *The Tragedy of Alphonsus, Emperor of Germany* (ca. 1590) is set during the disputed imperial election of 1257 in which the King of Bohemia, Přemysl Otakar II, Alfonso X of Castile, and Richard, earl of Cornwall, contended for the title of Holy Roman Emperor. In *Old Fortunatus* (1600) and *The Masque of Queens* (1609) Thomas Dekker and Ben Jonson, respectively, portray Bohemia as a pagan land free of tyranny. In *Old Fortunatus* Fortune singles out Primislaus—the peasant founder of the medieval dynasty of Czech kings—among those commoners whom she has elevated to a position of power and influence.

These references reflected Bohemia's strategic importance and symbolic significance in the minds of informed English men and women. The traditional assumption that Bohemia was a faraway country of which Shakespeare's English contemporaries knew nothing is not only untrue; it anachronistically reproduces a modern map of Europe created by the Versailles Treaty of 1919. About the same time that *The Winter's Tale* was being written, the emperor Rudolf's residence was not in Vienna but in Prague, where he gathered about him an international array of scholars, artists, and alchemists, and where he amassed one of the greatest art collections the world has ever seen. Like Paulina's private gallery, where the "statue" of Hermione miraculously comes to life at the end of the play, Rudolf's *Kunstkammer* was a testament to the acquisitive spirit of the age.

Prior to the fateful Battle of the White Mountain in 1620, which ended an era of religious tolerance in central Europe and set the stage for the Thirty Years' War, the Habsburg rulers Maximilian II and his son Rudolf II pursued an ecumenical policy toward their Protestant subjects in the Holy Roman Empire. In Bohemia Catholics, Protestants, and Jews lived and worshiped in mutual tolerance. Tolerated by the Habsburgs, the large Jewish population of Prague enjoyed a veritable golden age in the late sixteenth and early seventeenth century. This ecumenical climate provided a stark contrast with England, where religious nonconformity was severely punished. It has been estimated that there were as few as two hundred Jews living in Shakespeare's London. The Jews had been deported by Edward I in 1290 and did not begin to return until Cromwell's relaxation of the ban in 1656. The situation for English Catholics was not much better. Initially Elizabeth I had been tolerant toward her recusant subjects; but when Pope Pius V excommunicated her in his bull *Regnans in excelsis* (1570), the queen became increasingly suspicious and intolerant of them. An atmosphere of paranoia akin to that in King Leontes' kingdom of Sicilia prevailed. The Protestant nobleman Baron Waldstein, who visited England in the summer of 1600, reports in his diary that he and his companions were held up for three days in Dover, virtually under house arrest, before being allowed to travel on to London. Such was the suspicion in which even the Queen's co-religionists who came from abroad were held.

It would seem likely that Bohemia's role as a refuge from tyranny in *The Winter's Tale* reflected Shakespeare's sensitivity to the repressive nature of English society as well as the utopian allure of distant Bohemia. It might also suggest that the playwright was sympathetic to the plight of English Catholics. In recent years several Shakespeare scholars have argued that the playwright was himself an adherent of the old religion. Complicating this theory is the fact that *The Winter's Tale* and *The Tempest* (another romance in which the experience of exile is central to the plot) were among fourteen plays performed at court in 1613 during the festive season preceding the marriage of King James's daughter Elizabeth to the Calvinist Frederick V, Elector Palatine of the Rhine. Five years later Frederick was offered the crown of Bohemia by the Protestant Estates who had decided to reject the Habsburg claimant, Ferdinand of Styria. Frances Yates has suggested that the young couple Ferdinand and Miranda in *The Tempest* may be intended as fictional surrogates of Frederick and Elizabeth, who were seen to embody the hope for a bright new future of European peace and harmony in contrast to the disillusioned older generation of Prospero.[2] In linking the future Calvinist king and queen of Bohemia with Shakespeare's Ferdinand and Miranda, Yates suggests that Shakespeare was well disposed to the Protestant cause, an assertion that complicates the claim of more recent scholars that the drama encodes pro-Catholic sentiments. It is not my intention in this chapter to take sides in this massively complex debate. Rather than trying to divine Shakespeare's private beliefs, I will seek to explain the wish-fulfillment ending of *The Winter's Tale* as evidence of his ecumenical hopes for a world in which Catholics and Protestants might live together in peace and harmony.[3] I shall suggest that the embodiment of these utopian hopes for many disaffected English men and women was the kingdom of Bohemia. But before turning to *The Winter's Tale*, I shall provide a political and religious context for a deeper understanding of its complexities by tracing the fortunes of English Catholics and Protestants in Renaissance Prague.

Sir Philip Sidney

Shakespeare may have received favorable first-hand reports about Bohemia from English actors who had been touring the towns and villages of the Holy Roman Empire since the 1590s.[4] But the perception of Bohemia as a repository of English hopes for a peaceful Europe goes back to 1575 when Elizabeth I appointed the twenty-two-year-old Sir Philip Sidney as her special ambassador to Prague.[5] The mission was ostensibly a polite expression of condolence to the new Emperor

---

[2] Frances Yates, *Shakespeare's Last Plays* (London, 1975), 93.

[3] For Shakespeare's ecumenicism, see Arthur F. Marotti, "Shakespeare and Catholicism," *Theatre and Religion. Lancastrian Shakespeare,* ed. Richard Dutton, Alison Findlay, and Richard Wilson (Manchester, 2003), 218–41.

[4] See Zdeněk Stříbrný, *Shakespeare and Eastern Europe* (Oxford, 2000), chap. 1.

[5] For Sidney's mission to Prague, see Katherine Duncan-Jones, *Sir Philip Sidney, Courtier Poet* (New Haven, 1991), 120–30, and Alan Stewart, *Philip Sidney—A Double Life* (London, 2001), 173–78.

Rudolf on the recent demise of his father, Maximilian II. But the underlying reason for the visit was more pragmatic. In an attempt to overcome England's political and religious isolation, Elizabeth regarded the Austrian Habsburgs as potential allies against Catholic France and Spain. Emperor Charles V's younger brother Ferdinand I and his nephew Maximilian II had been remarkably tolerant of Protestants living in their dominions. Ferdinand was known for his humanist inclinations and his court included a number of advisers who displayed pronounced Erasmian sympathies. His successor Maximilian was even more tolerant of religious diversity in his domains and was so well disposed to his Lutheran subjects that he was even suspected of apostasy. Moreover, he maintained frigid relations with the pope and his own cousin Philip II of Spain.[6]

The choice of Sir Philip Sidney as ambassador to the Habsburg court was highly judicious. The brilliant young courtier was well traveled and fluent in French and Latin. Furthermore, Sidney had already visited Poland and Bohemia the previous year. Accompanied at that time by his humanist mentor, the Huguenot Hubert Languet, Sidney traveled to Cracow and then to Prague, where he spent nine days and where the Emperor Maximilian was holding his court for the meeting of the Estates.[7] Before arriving in the Bohemian capital, the two men stopped at Ivančice in Moravia, the site of the press of the Bohemian Brethren (*Unitas Fratrum*), which a decade earlier had produced the celebrated Ivančice Hymnbook (1564) and in 1577 saw the publication of the renowned Kralice Bible in the nearby town of that name. This translation, a triumph of humanist learning, was the central European counterpart to the King James Bible (1611). But it was also an exercise in confessional collaboration. In addition to the Latin and Greek translators, the editorial board consisted of two Jewish scholars recruited to offer advice on the ancient Hebrew texts. Ivančice was already known to Languet, who had been instrumental in bringing the German printer Esrom Rüdiger there from an intolerant Wittenberg in 1574.[8] It is likely that Languet wished to acquaint his English protégé with this enlight-

---

[6] R. J. W. Evans, *The Making of the Habsburg Monarchy 1550–1700* (Oxford, 1979), 19–20. See also Paula Sutter Fichtner, *Emperor Maximilian II* (New Haven, 2001), chap. 3.

[7] Stewart, *Philip Sidney*, 135.

[8] See R. J. W. Evans, *Rudolf II and His World. A Study in Intellectual History* (Oxford, 1973), 100.

ened community of nonsectarian Protestants in the heart of Europe. Moravia was clearly no cultural wilderness but, as R. J. W. Evans has pointed out, a vibrant center of humanist learning and scholarship.

When he was appointed ambassador to the imperial court the following year, Sidney launched into a rigorous program of academic and intellectual preparation. Much time was spent with the Queen's astrologer, Dr. John Dee, studying chemistry and reading Livy under the guidance of the Cambridge classicist Gabriel Harvey, the adviser to Sidney's uncle, the earl of Leicester.[9] These activities were not purely academic but were directly related to Sidney's mission to the court of Rudolf II. John Dee had been at Prague in 1564 where he dedicated his *Monas Hieroglyphica* (a philosophical-alchemical treatise) to Maximilian II.[10] The frontispiece of the treatise displays the geometric shape of a perfect circle. (Significantly "perfect" is the word used to introduce Bohemia in act 3 of *The Winter's Tale*.) Dee thought of these astronomical symbols as the relics of a long-lost universal language which predated and transcended political and religious barriers. This utopian vision came to influence John Amos Comenius' *Pansophia*, the belief that all human knowledge can be reduced to a set of interconnected universal principles. Comenius' textbook for schoolchildren, *Orbis Pictus* (*The World in Pictures*), first printed in Nuremberg in 1658, includes a map of Europe at the heart of which Bohemia is depicted in the form of a perfect circle.

Sidney must have been aware of the new emperor's interest in alchemy and presumably regarded Dee as a valuable source of information concerning Rudolf's passion for the sciences. Moreover, his reading of Livy on Roman history was perfectly appropriate for a diplomat preparing to visit the court of a latter-day Caesar. Sidney and his party left England in late February and traveled through Germany, where he met several Lutheran princes in an effort to strengthen the Protestant alliance. The English embassy finally arrived in Prague on Maundy Thursday, April 4, 1576. The next four days were taken up with the celebration of Holy Week during which Sidney and the emperor attended Mass in the St. Vitus Cathedral and heard a sermon delivered by Edmund Campion, who had entered the priesthood in

---

[9] Ibid., 168–69.
[10] Duncan-Jones, *Sir Philip Sidney*, 116.

Figure 12. Emperor Rudolf II (1552–1612), Schloss Ambras, Innsbruck, Austria. Erich Lessing/Art Resource, New York.

Prague. On Easter Monday Sidney had a brief audience with the emperor which was probably held in the late medieval Vladislav Hall. In his report home, Sidney seems to have found the meeting rather disappointing. Rudolf was not the great embodiment of classical learning the idealistic young Englishman had come to expect: "He answered me in Latin with very few words . . . the Emperor is wholly by his inclination given to the wars, few of words, sullen of disposition, very secret and resolute, nothing the manner of his father had in winning men in his behaviour, but yet constant in keeping them."[11] The truth of the encounter is hard to distinguish from Sidney's account of it. If Sidney was unimpressed by Rudolf, it is equally possible that the emperor was unmoved by the young Englishman's rhetorical blandishments. After all, he had a far more brilliant rhetorician of his own in the person of Edmund Campion.

Edmund Campion

After being received into the Society of Jesus at Rome, Edmund Campion had visited Prague in 1574 in the company of James Avellanedo, the newly appointed confessor to the empress, as part of the Austrian Jesuit Province. Campion's assignment to Bohemia was part of a larger confessional project encouraged by Emperor Ferdinand I who had founded a Jesuit academy in Prague in the early 1560s, and which soon became the focus for a Tridentine mission among the local people.[12] In the perception of the Catholic authorities Bohemia was "infected" by the heresiarch Wyclif, so that Campion's mission was regarded as an act of English penance for the sins of an earlier Englishman. Responding to his tutor's curiosity about Bohemia, Campion acknowledges this fact: "Do you want to know about Bohemia? . . . A mixen and hotch-pot of heresies. But all the chief people are Catholics. The lower orders promiscuous. A pleasant and diversified harvest. For my part, I labour in it with more pleasure since an Englishman, Wycliffe, infected the people."[13] The utopian notion of a land free from "infection" finds expression in John of Gaunt's famously patriotic paean to a lost England in act 2, scene 1, of *Richard II*. Campion's perspective is simi-

[11] Quoted ibid., 127.
[12] Evans, *Rudolf II*, 34.
[13] Quoted from Richard Simpson, *Edmund Campion: A Biography* (London, 1896), 123. In his hagiographical life of Campion, William Cardinal Allen alludes to Wyclif's "infection" of Bohemia in a conversation held with Campion in Rome before the latter's fateful mission to England: "You owe more duty to England than to Beameland [Bohemia], and to London than to Prage; though it liketh me well that you have made some recompence to that countrey for the old wound it received by us." William Cardinal Allen, *A Briefe Historie of the Glorious Martyrdom of Twelve Reverend Priests Father Edmund Campion and His Companions* (London, 1908), 7.

larly utopian in its nostalgia for a time when Bohemia had been free of Wyclif's infection.

Campion's residence in Prague was of short duration; within two months of his arrival there, on October 10, 1573, he was sent east to Moravia where the prospects for Catholicism were even bleaker than in Bohemia. Less than a year later, on September 7, 1574, Campion returned to Prague with the novice-master John Paul Campanus in the coach of Chancellor Pernstein. He was appointed professor of rhetoric at the Jesuit Clementine College. At the beginning of the autumn term in 1577, Campion delivered a panegyric of St. Wenceslas, the patron saint of Bohemia whose feast day it was.

During his six years in Prague (1574–79), Campion occupied various important pedagogical positions. He was noted for his eloquent sermons, his oratorical gifts, and his religious dramas. In 1577, his tragedy on the subject of tyrannical King Saul was staged with great splendor before the empress and Elizabeth, widow of King Charles IX of France. It played for six hours and was repeated the next day at the request of Emperor Rudolf. Campion also wrote and produced at the Clementine College the play *Ambrosia*. This drama relates important events in the life of the early Church Father St. Ambrose who confronted and defeated Empress Ambrosia, defender of the Arian heresy. In the earlier mentioned poem "Collyn Clout" by John Skelton, the Arian heresy is explicitly linked with Wyclif and Hus. Campion's *Justina* thus alluded not only to English Protestantism but also to the local Czech legacy of Jan Hus. Justina was clearly meant to refer to Elizabeth I and the Arian heresy to the reformed religion of England. Perhaps Campion identified with Ambrose. Several years later he confronted Elizabeth and defended the tenets of the Catholic religion during his interrogation in the Tower.

On August 6, 1577, Campion wrote from Prague to his fellow Jesuit Robert Arden in Warwickshire: "For this at least we are indebted to those by whose heresy and persecution we have been driven forth and cast gently on a pleasant and blessed shore . . ."[14] Since in *The Winter's Tale* Bohemia becomes a refuge for Perdita as it did for Campion and his fellow exiles from England, it is intriguing to speculate whether Shakespeare knew about Campion's letter, especially since its recipi-

---

[14] Simpson, *Edmund Campion*, 121.

ent, Robert Arden, may have been a relative of Shakespeare's mother. In the early-modern period letters were frequently intended as public documents to be read by or to a group of people, often members of the same family; so it is not impossible that Shakespeare had been exposed to Campion's letter in some form or other. If Stephen Greenblatt and others are correct that Shakespeare met Campion either in Warwickshire or Lancashire during the latter's fateful mission to England in 1580–81, the young playwright may have heard the Jesuit deliver a sermon in which Bohemia is presented as a "blessed shore." But even if Shakespeare did not meet Campion, it is possible that he heard of Bohemia's reputation as a safe haven for exiled Catholics among members of the recusant community in England.

Certainly the tribulations of exile were to become a major theme of Shakespeare's drama. In *Richard II* Thomas Mowbray, duke of Norfolk, is banished from England and sentenced to perpetual exile on the Continent. This was the fate of many Catholics in Elizabethan England, especially following Campion's execution in 1581 when the persecution of recusants intensified. The reference to the exile of the duke of Norfolk must have resonated with the audience when *Richard II* was performed: Thomas Howard, the fourth duke of Norfolk and the most prominent recusant during Elizabeth's reign, had been beheaded for his role in the Ridolfi plot, an attempt to depose Elizabeth and place her cousin, Mary Queen of Scots, on the English throne. *Richard II* reflects the political and religious situation in late Elizabethan England. Like the exiled recusants of Elizabeth's reign, Mowbray is faced not only with the loss of his homeland but the loss of his native tongue as well since English was at this time a purely insular language not spoken or understood on the European mainland:

> The language I have learnt these forty years,
> My native English, now I must forgo;
> And now my tongue's use is to me no more
> Than an unstringèd viol or a harp,
> Or like a cunning instrument cased up
> Or, being open, put into the hands
> That knows no touch to tune the harmony
> (1.3.159–65)[15]

[15] *Riverside Shakespeare*, 810.

Elizabeth Jane Weston

One such recusant was Elizabeth Jane Weston (1581–1612). A highly gifted linguist, Elizabeth composed accomplished poetry in Latin and was proficient in Greek, Italian, German, and Czech. In 1583—two years after Campion's martyrdom at Tyburn and at the height of the persecution of English Catholics—her mother, Joan Cooper Weston, her stepfather Edward Kelley, and Dr. John Dee, the queen's astrologer and Kelley's associate in angelic séances, left England for the Continent. Joan's children by her deceased first husband John Weston, John Francis and Elizabeth Jane, stayed behind in England until December 1584. After spending some months in Poland, where they were engaged in séances under the patronage of the Polish landowner Albrecht Łaski (1536–1605), Dee and Kelley departed Cracow on August 1, 1584, leaving their spouses and children until they had found suitable accommodation for them in Prague.[16] The three-hundred-mile journey from Cracow to Prague took eight days as the two Englishmen traveled along the course of the Vistula River, skirting the foothills of the Carpathian Mountains. Soon afterwards both families settled in Bohemia where Elizabeth Jane's brother was educated at the Jesuit Clementine College, the same seat of learning where Edmund Campion had taught the previous decade.

In spite of being granted a private audience with the Emperor Rudolf at Prague, Dee was eventually banished from the city on charges of spying for the British government; and on September 14, 1586, he settled in southern Bohemia under the protection of the regional magnate Lord William of Rožmberk. Here he was provided with a laboratory in order to carry out his ultimate utopian experiment: the alchemical transformation of base metals into gold. Dee collaborated with Kelley on these experiments and their renowned angelic séances. By this time Kelley's fame as an alchemist had surpassed that of his partner and he was invited back to Prague by the emperor where he was knighted in 1589, the same year that Dee returned to his home in Mortlake near London.

Kelley's fame as an alchemist must have contributed to Bohemia's

---

[16] Benjamin Woolley, *The Queen's Conjurer. The Science and Magic of Dr. John Dee, Adviser to Queen Elizabeth I* (New York, 2001), 221. For Dee's career in Poland and Bohemia, see Evans, *Rudolf II*, 218ff.

glamorous reputation in Shakespeare's England. It may also have made his patron, Rudolf, a figure of mythic fascination. In many ways the magus Prospero in *The Tempest* recalls the eccentric Rudolf. His famous epilogue speech beginning with the words "Now my charms are all o'erthrown" has often been seen as a veiled articulation of Shakespeare's own farewell to the stage. Intriguingly, however, Katherine Duncan-Jones has proposed that Shakespeare may have been thinking of Emperor Rudolf when he makes Prospero declare:

> The government I cast upon my brother,
> And to my state grew stranger, being transported
> And rapt in secret studies.[17]
>
> (1.2.75–77)[18]

Rudolf had abdicated in favor of his younger brother Matthias in 1608 just as Prospero relinquishes his power to his brother Antonio. Like Prospero, he had turned his back on matters of state, immersing himself in his intellectual pursuits of alchemy, astrology, and art collecting. Thus Prospero's famous valedictory could be interpreted as a swansong of the long reign of Rudolf.

Several years earlier Kelley had moved to the town of Jílov, in South Bohemia, where he had mining interests given to him by his new patron and William of Rožmberk's successor, Lord Peter Vok of Rožmberk. It was here that his stepdaughter Elizabeth Jane Weston was taught to read by the humanist John Saršan Vodňanský. When Kelley was imprisoned for debt in 1591, the family moved to the town of Most, where Elizabeth continued her education under the tutelage of another English exile, the Oxford scholar John Hammond. Elizabeth became fluent in the composition of Latin by the age of fourteen, an achievement impossible for women in Protestant England due to the increasing association of Latin learning with popishness.

When Edward Kelley died in 1597, his widow and stepchildren found themselves destitute. Young Elizabeth and her mother went to Prague in the hope of enlisting the patronage of the Emperor Rudolf. Here she excelled by her learning and her Latin verse and was praised

---

[17] Duncan-Jones, *Sir Philip Sidney*, 127.
[18] *Riverside Shakespeare*, 1612.

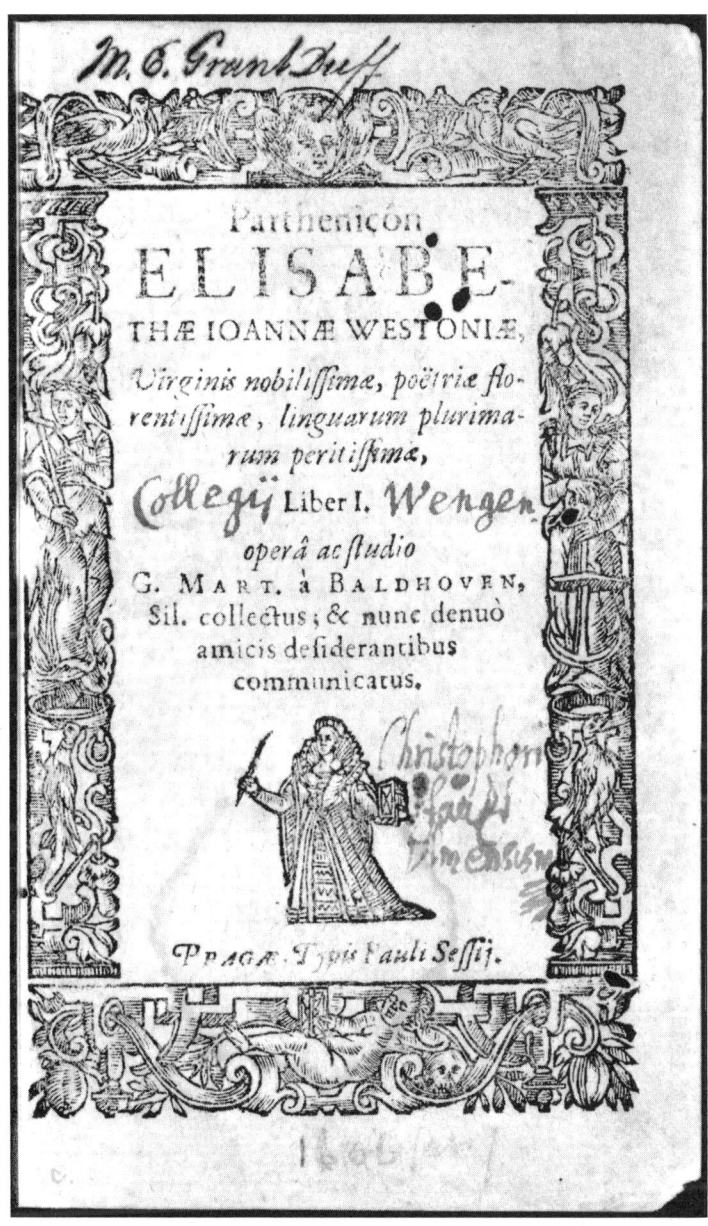

Figure 13. Elizabeth Jane Weston: *Parthenicon*, printed in Prague, 1606. By permission of the Houghton Library, Harvard University.

for her facility in Greek, Italian, Czech, and German. She corresponded with many of the leading scholars of her day. Her poems were collected and printed at Frankfurt an der Oder by the Silesian nobleman Georg Martin von Baldhoven with the florid title *Parthenicon Elisabethae Joannaie Westoniae, virginis nobilissimae, poetriae florentissimae, linguarum plurimarum peritissimae* (figure 13). Editions were printed in 1606 at Prague, in 1609 at Leipzig, in 1712 at Amsterdam, and in 1723 at Frankfurt. Many of her poems take the form of addresses to princes such as James I. She also wrote epigrams, epistles to friends, and a poem in praise of printing, and translated some of Aesop's fables into Latin verse. Her English contemporaries compared her favorably with Sir Thomas More; and her reputation on the Continent was even higher. Around 1602, she married a German lawyer, Johann Leon, agent at the imperial court for the duke of Brunswick and the prince of Anhalt. She had four sons, all of whom predeceased her, and three daughters. She died in Prague in 1612 and was buried in the cemetery of the Augustinian church of St. Thomas in the Lesser Town. She has remained one of the outstanding writers—and the only female writer—of humanist Latin verse from Rudolfine Bohemia.

One of the most striking poems in the *Parthenicon* is "De inundatione Pragae" ("On the Flood of Prague"), which describes the devastation wrought by the flooding of the river Vltava after several days of heavy rain. By a prodigious act of poetic imagination Weston transforms a real event into a fantasy of primordial destruction in which the imperial city is threatened with total inundation and seems about to disappear beneath the waves of the almighty sea:

> Headlong the foaming whirlpool sweeps all that is before it:
> Desperately all are carried by the maddened waters.
> Here grain, here wasted fruit are flooded by the waves;
> There a man, there a bed, and a woman swim.
> Look, timber, pine, and swimming rooftops, look;
> Prodigious things are swirled in the rapid flood.
> Far and wide stand walls submerged in tempestuous eddies,
> So everything submerged is destroyed by the deep.
> A small boat plows the forum; fish defile the holy
> Places; and an altar is soaked by the receding waves.
> A crowd, their clothing drenched, stand and watch astonished

And grieve for all destroyed by unrestrained evils.
Thus it was to see the face of furious Moldau,
Its waters seemed like those of Deucalion's flood.
Oh you who quiet the monsters of the sea and raging storms,
Jehovah, with your nod, submerge so many evils.[19]

The pagan setting of Weston's inundated Prague is intriguingly reminiscent of Shakespeare's Bohemia as a mythic pre-Christian land with a coastline in *The Winter's Tale*. It is not impossible that the playwright had heard of Weston's *Parthenicon* through the humanist circles at the Jacobean court where, as we shall see, Bohemia seems to have acquired a reputation as a pagan utopia.

Elizabeth Stuart ("The Winter Queen")

If Rudolfine Bohemia was a congenial place for Catholic exiles like Elizabeth Jane Weston, it was equally appealing to Protestant visitors. Bohemia had been predominantly—if not exclusively—Protestant for several generations and its nobility enjoyed the kind of religious liberties unavailable to its English counterpart. Under the rule of Maximilian II and Rudolf II a modus vivendi was established between the Catholic emperor and his Protestant subjects. But after Rudolf's death in 1611 the situation began to deteriorate. The new emperor Ferdinand was less well disposed to his nonconformist subjects and began to reverse many of the privileges enjoyed by the Bohemian nobility. The result was religious conflict and the beginning of the end of the Bohemian reputation as an ecumenical utopia. In 1618 angry members of the Protestant Estates entered the Prague Castle and, following a heated argument, threw the emperor's two regents—along with their hapless secretary—from the window of the council chamber into the castle moat (figure 14). Miraculously, the three men escaped relatively unscathed.

The following year the rebellious Estates formally deposed Ferdinand and offered the crown of Bohemia to Frederick, Elector Palatine,

---

[19] Quoted in Louise Schleiner, *Tudor and Stuart Women Writers* (Bloomington, 1994), 105.

Figure 14. The Defenestration of Prague, May 23, 1618. Kunstbibliothek, Staatliche Museen zu Berlin. Bildarchiv Preussicher Kulturbesitz/Art Resource, New York.

and his wife Elizabeth Stuart. The carefree and happy pair, who had once enjoyed watching Shakespeare's plays at their nuptials and perhaps saw themselves allegorically represented as Ferdinand and Miranda, were now projected onto the far less appealing stage of European politics. The royal couple left their Palatine seat of Heidelberg on Monday, October 7, for their new capital of Prague. After a leisurely progress through Bohemia, their triumphal entry into Prague took place on October 31, 1619. The ceremonies began at the summer residence six miles west of the river Vltava known as the Hvĕzda ("the Star"). This fantasy palace had been built in the form of a six-rayed star by Rudolf's uncle Ferdinand of Tyrol (1529–95).[20] Baron Bohuslav Burka, Grand Chamberlain of Bohemia, accompanied by the burgesses of Prague and an impressive assembly of Bohemian, Moravian, Silesian, and Lusatian nobility, came to this hunting lodge to welcome

[20] Evans, *Rudolf II*, 27.

their new king and queen. Baron John of Tallenburg opened the proceedings with a speech in Czech, which was translated for the benefit of the royal couple. Frederick answered in German since he did not speak a word of his subjects' native language.[21]

The entry of Frederick and Elizabeth into Prague resembled a Roman triumph and lasted over three hours. The new king and queen entered the Castle through the Strahov Gate. The king's coronation took place in the St. Vitus Cathedral, suitably stripped of all popish ornament, on November 4 (N. S.). Three days later Elizabeth was crowned in the same cathedral in a separate ceremony. The banquet to celebrate the coronations took place in the beautiful Vladislav Hall within the precincts of the royal palace. Ominously, Elizabeth's father, King James, had refused to send any English representatives to witness the ceremonies since he still demurred to acknowledge the legality of the Bohemian election.

Twelve days after these momentous events, a series of Bohemian deputations arrived at the Castle. On the Queen's name day—the feast of St. Elizabeth, November 19—the most prominent Protestant ladies of Prague crossed the river from the Old Town to present gifts to their heavily pregnant sovereign. These consisted of loaves of bread baked in the shape of flowers in memory of the legend of St. Elizabeth of Hungary who had smuggled loaves of bread out of her castle against her husband's command to feed the poor; just before these were discovered by her husband, they were transformed miraculously into roses. November 19 (N. S.) actually commemorated the mother of John the Baptist and not Elizabeth of Hungary, but it was probably deemed more appropriate to recall the new Queen's regal namesake rather than the infertile Elizabeth of the New Testament.[22]

By all accounts the event was not a great success. Elizabeth seemed unmoved by the gesture and unappreciative of the gifts. Perhaps the Calvinist queen was offended by the allusions to a Catholic saint and the strangely humble offerings of the Prague ladies. When a second deputation arrived at the Castle sometime later, the event seems to have proceeded more smoothly. The gift for the Queen was more suitably magnificent: an ivory cradle studded with gems, and a casket to

---

[21] Carola Oman, *The Winter Queen. Elizabeth of Bohemia* (London, 1938; rev. ed., 2000), 188.
[22] Ibid., 199.

match, containing a complete set of infant's clothes. This time the Queen reacted with greater enthusiasm. Perhaps tutored by her Bohemian chamberlain in local etiquette, she warmly squeezed her subjects' right hands—much to their amazement—and even managed to speak a sentence of thanks in Czech.[23]

On the night of December 17, the queen gave birth to a strong male child. The citizens of Prague hoped that their new prince would be named Přemysl in memory of ancient dynasty of Czech kings. But the boy was christened Rupert in honor of his ancestor, Rupert III, Elector Palatine, who had been elected emperor on the deposition of Wenceslas IV in 1400. Prince Rupert (1619–82) was later to achieve fame in England as the dashing cavalry commander who fought on the side of his uncle, King Charles I, in the English Civil War.

The bestowal of a German name on their son was not the only faux pas of the new king and queen. When Frederick decided to go swimming among the ordinary citizens of Prague in the river Vltava, his utopian gesture was deemed inappropriate and unseemly for a king. The Calvinist Frederick also misjudged the ecumenical mood of his people when he ordered the crucifix adorning the Charles Bridge to be removed. As the king swam in the river Vltava, Count Schlick arrived to inform him that an indignant crowd was on its way to the Castle to protest the removal of the cross. Frederick quickly reversed the decision, but the damage had already been done. According to an Irish Jesuit propagandist resident in Prague, the presence of the cross, erected in the reign of Rudolf II on the site of an earlier crucifix, was the reason why the new queen had so far not condescended to traverse the bridge and visit the Old Town.[24]

John Harrison

In England a war of propaganda on behalf of the new king and queen of Bohemia was being fought, albeit without great practical results. Sir Thomas Roe wrote a pamphlet extolling the righteousness of the Bohemians' actions and sent a copy to Queen Elizabeth, who thanked

---

[23] Ibid., 200.
[24] Ibid., 209–11.

"honest Thom Roe" in a personal letter. A former groom to Elizabeth, John Harrison, wrote the first English history of Bohemia (1619–20). This work stresses the Bohemian tradition of Protestantism and celebrates the kingdom's defiance of popes and emperors: "It has had more wars with the Pope and won more victories against him, and his partakers, than any other nation. (The Bohemians) have kept the faith in Christ better and purer than any other nation; they have stoutly defended it and many of them have died for it; they maintained it against the Pope; and all the Kings of Europe who were then the slaves to the Pope and not one of them so free as the King of Bohemia."[25]

In 1619 Harrison published a pamphlet with the elaborate title *A Short Relation of the Departure of the high and mightie Prince Frederick King Elect of Bohemia with his royall and virtuous Ladie Elizabeth; and the thryse hopefull young Prince Henrie, from Heydelberg towards Prague, to receive the Crowne of that Kingdom.* The first half of the pamphlet is devoted to an account of the preparations for the royal family's departure for their new kingdom; the second half is a short account of the coronation of King Frederick I of Bohemia on October 25, 1619, followed by the coronation of Queen Elizabeth three days later, on October 28. Harrison compares Elizabeth with her namesake, Elizabeth I, and likens her heroic departure for Prague with Elizabeth's defiance of the Spanish Armada at Tilbury in 1588: "Gonne is this sweete Princesse, with her now-more-than-princlie houseband ... towards the place whear his armie attendeth, to march forward: showing herself like that virago of Tilburie in eightie eight: another Queen Elizabeth, for so now she is; and what more she may be in time, or her royall issue, is in gods hands to dispose to his glorie ..."

A year later appeared *The Bohemian Lawes or Rights Defended against the Informer*, a translation of *Bohemica Jura defensa*, which affirmed the Bohemian Estates' historic right to elect their rulers. This pamphlet was a retort to an anonymous Catholic tract attacking the Bohemians' deposition of the Habsburg Frederick of Styria. Like *The Winter's Tale*, Harrison's pamphlet mingles history and myth, fact and fiction, in presenting the foundational figures Čech (Czechius), Krok (Crocus) and Libuše (Libussa) as the first legitimate rulers of Bohemia.

In his *The Masque of Queens*, which was performed by Anne of Den-

---

[25] Quoted in Josef V. Polišenský, *Britain and Czechoslovakia* (Prague, 1968), 32.

mark and her ladies at Whitehall on February 2, 1609, Ben Jonson introduces the pagan Amazon Valasca. Better known in the Czech sources as Vlasta, this formidable lady leads a female rebellion against the patriarchal rule of Přemysl (Primislaus) after the death of Libuše. Embodiments of the virtues of courage and freedom, the rebellious Vlasta and her female followers were probably intended to symbolize the independence of the Bohemian nobility whose ancient liberties were confirmed by the so-called Letter of Majesty, an edict of tolerance issued by Rudolf II to his Protestant subjects in the same year as Jonson's masque was performed at Whitehall: "The eleventh was that brave Bohemian queen, Valasca, who, for her courage, had the surname of Bold; that, to redeem herself and her sex from the tyranny of men, which they lived in under Primislaus, on a night, and at an appointed hour, led on the women to the slaughter of their barbarous husbands and lords; and possessing themselves of their horses, arms, treasure, and places of strength, not only ruled the rest, but lived many years after with the liberty and fortitude of amazons."[26]

As in Thomas More's *Utopia*, the foundational figures of Bohemia embody prefeudal liberties.[27] In Renaissance thought generally paganism is frequently synonymous with political liberties. It is significant in this respect that Přemysl the Plowman, who is elevated to the ducal throne, is not a nobleman but a commoner. Harrison's tract presents the election of the peasant-prince as a constitutional precedent for the nonhereditary status of the crown of Bohemia. Although the Habsburgs had been de facto hereditary rulers of Bohemia since 1526, their title was technically subject to confirmation by the Estates. Harrison's vision of the Bohemian polity is thus a utopian tabula rasa upon which feudal law has never left its trace. Harrison also refers to pagan Bohemia as a "desert," an image which brings to mind *The Winter's Tale*. Harrison's conceit indicates that the utopian reputation enjoyed by Bohemia was not confined to English recusant circles but formed part of a more general discourse of religious and political freedom. The peasant-princess Perdita in *The Winter's Tale* personifies these ideals. A female counterpart to the peasant-prince Primislaus, she gives voice to the egalitarian sentiment: "The self-same sun that shines upon his court / Hides not his visage from our cottage, but / Looks on alike" (4.4.444–46). Not

---

[26] Ben Jonson, *The Masque of Queens*, in *Court Masques. Jacobean and Caroline Entertainments 1605–1640*, ed. David Lindley (Oxford, 1995), 35–53 at 50.

[27] Susan Bruce, *Three Early Modern Utopias* (Oxford, 1999), ix.

only do these lines serve as a retort to Polixenes' threats; they also provide an implicit contrast between the pastoral innocence of Bohemia and the treacherous world of Leontes' court. And even the status-conscious King Polixenes unconsciously undermines his own case against the marriage of a prince with a shepherdess in affirming that a princess, in spite of her royal rank, is still a child of nature.

John Taylor

Another Englishman with Bohemian-Protestant sympathies was John Taylor (1580–1653), the self-styled "Water Poet." A native of Gloucester who found modest employment as a bargeman on the river Thames, Taylor was commissioned to arrange the details of the water pageant at the marriage of Princess Elizabeth in 1613, and was afterwards kindly entertained by the queen in Bohemia. Taylor wrote two short pamphlets about his travels in Bohemia. The first one was titled *An English-man's Love to Bohemia with a friendly farewell to all the noble souldiers that goe from Great Britain to that honorable expedition* (1620). It is written entirely in a high-flown patriotic vein, appealing to British men to honor their brave English and Scottish ancestors by fighting on behalf of the Protestant cause in Bohemia:

> And true borne Britaines, worthy countrymen,
> Resume your ancient honors once agen.
> I know your valiant minds are sharpe and keene
> To serve your Soveraignes daughter, Bohems Queene.

Like Africa and America, Bohemia is regarded as a valuable colonial prize to be gained by conquest:

> Through all the coasts of tawny Affrica,
> And through the bounds of rich America.
> And as the world our worths acknowledge must,
> Let not our valour sleeping lye and rust:
> But to immortalize our Britaines name,
> Let it from imbers burst into a flame.[28]

[28] Houghton Library, Harvard University.

The pamphlet ends with an evocation of Bohemia as a utopian land of bounty and freedom:

> The Kingdome of Bohemia is well peopled with many brave horsemen and footmen: rich, fruitfull, and plentifully stored (by the Almightes bounty), with all the treasures of nature fit for the use and commodity of man; it hath in it of Castles and walled townes, to the number of 780 and 32000 villages; by a grant from the Emperor Charles the fourth, it was freed for ever of the payments of all contributions to the Empire whatsoever; Moravia, Silesia, and Lusatia are as large as Bohemia, well replenished with stout horsemen and footmen.

Taylor's second pamphlet about Bohemia is a booklet of alternating prose and verse titled *Taylor his Travels: from the City of London in England, to the City of Prague in Bohemia* (1621). In this booklet Taylor continues to evoke Bohemia as a plentiful paradise akin to the mythic land of Cockaigne:

> When we had thus footed it and travelled past the hills and woods, (being at the least 4 houres toyle) and that we might looke down the mountaines, into the fruitfull land of Bohem, never did sight more rejoyce us, the lower hills being full of Vineyards, and the vallies, corne and pasture; not an English mile distance, but a village every way; and twenty, thirty, or forty reecks or stacks of corne which their barnes cannot hold, in the space of every hours iourney: in a word, everything that belonged to the use and commodity of man, was and is there, and all the delightfull objects to satisfie there is abundantly, so that nature seemed to make that country her storehouse or granary, for there is nothing wanting except mens gratitude to God for such blessings.[29]

At the outskirts of Prague, Taylor witnesses a scene completely opposite to the pastoral idyll of the Bohemian countryside: a Golgotha of executed prisoners:

> Within halfe a dutch mile is a fearfull place, being frequented with inhumane and barbarous murderers, that assault travellers, first shoot-

[29] Ibid.

ing and murdering them, and after searching their pockets, where if they have money or not, all is one, it is but so many slaine; for these villaines have a wood, and a deepe valley to shelter themselves in, that they are hardly taken afterwards; but if they chance at any time to be but apprehended, they are racked and tortured to make them confesse, and afterwards their executions are very terrible . . . and we saw in our iourney above seaven score gallowes and wheeles, where thieves were hanged some fresh, and some half rotten, and the carkasses of murtherers, broken limb after limb on the wheeles . . .

Taylor arrived in Prague on Thursday, September 7, 1620. He mentions the "faire stone bridge" across the Vltava (the Charles Bridge) with a tower at either end. He is impressed by the large number of churches and the harmonious coexistence of Catholics, Protestants, and Jews: "There is said to bee in it of Churches and Chappells, 150. For there are great numbers of Catholiques, who have many Chappells dedicated to sundry Saints, & I was there at foure severall sorts of divine exercises, viz. at good sermons with the Protestants, at masse with the Papists, at a Lutherans preaching and at the Iewes Synagogue, three of which I saw and heard for curiosity, and the other for edification."

Taylor estimates that there are between fifty and sixty thousand Jews living in Prague, who "Do all live by brocage and usury upon the Christians, and are very rich in money and Iewells, so that a man may see tenne or twelve together of them, that are accounted worth 20. 30. or 40000 l' a piece; and yet the slaves go miserably attired, that 15. of them are not worth the hanging for their whole wardrobes." Prague's importance as a major center of Jewish religion and culture is confirmed by an earlier English traveler to Bohemia, Fynes Moryson. In his *Itinerary* (1617) Moryson attests to the religious pluralism of Habsburg Bohemia: "Generally in all the kingdome there was great confusion of Religions, so as in the same Citty some were Calvinists, some Lutherans, some Hussites, some Anabaptists, some Picards, some Papists, not only in the Cheefe Citty Prage, and other Cittyes of Bohemia. . . . And as the Jewes have a peculiar Citty at Prage, so they had freedome throughout the kingdome."[30]

---

[30] *Shakespeare's Europe: A Survey of the Condition of Europe at the end of the 16th century*, ed. Charles Hughes, 2nd ed. (New York, 1967), 275.

Established in Prague since the High Middle Ages, the Jews had undergone rising and falling fortunes; but the years between 1564 and 1612 witnessed the golden age of Prague Jewish culture. The improvement of the conditions of the Jews began with the reign of Maximilian II (1564–76) and continued through the reign of his son Rudolf II. In 1567 Maximilian confirmed the privileges granted to Jews already settled in Prague and throughout the kingdom. Under Rudolf things became even better. In 1577 he confirmed their privileges and promised that they would not be expelled from either Prague or the Czech kingdom. In 1611 the Emperor Matthias confirmed the privileges accorded to the Jews by his predecessors. This tolerant political climate was accompanied by a growth in Jewish prosperity and the number of synagogues in Prague increased. In 1592 the new Meisl Synagogue was completed; and in 1599 the Munk Synagogue, later renamed Wechsler's Synagogue, was built on the south side of Židovská (later Široká) Street. The Cikánova Synagogue, named after its founder Šalomon Cikán, was founded sometime before 1613.

Taylor visited the Prague Castle daily for twenty days. He compares its capacious precincts favorably with the less spacious Tower of London: "The Castle where the King and Queene doe keepe their Court, is magnificent and sumptuous in building, strongly situated and fortified by nature and art, being founded on a high hill, so that at pleasure it keepes the town in command, & it is much more spacious in rooms for receipts in gardens & orchards then twice the bounds of the Towre of London." One of the most delightful sections of this little book is the account of Taylor's reception by the king and queen of Bohemia. He tells us that he was permitted to hold the queen's youngest child, Prince Rupert, and confesses in a humorous aside:

> There (for a token) I did thinke it meet,
> To take the shooes from off this Prince his feet:
> I doe not say I stole, but I did take,
> And whilst I live Ile keepe them for his sake:
> Long may his Grace live to be stylde a man,
> And then Ile steale his boots too if I can.

Taylor ends his travelogue with a rhapsodic paean to the Bohemian capital which again stresses its richness and abundance:

> Prague is a famous, ancient, Kingly seat,
> In scituation and in state compleat,
> Rich in abundance of the earths best treasure,
> Proud and high minded, beyond bounds or measure:
> In Architecture stately: in attire
> Bezonians and Plebeians do aspire,
> To be apparel'd with the stately port
> Of worship, honor, or the royal court . . .

Another English adherent of the Bohemian cause, Sir Henry Wotton, British ambassador to the imperial court at Prague, wrote a poem to Queen Elizabeth titled "On his Mistris, the Queen of Bohemia." Beginning with the famous line "You meaner beauties of the night," Wotton's eulogy is one of the most memorable English poems of the Jacobean era and an eloquent testimony of a courtier's personal devotion to his mistress. Just as Shakespeare emphasizes Perdita's natural virtue more than her noble birth, so does Sir Henry Wotton characterize his royal mistress as virtuous first and royal second. Notable in the phrasing of Elizabeth's royal title is the word "choice," a reference to her election by the Bohemian Estates:

> So, when my Mistris shal be seene
> In form and Beauty of her mind,
> By Vertue first, then Choyce a Queen,
> Tell me, if she were not design'd
> Th'Eclypse and Glory of her kind.[31]

But these expressions of religious and personal loyalty amounted to very little as long as King James refused to recognize the legality of the Bohemian election and provide his beleaguered daughter and son-in-law with military assistance in defense of their kingdom. Finally, after several months, James at last sent ambassadors in an attempt to broker a peace and avoid a full-scale war between the Bohemian Estates and the Catholic emperor.

---

[31] *The Metaphysical Poets,* ed. Helen Gardner (Harmondsworth, 1957), 46.

The Battle of the White Mountain

On November 8, 1620, King Frederick was entertaining these ambassadors when news arrived that his army had been attacked and scattered at the White Mountain on the outskirts of the city. The ill-disciplined Protestant force disintegrated within an hour of engagement with the enemy. Their lack of morale was hardly helped by the absence of their king, who now hurried—too late—to rally the panicked and fleeing troops. Prague was in chaos as retreating soldiers flocked into the city and the citizens began to fear savage reprisals from the triumphant imperial army. Frederick and Elizabeth were forced to make a hasty and undignified departure from the Prague Castle and crossed into the Old Town to avoid capture by the pursuing Catholic army. Jesuit propagandists derived great satisfaction from the fact that the Calvinist queen was now forced to behold the crucifix she had so abhorred as her carriage crossed the Charles Bridge into the Old Town. From there the couple and their entourage fled toward the Silesian border, never to return to their kingdom and soon to lose their Palatine lands as well. The Jesuits derisively dubbed Frederick and his consort "The Winter King" and "The Winter Queen," so named since their presence in Bohemia had lasted no more than a year—from November 1619 to November 1620.

The aftermath of the Battle of the White Mountain was terrible indeed. On June 21, 1621, the twenty-seven leaders of the Protestant rebellion were executed on the Old Town Square in Prague, among them three noblemen, seven knights, and seventeen leading burghers; their heads were impaled on the towers at both ends of the Charles Bridge as a deterrent to others. These gruesome events signaled the beginning of a widespread campaign of persecution in which Bohemian nonconformists were forced either to convert to Catholicism or to leave their homeland forever. Philip Massinger's tragedy *The Picture* (1629) reflects Bohemia's lurch into violence. Forming the background to a drama of jealousy and revenge, his Bohemia recalls Robert Greene's gloomy kingdom rather than Shakespeare's bucolic idyll.[32] The English love affair with Bohemia was finished.

---

[32] *The Plays of Philip Massinger*, ed. Philip Edwards and Colin Gibson, vol. 3 (Oxford, 1976).

The Winter's Tale

The cataclysmic events of 1620 still lay in the future when *The Winter's Tale* was performed before the court at Whitehall in 1613. The theme of reconciliation which informs the play reflected the ecumenical optimism of the Jacobean court and the king's self-image as "the Great Peacemaker." Just as James avoided taking sides in the growing European conflict, so is Shakespeare's play assiduously noncommittal in its religious sympathies. In recent years scholars have become increasingly sensitive to the religious subtexts of *The Winter's Tale*; but they rarely look beyond England in an attempt to understand these subtexts. According to Julia Reinhard Lupton, Bohemia encodes cultural and religious references to England's pre-Reformation past in the form of a "rustic English paganism, the country remains of Catholic syncretism."[33] I would concur that Shakespeare's Bohemia to some extent evokes a lost Catholic England; its deserts and seacoast, for example, may even have been linked in the playwright's imagination with the wetlands of recusant Lancashire where, some scholars believe, he spent the so-called "lost years" of his youth. But we must remember that Shakespeare's Bohemia is not a Christian but a pagan land. To this extent his Bohemia is neither Catholic nor Protestant but a congenial alternative to both religious extremes.

Bohemia plays a crucial role in providing Shakespeare with the necessary denouement of reconciliation, since it is there that Perdita finds the safe haven which permits her eventual return home sixteen years later. It also functions as a transition from the repressive kingdom of Sicilia (in acts 1 and 2), where personal accusations of adultery coexist with Protestant fears of idolatrous representation, to act 5 in which Leontes is reunited and reconciled with his wife and daughter. Scholars of the play have pointed out that the statue of Hermione may allude to the new marble funerary effigies of Elizabeth I and King James's mother, Mary Queen of Scots, at Westminster Abbey (1605–12).[34] If these monuments were in Shakespeare's mind, they would reinforce the theme of expiation and reconciliation fundamental to the

---

[33] Julia Reinhard Lupton, *Afterlives of the Saints: Hagiography, Typology, and Renaissance Literature* (Stanford, 1996), 197.

[34] See Richard Wilson, *Secret Shakespeare. Studies in Theatre, Religion and Resistance* (Manchester, 2004), 246.

play's ending: in bringing together the tombs of Elizabeth and Mary—the latter for Catholics a martyr, for Protestants a traitor—in the royal mausoleum at Westminster, James was attempting to heal the rift between the religious denominations.

Perdita's departure from Bohemia after sixteen years in exile offers an intriguing parallel with Campion's return from Prague to England in 1580. If Campion was indeed on Shakespeare's mind, his decision to make Perdita the instrument of her parents' reconciliation after so many years of estrangement and separation can be read as a poignant allegory of Shakespeare's hoped-for reconciliation between Catholics and Protestants. But unlike the wish-fulfillment of the play's ending, Campion's return did not bring reconciliation. On the contrary, it made things far worse. According to Stephen Greenblatt, his horrific execution at Tyburn (where he was hanged, drawn, and quartered) may have traumatized many of Shakespeare's Catholic contemporaries into distancing themselves from the "nightmare of persecution, torture and death."[35]

If *The Winter's Tale* avoids taking sides in the great religious debate of its time, I suspect that the reason is less conspiratorially covert than genuinely ecumenical. Shakespeare's utopian vision of Bohemia is certainly consistent with the likelihood that—whatever his personal religious beliefs may have been—the mature playwright was sympathetic to irenicism, a pan-European phenomenon extending from Jacobean London to Habsburg Vienna and Prague.[36] The courts of Maximilian II and Rudolf II provided a particularly favorable setting for irenicism and boasted some of the most progressive minds of the confessional age.[37] According to Hugh Trevor-Roper, Rudolf's court at Prague was "neither Catholic nor Protestant. Indeed, it was not religious at all."[38] In the spirit of *The Winter's Tale* and *The Tempest*, it was:

> A magical world, a world of neo-Platonist "natural" magic, whose philosophers looked beyond the multitudinous visible phenomena of

---

[35] See Stephen Greenblatt, *Will in the World. How Shakespeare Became Shakespeare* (New York, 2004), 116.

[36] For the claim that the older Shakespeare adhered to the irenicism of the Jacobean court, see Marotti, "Shakespeare and Catholicism."

[37] Howard Louthan, *The Quest for Compromise. Peacemakers in Counter-Reformation Vienna* (Cambridge, 1997).

[38] Hugh Trevor-Roper, *Princes and Artists. Patronage and Ideology at Four Habsburg Courts 1517–1633* (London, 1991), 90.

nature and found a vast system of divinely ordered harmony, discoverable by research, intelligible by human reason, operable by the adept, the magus. This magical world repudiated the formal cosmology of medieval Christendom, and transcended differences between orthodox Catholicism and orthodox Protestantism, both of which had returned to that cosmology. At its core, it was ecumenical, tolerant, contemplative, scientific; at its periphery, it ran out into alchemical fantasies, astrological calculations, Pythagorean numerology.[39]

The ecumenical foundation of Rudolf's court was laid at his father's court at Vienna. One of the key irenicists at Maximilian's court was his chief architect Jacopo de Strada, a former pupil of Giulio Romano.[40] It may be a pure coincidence that the magical statue of Hermione which comes to life at the end of *The Winter's Tale* is ascribed to Romano. More likely is the fact that Shakespeare was evoking a spiritual *renovatio* of humanist tolerance redolent of the Jacobean and Habsburg courts in contrast with the intolerance of Elizabeth's reign, symbolized by the paranoia and hatred of acts 1 and 2. By emphasizing the classical pedigree of the Holy Roman Empire, Strada tried to look beyond the confessional tensions of the age. For him, as for Shakespeare, art in an age of religious conflict should attempt to bring people together, not divide them. *The Winter's Tale* was written and performed in that ecumenical spirit. It is not the work of a man entering benign old age but the aspiration of a tolerant artist anxious to maintain a fragile European peace. In our own world of increasing religious extremism this is surely an aspiration with which many of us can identify.

[39] Ibid., 91.
[40] Lonthan, *The Quest for Compromise*, 24–26.

Chapter 7

Three Men in a Boat

*Waldstein, Hollar, and Comenius
in Seventeenth-Century England*

In 1627 Emperor Ferdinand decreed that the Protestants of Bohemia and Moravia must convert to Catholicism within six months or else go into exile. This became the fate of John Amos Komenský (Comenius) (1592–1670). After years of wandering, Comenius eventually settled in Amsterdam. During his exile in Leszno, Poland, where he was the director of an important school for the children of the Bohemian Brethren, Comenius made a voyage to England where he stayed for several weeks. The central European Protestants who came to England before and after the Battle of the White Mountain in 1620 brought with them a humanist vision of the world which shaped their perception of England. The three such travelers I shall focus on in this chapter—Baron Waldstein who toured southern and eastern England in 1600; the engraver Wenceslas Hollar who arrived in London in the entourage of Thomas Howard, earl of Arundel, and settled in England; and Comenius who visited England in 1641—shared an empiricist belief that reality could be directly apprehended in writing and art and that human knowledge could be classified in terms of universal principles. In an age noted for its geographical explorations and munificent art collections—the age of Sir Walter Raleigh and Rudolf II—these three exiles viewed England as a rich treasure-house from which to

Three Men in a Boat   197

garner knowledge concerning the nature of the world around them. And yet, as we shall discover, their Renaissance perspective on the world is not so very different from the legacy they inherited from their medieval forebears. Just as in the fifteenth-century travelogues discussed in chapter 5 where real experience is difficult to distinguish from what was found in books, so too Waldstein's and Comenius' unmediated encounter with England is belied by a complex fabric of citation and secondary sources which undercuts their empiricist investment in the immediacy of the human senses.

Baron Waldstein

The earliest of our three visitors to England was Baron Zdeněk Brtnický of Valdštejn, usually known by his German name Waldstein (1581–1623). Waldstein was a relative of the great military commander Albert of Wallenstein.[1] After the death of his uncle Hynek, chief justice of Moravia, Waldstein inherited his estates near Budějovice in the south of Bohemia at the age of fourteen. Soon after he matriculated at the age of fifteen at Strasbourg University, a popular seat of learning for the sons of Protestant families, Waldstein began to keep a diary on January 1, 1597. During these student years Waldstein conscientiously recorded his daily timetable of studies. Only occasionally are his entries interesting, for example, when he refers to ten plays he saw performed by a troupe of English actors at the end of July and the beginning of August, 1597. One of these was probably Christopher Marlowe's drama *Doctor Faustus,* which Waldstein refers to simply as *de Fausto.*

Soon after his eighteenth birthday Waldstein left Strasbourg for the grand tour of Europe which was to occupy him for the next three years. He began by touring through France and spent a few weeks studying in Paris. His next trip was to the Netherlands, where he spent two months visiting all the major cities. He returned to France where he

[1] See *The Diary of Baron Waldstein. A Traveller in Elizabethan England,* trans. G. W. Groos (London, 1981). All subsequent citations of the diary are from this edition. For Bohemian and Moravian travelers to England at this period, see Otakar Odložilík, "Cesty z Čech a Moravy do Velké Britanie v letech 1593-1620," *Časopis Českého Muzea* 59 (1935): 241–320.

stayed for a while in Orleans (for a brief period of study), Provence, the Loire region, Chartres, and Paris. From the French capital he proceeded to Calais, the port of departure for England.

The party arrived at Dover around noon on Monday, June 26, 1600. Their departure from Dover was delayed by a recent regulation that required all foreigners to register with the local magistrates and await clearance from the authorities in London. According to Waldstein, this rule had been introduced because certain influential aliens had been allowed to travel in England incognito and had posed a threat to the life of the elderly queen. There had been several plots against Elizabeth; and the infamous rebellion of the earl of Essex in 1601 can only have intensified the authorities' fear of sedition. This, then, was the England encountered by Waldstein: regulated, suspicious, and xenophobic. All this provided a stark contrast with the capaciously tolerant world of Renaissance Prague witnessed by Sir Philip Sidney just a quarter of a century earlier.

Waldstein and his party were held up in Dover for three days waiting for permission to resume their journey. By Thursday, June 29, they were so desperate they went to see the governor of the castle and begged for permission to leave. After lunch on the same day they were finally allowed to ride to Canterbury, the first stop on the high road to London. Unlike his fifteenth-century predecessors, whose tour of southern England was organized around the important pilgrimage sites of St. Thomas at Canterbury and St. Osmund at Salisbury, Waldstein's itinerary was purely motivated by the interests of a Protestant humanist. He lists his observations in an encyclopedic and systematic fashion much in the way that his co-religionist and fellow Moravian Comenius organized human knowledge in his textbook *Orbis Pictus*. Whereas Waldstein's Catholic predecessors saw England as a series of pilgrimage sites, Waldstein experienced England as a vast library of undiscovered knowledge. For him truth was revealed through the literal word of Scripture, not through the Word of the Incarnation. Wherever Waldstein goes, he transcribes learned epitaphs and inscriptions—usually in Latin, occasionally in French—on tombs and chapel walls. In most instances Waldstein does not comment on these writings but records them mechanically as if he were cataloguing artifacts in his personal collection. Even monuments are treated as facts rather than as physical objects. In Canterbury Cathedral, for example, the diarist provides an abbreviated list of tombs he finds: "The tomb of Henry IV of England and his Queen is to be seen here, and here also lies the body of the Ambassador of the King of France, Cardinal Chatillon, who died of poison in England. We saw too the tomb of Bishop William Bruchelle together with his death mask. By the entrance to the door is a fine painting of the story of the Revelation" (31). The entire diary assumes the form of a list or catalog of random details, presumably preparatory jottings for subsequent sorting into meaningful categories. The procedure is scientific but not scrupulously so. Errors creep in: inscriptions are frequently mistranscribed and titles misattributed (Bruchelle, for example, was not a bishop but a judge). A more egregious error is mistaking Thomas Aquinas for Thomas Becket. The editor of Waldstein's diary claims that this was a slip of the pen, but we have to remember that Waldstein was still a teenager and hardly an erudite scholar. Moreover, he was presumably reliant on local guides who probably spoke only broken Latin (Waldstein did not speak English and attended church services in French both in Canterbury and in London).

The crucial difference between Waldstein's time and that of his fifteenth-century predecessors was the dissolution of a unified Western Christendom. For Lord Rožmitál and his companions Catholic England had been more or less familiar territory and its sites of pilgrimage and churches represented a continuity of, rather than a rupture with, the mainstream religious culture of continental Europe. By the time of Waldstein's visit England had sundered its religious affiliations with Catholic Europe. The shrine of St. Thomas Becket at Canterbury had been destroyed and its treasures carted off to London. This physical destruction was accompanied by a major shift in religious sensibility. Whereas the shrine at Canterbury had been a source of wonder and admiration to Rožmitál and his travel companions, for Waldstein it has become a mere antiquarian detail, an arcane footnote within a document crammed—like some Renaissance *Kunstkammer*—with numerous strange curiosities. Gone is the familiarity with but also the wonder at miraculous relics and glittering shrines: the cultural landscape of England has irrevocably changed.

Waldstein's stay in London is among the most interesting sections of the diary. But unlike Šašek, he is oblivious to aspects of everyday life and entirely preoccupied with the establishment culture of the court and the universities. He dutifully records inscriptions on plaques and monuments in exhaustive detail yet leaves the reader ignorant of the more dynamic and vibrant features of Elizabethan life. A trip to the theater is reported in a few tantalizingly brief words: "Monday, July 3. Went to see an English play. The theatre follows the ancient Roman plan: it is built of wood and is so designed that spectators can get a comfortable view of everything that happens in any part of the building" (37). Waldstein tells us nothing at all about the experience: was this theater the newly opened Globe, the Rose, or the Swan? Which play had he come to see? To appreciate Waldstein's perspective, we might imagine how a modern American or British visitor to Prague would respond to a play performed in Czech at the National Theater. In relating the experience to friends at home, the foreign visitor would be more inclined to describe the physical setting of the production than the performance itself. But even if Waldstein was witnessing an early performance of a Shakespearen play (something we would certainly like to imagine), the playwright's name would have meant nothing at all to him.

On the way to Cambridge Waldstein stopped at Theobalds, the residence of Sir Robert Cecil about twelve miles from London which was built by his father William Cecil, Lord Burghley. Waldstein's tour of the house reads like an inventory of its furnishings and effects and is typical of the acquisitive mentality of the Rudolfine era: "In a different part of the house there is a room containing valuable hangings and various other bed-furnishings: one bed has its coverlet woven of gold, another is made of ostrich feathers, and there are hangings which are made—with wonderful skill—out of multi-coloured straw. There is a draughts board with all the pieces made of gold and silver, an oil-lamp made of gold, and a painting on the wall of Queen Elizabeth's coronation" (85).

In spite of the impression of immediacy suggested by this list-like attention to material detail, Waldstein is often dependent on previous written accounts of places and monuments. This is particularly true of his descriptions of the ancient universities of Oxford and Cambridge, which are modeled almost verbatim on Camden's *Britannia*. Here his insights are frequently citational and derivative. His account of Cambridge University includes an exhaustive list of its sixteen colleges and their founders, all of whom are correct apart from the founder of Trinity Hall: William Bateman, bishop of Norwich.

On his return trip from Oxford to London, Waldstein visited Richmond, the site of Anne of Bohemia's residence of Sheen and the place where she died of the plague in 1394. Waldstein erroneously refers to Queen Anne as the daughter of Wenceslas IV rather than Charles IV. He also adds that Queen Anne introduced to England the practice of riding sidesaddle. The high point of Waldstein's diary is his audience with Elizabeth I at Greenwich Palace. In his diary entry of Sunday, July 9, 1600, the Moravian describes how he and his companions took a small boat to Greenwich. His description of the audience is remarkable and provides a fascinating insight into the protocol of the Elizabethan court:

> A procession came first, led by the Chancellor carrying a gold-embroidered purse bearing the royal insignia and a Knight of the garter holding a sword before him, and Secretary Cecil following; then she herself, glittering with the glory of majesty and adorned with jewellery and precious gems, entered into the view of the whole assembly and stretched her arms out wide as if to embrace everybody present. At her entry everyone knelt. (73)

Several of the English courtiers gave up their places for Waldstein and his entourage. It is perhaps surprising to find such respect being shown to a young foreigner with no diplomatic credentials. We must remember, however, that in 1600 Prague was still the capital of the Holy Roman Empire and the residence of the emperor. Bohemian visitors to England would have been regarded as representatives of an important European state.

Waldstein's fame today rests less on his diary than on his subsequent political fortunes as one of the Moravian directorate and chamberlain to the ill-fated "Winter King." Spared execution after the battle of the White Mountain, he was imprisoned in Spilberk Castle in Brno, and despite pleas for his release when he fell sick, died there on June 24, 1623, at the age of forty-two.

Wenceslas Hollar

By the 1630s relations between England and the Empire had sufficiently improved to encourage King Charles I to send an embassy to the court of Emperor Ferdinand at Vienna to negotiate the reinstatement of Frederick's son and heir (and his own nephew) Charles Louis (1617–80) as Elector Palatine. The embassy was led by Thomas Howard, earl of Arundel. The mission began at The Hague, where Frederick's widow, Elizabeth Stuart, was living in exile. The queen received Lord Arundel, who stayed overnight. The English embassy then continued its journey by boat down the river Rhine. As Arundel was passing through Cologne en route to Vienna, he met a young Bohemian artist named Wenceslas Hollar (1607–77). Hollar had left his homeland in 1627 to seek his fortunes as a skilled engraver in Germany. Having made the acquaintance of the earl of Arundel at Cologne, Hollar joined the English party with the task of illustrating the rest of the journey along the Rhine to Prague and Vienna. These drawings were intended to illustrate the travel diary of Arundel's secretary, William Crowne.

After being received by Emperor Ferdinand in Vienna, the English embassy traveled north by coach through Moravia to Prague where they spent one week. As a native of the city, Hollar acted as the personal guide to the earl. Crowne's account of the English embassy in Prague is interesting because at that time Emperor Rudolf's fabulous art collection had not yet been dispersed by war and plunder. Crowne provides a typically elaborate inventory of Rudolf's famous *Kunstkammer*:

> In the first roome was cup-boords placed in the walls on our right hand; the first was of corall; the second, of Purslaine; the third, of mother of pearle; the fourth, of curious brasse-plates engraven; the fifth and sixth, Mathematicall Instruments; the seventh, Basons, Ewers, and cups of Amber; the eighth, cups of Aggets, Gold and Chrystall; the ninth of rocks; the tenth of Mozaique worke in stone; the eleventh, cups of Ivorie, and a great Unicornes horne a yard in length; the twelfth, of imbossing worke; the thirteenth of Brasse pictures; the foureteenth, of antick things cast in silver; the fifteenth, cabinets of Bohemia Diamonds, and little chests of Bohemia pearle; the sixteenth, things belonging to Astronomy; the seventeenth and eighteenth, Indian worke; the nineteenth, Turkey-worke; the twentieth, of a lively statue of a women covered with taffatie.[2]

[2] William Crowne, *Travels of Thomas Lord Howard. London 1637*, The English Expe-

Figure 15. "Sala regalis cum curia West-Monasterij, vulgo Westminster Haall." Engraving by Wenceslas Hollar. The New York Public Library/Art Resource, New York.

At the end of December 1636, Lord Arundel returned home, bringing Hollar with him. In 1637 Hollar etched his first plates in England, a series of views of Greenwich. Hollar spent the greater part of his life in England, where he is especially famous for his highly detailed and exquisitely delicate views of seventeenth-century London (figure 15). Like Waldstein's diary entries, these representations of London are detailed and empirical. The artist records what he sees accurately and dispassionately. Having launched into the world of Protestant philosophy that flourished in seventeenth-century London, Hollar had been exposed to the empiricist ideas of Bacon and Hobbes and the rationalism of Descartes. But he equally shared affinities with Comenius, whom the artist met during the latter's sojourn in England from September 1641 to August 1642.[3] Like Comenius, Hollar's range is encyclopedic and exhaustive, his temperament patient and ecumenical. He depicts not only monuments and buildings but also fashions in dress,

---

rience, 357 (Amsterdam, 1971), 28–29. For Rudolf's *Kunstkammer,* see Peter Marshall, *The Magic Circle of Rudolf II. Alchemy and Astrology in Renaissance Prague* (New York, 2006), chapter six.

[3] Vladimír Denkstein, *Hollar's Drawings* (London, 1977), 17; Katherine S. Van Eerde, *Wenceslaus Hollar. Delineator of His Time* (Charlottesville, 1970), 22–23. See also Johannes Urzidil, "Comenius' Meeting with Hollar in London," in *Comenius,* ed. Vratislav Bušek (New York, 1970), 135–39.

animal life, and fauna. In fact, our present-day understanding of what seventeenth-century London actually looked like is largely mediated through the meticulous engravings and etchings of this remarkable Bohemian artist.

Comenius

As a Moravian student at Heidelberg in 1618, Comenius witnessed Elector Frederick's triumphal entry into the capital of the Palatinate. He was also present at his coronation in St. Vitus Cathedral at Prague a year later. Comenius shared with his co-religionists the utopian dream of a golden age under the enlightened rule of the new Protestant king of Bohemia. But these hopes were soon to be cruelly dashed. After the defeat of the Protestant cause at the Battle of the White Mountain in 1620, Comenius fled his parish at Fulnek, which was sacked by marauding imperial troops, and took refuge on the lands of the Protestant lord Charles of Žerotín at Brandýs nad Orlicí. After losing his pregnant wife and child to the plague, Comenius reached his safe haven in a state of spiritual and physical exhaustion. It was this state of mind and body which gave rise to his nightmarish vision of a city populated by a dehumanized and alienated citizenry—the dark antithesis of Augustine's *De Civitas Dei*—in *The Labyrinth of the World and the Paradise of the Heart* (1623).

In the second half of chapter 9 of *The Labyrinth*, Comenius provides an unexpected description of a tempestuous sea voyage: "Indeed, the storm grew so violent that not only we, but the depths beneath were shaken; and terror entered our hearts. The sea rolled with such waves on all sides that we were thrown as if onto high mountains and into deep valleys, now upward, now downward. Sometimes we were shot so high that it seemed as if we could reach the moon; then again we descended into the abyss. Then it seemed that a wave, coming against us or the sides of the boat, would rush upon us and sink us on the spot."[4] This description was later added to the 1663 edition of the text published in Amsterdam but was not included in the original manu-

---

[4] John Amos Comenius, *The Labyrinth of the World and the Paradise of the Heart*, trans. Howard Louthan and Andrea Sterk (New York, 1998), 90–91.

script or in the first printed edition of 1631. It provides a lively and dramatic account of Comenius' voyage to England in 1641. Yet the description is not based on his personal experience but derives from the great Moravian's reading of the *Peregrinatio* by his co-religionist and compatriot Jan Laetus-Veselský (1609–56). This Latin account was itself based on a trip undertaken with Andrew Rej of Nagłowice, ambassador to the Polish-Lithuanian king Vladislav IV.[5] Just as the impressions of England provided by the fifteenth-century Bohemians discussed in chapter 5 were colored by the world of courtly romance, so is Comenius' description of his tempestuous voyage reliant upon seventeenth-century seafaring narratives. In fact, the sea voyage description is not the only citational part of Comenius' masterpiece: this is especially true of final passages of *The Paradise of the Heart* which are woven together from various sources such as the psalms and Augustine's *Confessions*. Paradoxically, the more text appears to shed the perspective of the world and internalize the longings of the narrator's heart, the more dependent it becomes on the words of others.[6]

By the time the Amsterdam edition of *The Labyrinth* appeared in 1631 Comenius had established an international reputation as the most progressive pedagogue of his day. It was above all his utopian system of Pansophia—the belief that all human knowledge could be quantified and codified into a universal system—which appealed to his English admirers. According to R. J. W. Evans, the ideas of the English alchemist Dr. John Dee were an important influence on Comenius' Pansophia: "Dee's broad metaphysical position was characteristic of an intellectual of his time: he believed in the theory of the microcosm, in hidden forces underlying the visible world, in cosmic harmony.... At the same time he believed ... that access to these mysteries could be achieved through such things as symbols, intellectual 'keys,' and combinations."[7] It was Comenius' belief in a universal set of principles governing all knowledge that endeared him to Dee's English intellectual descendants. Among these was Samuel Hartlib (1595–1662), a German-born philanthropist and scientific enthusiast residing in Lon-

---

[5] Josef Polišenský, *Komenský. Muž Labyrintů a Naděje* (Prague, 1996), 62.

[6] See Alfred Thomas, *The Labyrinth of the Word. Truth and Representation in Czech Literature* (Munich, 1995), 70.

[7] R. J. W. Evans, *Rudolf II and His World. A Study in Intellectual History* (Oxford, 1973), 219.

don. Hartlib's correspondence with Comenius dates back to 1632. He had heard about the Moravian scholar through his younger brother, George, who had studied at Heidelberg at the same time as Comenius. Contact with Comenius (who was still exiled at Leszno in Poland) was provided by two Czech students who came to England to study at Cambridge University. The first, Samuel Benedict, was enrolled at Sidney Sussex College; the following year Daniel Erastus, the son of a bishop of the Bohemian Brethren, matriculated at St. Catharine's College. Comenius had given these young men letters of introduction to Hartlib.[8]

In 1637 Comenius sent Hartlib an extended description of his latest pansophic treatise, the *Janua Rerum* (*The Gate of Things*), a sequel to his universally acclaimed language textbook *Janua Linguarum Reserata* (*The Gate of Languages Unlocked*). Without obtaining Comenius' approval, Hartlib arranged for this new work to be printed at Oxford with the title *Pansophiae Prodromus* (*Introduction to Pansophy,* or the *Prodromus,* as it was referred to at the time). The *Prodromus* was generally received with great enthusiasm in England and elsewhere, although it met with the criticism of the French philosopher René Descartes, who objected to its merging of philosophy and theology.[9] But it was precisely this syncretic approach to science, philosophy, and theology that appealed to Hartlib and his associates in London. They envisaged a utopian pedagogical system that would produce a great measure of nonconfessional uniformity in culture and religion, no vain aspiration in an age of widespread religious violence and war.[10] It was hoped that a whole generation of European schoolchildren would be trained in a spirit of nonsectarian tolerance. More than three hundred years before the foundation of the European Union, the pansophic ideals of Comenius, Hartlib, and others aimed to use education to avoid the pain of religious conflict and the consequent horrors of future wars.

Comenius' correspondence with Hartlib paved the way for the great man's much-awaited trip to England in 1641. The group that invited Comenius consisted of members of the two houses of the Puritan Long Parliament. Among these were John Williams, bishop of

---

[8] Mathew Spinka, *John Amos Comenius: That Incomparable Moravian* (Chicago, 1943), 63.
[9] Ibid., 64–68.
[10] Ibid., 71.

London, later to become archbishop of York, Lord Selden, and Lord Brooke. At this time Comenius was still rector of the school of the Bohemian Brethren in Leszno. Having obtained permission from his brethren at the school to take an extended trip, Comenius sailed from Skagerrak, a port on the Baltic Sea coast. Unfortunately his ship was driven by strong winds back to Danzig. It was this experience that provided the basis for the dramatic description of the sea voyage in *The Labyrinth of the World*.[11]

After a calmer second crossing, Comenius arrived in London on September 21, 1641. He attended a dinner hosted by Bishop Williams, who invited Comenius to settle in England with his second wife and children. Comenius considered the offer seriously and even solicited the advice of his brethren back in Poland. Comenius' wife was distraught at the idea of having to move to England and learn a new language. In any event, the proposal was brought to an end by the outbreak of the English Civil War on August 22, 1642. Although Hartlib's utopian dream of founding a Pansophic College in England based on the ideas of Comenius did not materialize, Comenius' visit to London suggests that for both men England could become the home of educational ideals which would bring peace and harmony to a Europe divided and traumatized by war.

A more immediate consequence of Comenius' sojourn in England was an increase in his fame in the English-speaking world. It was at this time that Comenius is said to have met John Winthrop, the governor of Massachusetts. According to Cotton Mather in his *Magnalia Christi Americana*, Winthrop invited Comenius to take up the presidency of Harvard College (founded 1636) in New England.[12] The story cannot be substantiated and is probably apocryphal. It is not even clear whether Winthrop met Comenius at all. Moreover, the presidency of Harvard was not vacant at the time it was supposedly offered to Comenius. More importantly, however, Comenius' works were known and appreciated in New England. Whether the Harvard story is true or not is perhaps less significant than the admiration for Comenius and his utopian ideals evinced in Mather's memorandum:

---

[11] Ibid., 75.
[12] Ibid., 84–85.

> That brave old man, Johannes Amos Comenius, the fame of whose worth hath been trumpeted as far as more than three languages (whereof everyone is indebted to his *Janua*) could carry it, was indeed agreed withall, by our Mr. John Winthrop in his travels through the low countries, to come over into New-England, and illuminate this College and country in the quality of a President. But the solicitations of the Swedish Ambassador, diverting him another way, that incomparable Moravian became not an American.[13]

If the original invitation was a wish-fulfillment, the face-saving qualification that it was not accepted due to the solicitations of the Swedish ambassador is perhaps equally an imaginary projection on Mather's part. In spite of Comenius' well-attested interest in the conversion and education of the native Indians of New England, his true concerns lay with the fortunes of his beloved Unity of Brethren. Even if Winthrop met Comenius and was in a position to offer him the presidency of Harvard College, it is unlikely that the famous pedagogue would have accepted the invitation. Comenius never relinquished the hope that he might be able to return to his Moravian homeland and live in peace and religious harmony with his Catholic neighbors.

---

[13] Quoted ibid., 85.

Conclusion

Bohemian Paris, Berlin, and New York have all been identified at one time or another in the twentieth century as the home of the disaffected and deracinated post-Romantic artist. These venues have changed according to economic and political circumstance, yet the ideal informing their artistic status has remained constant and immutable. I have argued in this book that the same fluidity between the real and the ideal has characterized English perceptions of the kingdom of Bohemia in the pre-modern period. The English vision of Bohemia—whether positive or negative—was inevitably shaped by the cultural and political climate that prevailed at home. Chaucer's vision of Bohemia as a distillation of the most progressive and sophisticated trends of humanist learning was certainly influenced by his awareness of the glamorous and cultured Luxembourg dynasty which ruled whole swaths of late medieval Europe from Brabant in the west to Silesia in the east. But it was also influenced by Chaucer's England, a land ruled by a highly cultured but unstable king whose Bohemian spouse seemed to embody her quasi-mythical land of origin. For Chaucer and his English contemporaries Anne of Bohemia was the opposite of her irate husband: if he is capricious and vindictive, she is magnanimous and conciliatory; if he is unstable and volatile, she is poised and dignified, even in the ritualistic act of kneeling in intercession before the king and his overmighty subjects.

At the other end of this book's chronology—the early seventeenth century—Shakespeare's Bohemia is similarly synonymous with the qualities personified by "good Queen Anne": tolerance, compassion, and dignity. In stark contrast with Elizabethan and Jacobean England, where Roman Catholics were persecuted and Jews demonized, Rudolfine Bohemia was an ecumenical haven for religious nonconformists. In making Bohemia a safe haven for the abandoned infant Perdita, Shakespeare was not simply reproducing the trappings of Greek romance; he was fusing the bucolic and pastoral ideal of the romance genre with the confessional realities of central Europe in which the Habsburg rulers succeeded (for a time at least) in establishing a harmonious equilibrium between political stability and religious tolerance.

For sure, the English tendency to idealize Bohemia alternated at times with an opposite image. If Shakespeare's Catholic compatriots saw Bohemia as a utopian alternative to their own repressive homeland, after the disastrous Battle of the White Mountain in 1620 and the ensuing forced Catholicization of the Czech lands, English Protestants reverted to a dystopian vision of Bohemia which had prevailed in the fifteenth century when Hussite Bohemia was regarded by the orthodox English as synonymous with heresy and anarchy.

Part of the argument of this book has been that the English preoccupation with Bohemia—both as a good or a bad place—was reciprocated in equally ambivalent measure. If the fifteenth-century Bohemian traveler Šašek characterized the English as treacherous and cunning, his compatriot John Hus and his followers perceived England as the blessed homeland of their religious hero John Wyclif. In all these accounts—English and Bohemian—it is impossible to state with certainty where reality ends and ideal takes over. Even though Šašek's travelogue is putatively an eyewitness account, its inclination to reproduce what its author has read in books (such as the hugely popular *Travels of Sir John Mandeville*) makes its perspective on the Other not so much an objective description as a curious mélange of literary lore, encyclopedic data, and sporadic moments of spontaneous observation. The same is true of the accounts of Elizabethan and Jacobean visitors to Renaissance Prague. The Jesuit exile Edmund Campion refers to the "blessed shore" of Bohemia while the Protestant John Taylor evokes Bohemia as a cornucopian land of plenty. Both men view Bohemia through a lens tinted by their respective religious preconceptions but the impression made is equally positive. Thus the premodern relationship between England and Bohemia cannot be reduced to an objective set of factual observations but is a mirror-like formation in which each sees the other through the distorting and subjective effect of its own reflection.

What of Bohemia and east-central Europe today? Following the fall of communism in 1989, the Czech Republic, Slovakia, Poland, and Hungary have become fledgling members of an expanding European Union. According to Jacques Le Goff:

> Some historians reckon that after the collapse of the Soviet Union in 1989, the central Europe that had been formed in the Middle Ages reappeared. One is the Hungarian medievalist Gabor Klaniczay, who has helped to organize a department of medieval studies in the new Central European University.... What he has revealed is a central Europe which, as in the Middle Ages, constitutes an open, diversified and creative laboratory for a vast and limitless area extending from west to east: in his own words, a veritable European "Utopia."[1]

As this book has tried to demonstrate, this "vast laboratory" of central Europe survived the medieval period. Early modern Bohemia, Poland, and Hungary were also an integral part of Renaissance Europe, the intellectual playground of Englishmen like Sir Philip Sidney and Dr. John Dee. The ancient university towns of Prague, Cracow, and Budapest were not consigned to a shadowy and barbarous "eastern bloc" but represented the shared humanist values of an integrated Europe. Moreover, for many English visitors to the region, east-central Europe was a more congenial place than Elizabethan or Jacobean England. Until the cataclysmic events of 1620, which brought the Habsburg experiment in irenicism to an abrupt and violent end, central Europe was indeed a "veritable European Utopia." Tragically, this idealized repu-

---

[1] Jacques Le Goff, *The Birth of Europe,* trans. Janet Lloyd (Oxford, 2005), 92.

tation was obscured and eclipsed by a seemingly endless series of conflicts on a global scale: the Thirty Years' War; the Great War; World War II, and the Cold War. Now that these wars are behind us, we are better placed not only to reassess the potential of the European present but also to rediscover the rich legacy of its past.

Appendix:
"The Wycliffite Woman":
A Rhymed Translation

Harken to this wondrous tale
Of how a virgin, young and hale,
Was summoned by a Wycliffite
To visit her quite late at night
And study everything that's right.　　　5

She told the scholar: "Come to me,
But do so very quietly.
Then I will teach you what is true,
And if you follow what I do,
I'll show the Gospels, Old and New."　　10

The young lord said without delay:
"I'll come to your house straight away."
Ever anxious to be better,
He promised faithfully to let her
Teach him Scripture to the letter.　　　15

Eager now to be his keeper,
The Wycliffite urged him deeper:

"Come to me without a sound
When there is no one far around
And I'll disclose what I have found."   20

Whereupon she said good-bye
With certain knowledge he'd comply.
And sure enough, when all was dead,
He came to her with furtive tread
On Sunday after each had fed.   25

"Welcome, my most beloved guest,"
So she cried as she undressed,
"For whom my soul has deeply yearned,
For whom my heart has fiercely burned!
Come in and hear what I have learned."   30

"Please sit down and rest a bit,
While I reveal the Holy Writ.
As you will pretty soon discern,
Holy Scripture's your concern:
It's up to you to try and learn.   35

Here the wench revealed the Book
To the boy's delighted look:
Two lovely chapters round and bare,
Each one delicious like a pear,
And in his eyes so very fair.   40

The fearless youth stood up and cried:
"Just give them here, my precious bride!
And out he took his scholar's quill
And studied Scripture to his fill
Until the sun rose past the hill.   45

And when he glimpsed the light of day,
The boy prepared to slip away.
But now the woman grasped his sleeve,
And said: "Before you take your leave,
There're still the matins, I believe."   50

How joyous was their parting song
As well befits this courtly throng
. . . .
Their voices sweetly intertwined.   55

And when the matins had been sung
They said farewell with joyful tongue.
In the love they each other bore
There was no anger that I saw
But more bliss than the night before.   60

And therefore, pages fair and bold,
Take courage from the tale I've told.
If you should wish to find the light
You must consult a Wycliffite
And study with her every night.   65

For no one knows the Book as well—
From Genesis to Daniel;
The Song of Songs she can recite.
A priest is not so erudite!
So serve her like a faithful knight.   70

Her expositions, sweet and clear,
Resound like music in your ear.
Whoever serves this learned wife
Will swiftly find eternal life.
God make her fertile, round, and rife!   75

Bibliography

Primary Sources

Manuscripts and Early Printed Books

Bodleian Library, Oxford
Latin Liturg. F. 3 (Anne of Bohemia's Book of Hours).

Houghton Library, Harvard University
Harrison, John. *The departure of the high and mightie prince Frederick King Elect of Bohemia; And the thryse hopeful young Prince Henrie, from Heydelberg towards Prague, to receive the Crowne of that Kingdom.* London, 1619.
——. *The Bohemian Lawes or Rights Defended against the Informer.* London, 1620.
Taylor, John. *An English-man's Love to Bohemia with a friendly farewell to all the noble souldiers that goe from Great Britain to that honorable expedition.* London, 1620.
——. *Taylor his Travels: from the City of London in England, to the City of Prague in Bohemia.* London, 1621.
Weston, Elizabeth Jane. *Parthenicon Elisabethae Joannaie Westoniae, virginis nobilissimae, poetriae florentissimae, linguarum plurimarum peritissimae.* Prague, 1606.

Other Printed Books

Allen, William Cardinal. *A Briefe Historie of the Glorious Martyrdom of Twelve Reverend Priests Father Edmund Campion and His Companions*. London, 1908.

Bernt, Günter, ed. *Carmina Burana. Die Gedichte des Codex Buranus*. Zurich, 1974.

Blamires, Alcuin, ed. *Woman Defamed and Woman Defended. An Anthology of Medieval Texts*. Oxford, 1992.

Chapman, George. *Plays of George Chapman*. Edited by Thomas Parrott. 2 vols., New York, 1961.

Chaucer, Geoffrey. *The Riverside Chaucer*. Edited by Larry D. Benson. 3d ed., Oxford, 1988.

———. *The Legend of Good Women*. Edited by Helen Philips and Nick Havely. London, 1997.

Chelčický, Petr. *Drobné spisy*. Edited by Eduard Petrů. Prague, 1966.

Chrétien de Troyes. *Arthurian Romances*. Translated by William W. Kibler. Harmondsworth, 1991.

Christian. *Legenda Christiani*. Edited by Jaroslav Ludvíkovský. Prague, 1978.

Comenius, Jan Amos. *The Labyrinth of the World and the Paradise of the Heart*. Translated by Howard Louthan and Andrea Sterk with a preface by Jan Milič Lochmann. New York, 1998.

Crawford, Anne, ed. *Letters of the Queens of England 1100–1547*. Stroud, 1994.

Crowne, William. *Travels of Thomas Lord Howard. London 1637*. The English Experience, 357. Amsterdam, 1971.

Daňhelka, Jiří, ed. *Kronika trojánská*. Prague, 1951.

French, Alfred, ed. *An Anthology of Czech Verse*. Ann Arbor, 1977.

Gardner, Helen, ed. *The Metaphysical Poets*. Harmondsworth, 1972.

Gower, John. *Confessio Amantis*, Edited by Russell A. Peek. Toronto, 1980.

Harkins, William E., ed. *Czech Prose. An Anthology*. Ann Arbor, 1983.

Head, Thomas, ed. *Medieval Hagiography. An Anthology*. New York, 2000.

Hildesheim, John of. *The Three Kings of Cologne. An Early Translation of the Historia Trium Regum by John of Hildesheim*. Edited by C. Horstmann, Early English Text Society. London, 1886.

Hoccleve, Thomas. *Selections from Hoccleve*. Edited by M. C. Seymour. Oxford, 1981.

Hrabák, Josef, ed. *Staročeské satiry Hradeckého rukopisu a Smilovy školy*. Prague, 1962.

Hughes, Charles, ed. *Shakespeare's Europe. A Survey of the Condition of Europe at the end of the 16th century being unpublished chapters of Fynes Moryson's Itinerary (1617)*. 2nd ed., New York, 1967.

Hus, Jan. *Documenta Mag. Joannis Hus*. Edited by František Palacký. Prague, 1869.

Jonson, Ben. *The Masque of Queens*. In *Court Masques*, edited by Lindley, 35–53.

Klassen, John, ed. *The Letters of the Rožmberk Sisters. Noblewomen in Fifteenth-Century Bohemia.* Woodbridge, 2001.

Komenský, Jan Amos. *Orbis Pictus (Svět v obrazích).* Prague, 1941.

Lindley, David, ed. *Court Masques. Jacobean and Caroline Entertainments.* Oxford, 1995.

Machaut, Guillaume de. *Le Jugement du roy de Behaigne and Remede de Fortune.* Edited by James I. Wimsatt and William W. Kibler. Athens, 1988.

Massinger, Philip. *The Picture.* In *The Plays of Philip Massinger,* vol. 3, edited by Philip Edwards and Colin Gibson. Oxford, 1976.

Meissen, Heinrich von. *Leiche, Sangsprüche, Lieder,* vol. 1, edited by Karl Stackmann and Karl Bertau. Göttingen, 1981, 126–46.

Mézières, Philippe de. *Letter to King Richard II. A plea made in 1395 for peace between England and France.* Translated by G. W. Coopland. Liverpool, 1975.

"The Old Czech Life of St. Catherine of Alexandria." Translated by Alfred Thomas. In *Medieval Hagiography,* edited by Head, 763–79.

Pfaffe Konrad. *Das Rolandslied des Pfaffen Konrad.* Edited by Dieter Kartschoke. Frankfurt am Main, 1970.

Rožmitál, Leo of. *Des böhmischen Herrn Leo's von Rozmital Ritter-, Hof—und Pilger-reise durch die Abendlande 1465–67. Beschrieben von zweien seiner Begleiter.* Edited by Franz Pfeiffer. Stuttgart, 1844.

Shakespeare, William. *The Riverside Shakespeare.* Edited by G. Blakemore Evans. Boston, 1974.

Tepl, Johannes von. *Der Ackerman.* Edited by Willy Krogmann. Wiesbaden, 1954.

Tkadleček. Edited by František Šimek. Prague, 1974.

Usk, Thomas. *Testament of Love.* Edited by R. Allen Shoaf. Kalamazoo, 1998.

Vantuono, William, ed. *Pearl. An Edition with Verse Translation.* Notre Dame, 1995.

Vilikovský, Jan, ed. *Staročeská lyrika.* Prague, 1940.

Younger Wycliffite Mass. In *Urkundliche Beiträge zur Geschichte des Hussitenkrieges,* vol. 2, edited by František Palacký. Prague, 1873, 521–22.

Waldstein, Zdeněk Brtnický of. *The Diary of Baron Waldstein. A Traveller in Elizabethan England.* Edited and translated by G. W. Groos. London, 1981.

Zittau, Peter of. *Chronicon Aulae Regiae.* Edited by J. Emler, Fontes Rerum Bohemicarum, 4. Prague, 1884.

Secondary Sources

Aers, David, ed. *Culture and History 1350–1600. Essays on English Communities, Identities, and Writing.* Detroit, 1992.

———, "Walter Brut's Theology of the Sacrament of the Altar." In *Lollards and Their Influence,* edited by Somerset et al., 115–26.

Allmand, Christopher. *Henry V.* New Haven, 1992.

Ashley, Kathleen, and Sheingorn, Pamela, eds. *Interpreting Cultural Symbols. Saint Anne in Late Medieval Society*. Athens, 1990.

Astell, Ann W. *Political Allegory in Late Medieval England*. Ithaca, 1999.

Aston, Margaret. *Lollards and Reformers. Literacy and Imagery in Late Medieval England*. London, 1984.

Barr, Helen, and Hutchinson, Ann M., eds. *Text and Controversy from Wyclif to Bale. Essays in Honour of Anne Hudson*. Medieval Church Studies 4. Turnhout, 2005.

Barraclough, Geoffrey. *The Origins of Modern Germany*. Oxford, 1962.

Barratt, Alexandra. "Continental Women Mystics and English Readers." In *The Cambridge Companion to Medieval Women's Writing*, edited by Dinshaw and Wallace, 240–55.

Barron, Caroline M. *London in the Later Middle Ages. Government and People 1200–1500*. Oxford, 2004.

Bartlett, Robert, and Angus Mackay, eds. *Medieval Frontier Societies*. Oxford, 1989.

Bartoš, František M. *Husitství a cizina*. Prague, 1931.

——, *Petr Payne. Diplomat husitské revoluce*. Prague, 1956.

Bennett, Michael J. *Community, Class and Careerism. Cheshire and Lancashire Society in the Age of Sir Gawain and the Green Knight*. Cambridge, 1983.

——, *Richard II and the Revolution of 1399*. Stroud, 1999.

——, "Richard II and the Wider Realm." In *Richard II. The Art of Kingship*, edited by Goodman and Gillespie, 187–204.

Benson, Larry D. "The Occasion of The Parliament of Fowls" In *The Wisdom of Poetry*, edited by Benson and Wenzel, 123–44.

Benson, Larry D., and Siegfried Wenzel, eds. *The Wisdom of Poetry. Essays in Early English Literature in Honor of Morton W. Bloomfield*. Kalamazoo, 1982.

Biller, Peter, and Anne Hudson, eds. *Heresy and Literacy, 1000–1530*. Cambridge Studies in Medieval Literature, 23. Cambridge, 1994.

Biller, Peter, and A. J. Minnis, eds. *Medieval Theology and the Natural Body*. York Studies in Medieval Theology, 1. New York, 1997.

Binski, Paul. *Westminster Abbey and the Plantagenets. Kingship and Representation of Power, 1200–1440*. New Haven, 1995.

——, *Medieval Death. Ritual and Representation*. London, 1996.

——, "The Liber Regalis. Its Date and European Context." In *The Regal Image*, edited by Gordon et al., 233–46.

Blamires, Alcuin. *The Case for Women in Medieval Culture*. Oxford, 1997.

Boulay, F. R. H. du, and Barron, Caroline M., eds. *The Reign of Richard II. Essays in Honour of May McKisack*. London, 1971.

Boureau, Alain. *The Myth of Pope Joan*. Translated by Lydia G. Cochrane. Chicago, 2001.

Bowers, John M. "Chaste Marriage. Fashion and Texts at the Court of Richard II." *Pacific Coast Philology* 30 (1995): 15–26.

———. *The Politics of Pearl. Courtly Poetry in the Age of Richard II.* Woodbridge, 2001.

Bowsky, William M. *Henry VII in Italy* (Lincoln, 1960).

Bressie, Ramona. "The Date of Thomas Usk's 'Testament of Love.'" *Modern Philology* 26 (1928): 17–29.

Brewer, Derek, and Jonathan Gibson, eds. *A Companion to the Gawain-Poet.* Cambridge, 1997.

Briggs, Julia. "Tears at the Wedding. Shakespeare's Last Phase." In *Shakespeare's Late Plays,* edited by Richards and Knowles, 210–227.

Brock, Peter. *The Political and Social Doctrines of the Unity of Czech Brethren in the Fifteenth and Sixteenth Centuries.* The Hague, 1957.

Bumke, Joachim. *Courtly Culture. Literature and Society in the High Middle Ages.* Translated by Thomas Dunlap. Woodstock, 2000.

Burke, Peter. *Popular Culture in Early Modern Europe.* New York, 1978.

Bušek, Vratislav, ed. *Comenius.* New York, 1972.

Calin, William. *The French Tradition and the Literature of Medieval England.* Toronto, 1994.

Cannon, Christopher. "Monastic productions." In *The Cambridge History of Medieval English Literature,* edited by Wallace, 316–48.

Carruthers, Mary J. *The Book of Memory. A Study of Memory in Medieval Culture.* Cambridge, 1990.

Catto, Jeremy. "Religious Change under Henry V." In *Henry V. The Practice of Kingship,* edited by Harriss, 97–116.

Chism, Christine. *Alliterative Revivals.* Philadelphia, 2002.

Císařová-Kolářová, Anna. *Žena v husitském hnutí.* Prague, 1915.

Coleman, Joyce. *Public Reading and the Reading Public in Late Medieval England and France.* Cambridge, 1996.

Constable, Giles. *Three Studies in Medieval Religious and Social Thought. The Interpretation of Mary and Martha; The Ideal of the Imitation of Christ; The Orders of Society.* Cambridge, 1995.

Cooke, William R. "Peter Payne. Theologian and diplomat of the Hussite Revolution." Ph.D. diss., Cornell University, 1971.

Copeland, Rita. "Why Women Can't Read. Medieval Hermeneutics, Statutory Law, and the Lollard Heresy Trials." In *Representing Women,* edited by Heinzelman and Wiseman, 253–86.

———. *Pedagogy, Intellectuals, and Dissent in the Later Middle Ages. Lollards and Ideas of Learning.* Cambridge, 2001.

Cust, Mrs Henry. *Gentlemen Errant. Being the Travels and Adventures of Four Noblemen in Europe in the Fifteenth and Sixteenth Centuries.* London, 1909.

Davies, D. W. *Elizabethans Errant. The Strange Fortunes of Sir Thomas Sherley and His Three Sons.* Ithaca, 1967.

Davies, R. R. *The First English Empire. Power and Identities in the British Isles 1093–1343.* Oxford, 2000.

Deanesly, Margaret. *A History of the Medieval Church, 590–1500*. London, 1994.
Denkstein, Vladimír. *Hollar's Drawings*. London, 1977.
Dinshaw, Carolyn. *Getting Medieval. Sexualities and Communities, Pre- and Postmodern*. Durham, 1999.
Dinshaw, Carolyn, and David Wallace, eds. *The Cambridge Companion to Medieval Women's Writing*. Cambridge, 2003.
Dinzelbacher, Peter. *Heilige oder Hexen? Schicksale auffälliger Frauen in Mittelalter und Frühneuzeit*. Munich, 1995.
Dodd, Gwilym, ed. *The Reign of Richard II*. Stroud, 2000.
Duffy, Mark. *Royal Tombs of Medieval England*. Stroud, 2003.
Duncan-Jones, Katherine. *Sir Philip Sidney, Courtier-Poet*. New Haven, 1991.
———, *Ungentle Shakespeare. Scenes from His Life*. London, 2001.
Dutton, Richard, Alison Findlay, and Richard Wilson, eds. *Theatre and Religion. Lancastrian Shakespeare*. Manchester, 2003,
Eberle, Patricia J. "Richard II and the Literary Arts." In *Richard II. The Art of Kingship*, edited by Goodman and Gillespie, 231–53.
Elliott, Dyan. *Spiritual Marriage. Sexual Abstinence in Medieval Wedlock*. Princeton, 1993.
———. *Fallen Bodies. Pollution, Sexuality, and Demonology in the Middle Ages*. Philadelphia, 1999.
———. "Response to Alfred Thomas's 'The Wycliffite Woman. Reading Women in Fifteenth-Century Bohemia.'" In *Voices in Dialogue,* edited by Olson and Kerby-Fulton, 302–5.
Emden, Alfred B., *An Oxford Hall in Medieval Times*. Oxford, 1927.
Erler, Mary C., and Maryanne Kowaleski, eds. *Gendering the Master Narrative. Women and Power in the Middle Ages*. Ithaca, 2003.
Evans, R. J. W. *Rudolf II and His World. A Study in Intellectual History*. Oxford, 1973.
———. *The Making of the Habsburg Monarchy 1550–1700*. Oxford, 1979.
Fajt, Jiří, ed. *Magister Theodoricus. Dvorní malíř císaře Karla IV*. Prague, 1997.
Federico, Sylvia. *New Troy. Fantasies of Empire in the Late Middle Ages*. Medieval Cultures at Minnesota, vol. 36. Minneapolis, 2003.
Fichtner, Paula Sutter. *Emperor Maximilian II*. New Haven, 2001.
Fisher, Celia. "A Study of the Plants and Flowers in the Wilton Diptych." In *The Regal Image,* edited by Gordon et al., 155–63.
Foucault, Michel. "Of Other Spaces." *diacritics* 16 (1986): 22–27.
Fudge, Thomas A. *The Magnificent Ride. The First Reformation in Bohemia*. Aldershot, 1988.
Gibson, Gail McMurray. *The Theater of Devotion. East Anglian Drama and Society in the Late Middle Ages*. Chicago, 1989.
Godfrey, Richard T. *Wenceslaus Hollar. A Bohemian Artist in England*. New Haven, 1994.

Goodman, Anthony, and Gillespie, James L., eds. *Richard II. The Art of Kingship.* Oxford, 1999.
Gordon, Dillian. *Making and Meaning. The Wilton Diptych.* London, 1993.
Gordon, Dillian, Lisa Monnis, and Caroline Elam, eds. *The Regal Image of Richard II and the Wilton Diptych.* London, 1997.
Green, A. S., *Town Life in the Fifteenth Century,* vol. 1. London, 1894.
Greenblatt, Stephen. *Marvelous Possessions. The Wonder of the New World.* Chicago, 1991.
———. *Will in the World. How Shakespeare Became Shakespeare.* New York, 2004.
Hamburger, Jeffrey F. *The Visual and the Visionary. Art and Female Spirituality in Late Medieval Germany.* New York, 1998.
Harris, Sylvia, C. "The Historia Trium Regum and the Medieval Legend of the Magi in Germany." *Medium Aevum* 28 (1959): 23–30.
Harriss, G. L., ed. *Henry V. The Practice of Kingship.* Oxford, 1985.
Harvey, John H. "Richard II and York." In *The Reign of Richard II,* edited by du Boulay and Barron, 202–17.
Hawkesworth, Celia, ed. *A History of Central European Women's Writing.* London, 2001.
Heinzelman, Susan Sage, and Zipporah Batshaw Wiseman, eds. *Representing Women. Law, Literature, and Feminism.* Durham, 1994.
Heng, Geraldine. *Empire of Magic. Medieval Romance and the Politics of Cultural Fantasy.* New York, 2003.
Higgins, Iain Macleod. *Writing East. The "Travels" of Sir John Mandeville.* Philadelphia, 1997.
Höfler, Konstantin. *Anna von Luxemburg.* Vienna, 1871.
Howard, Donald R. *Writers and Pilgrims. Medieval Pilgrimage Narratives and Their Posterity.* Berkeley, 1980.
———. *Chaucer. His Life, His Works, His World.* New York, 1987.
Hudson, Anne, *The Premature Reformation. Wycliffite Texts and Lollard History.* Oxford, 1988.
———. "Laicus Litteratus. The Paradox of Lollardy." In *Heresy and Literacy,* edited by Biller and Hudson, 222–36.
———. "William Taylor's 1406 Sermon; A Postscript." *Medium Aevum* 64 (1995): 100–106.
Huizinga, Johan. *The Autumn of the Middle Ages.* Translated by Rodney J. Payton and Ulrich Mammitzsch. Chicago, 1996.
Jackson, W. H., and S. A. Ranawacke, eds. *The Arthur of the Germans.* Cardiff, 2000.
Jordan, William Chester. *Europe in the High Middle Ages.* Harmondsworth, 2003.
Justice, Steven. "Lollardy." In *The Cambridge History of Medieval English Literature,* edited by Wallace, 662–89.

Kantik, Ghosh. *The Wycliffite Heresy. Authority and the Interpretation of Texts.* Cambridge, 2002.
Kavka, František. *Život na dvoře Karla IV.* Prague, 1993.
Keen, Maurice. "The Influence of Wyclif." In *Wyclif in His Times*, edited by Kenny, 127–45.
Kendall, Paul Murray. *The Yorkist Age.* New York, 1965.
——, *Warwick the Kingmaker and the Wars of the Roses*, Aylesbury, 1973.
Kenny, Anthony, ed. *Wyclif in His Times.* Oxford 1985.
Kermode, Frank. *The Age of Shakespeare.* New York, 2005.
Kiening, Christian. *Schwierige Modernität. Der Ackermann des Johannes von Tepl und die Ambiguität des historischen Wandels.* Tübingen, 1998.
Kienze, Beverley Maine. "The Prostitute-Preacher. Patterns of Polemic against Medieval Waldensian Women Preachers." In *Women Preachers and Prophets*, edited by Kienze and Walker, 99–113.
Kienze, Beverley Maine, and Pamela J. Walker, eds. *Women Preachers amd Prophets through Two Millennia of Christianity*, Berkeley, 1998.
Klaniczay, Gabor. *The Uses of Supernatural Power. The Transformation of Popular Religion in Medieval and Early Modern Europe.* Translated by Susan Singermann and Karen Margolis. Princeton, 1990.
Klassen, John. "Women and Religious Reform in Late Medieval Bohemia." *Renaissance and Reformation* 5/4 (1981): 203–21.
——. *Warring Maidens, Captive Wives, and Hussite Queens. Women and Men at War and Peace in Fifteenth-Century Bohemia.* Boulder, 1999.
Knapp, Jeffrey. *Shakespeare's Tribe. Church, Nation, and Theater in Renaissance England.* Chicago, 2002.
Kopičková, Božena. *Historické prameny k studiu postavení ženy v české a moravské společnosti.* Prague, 1991.
Kopičková, Božena, and Anežka Vidmanová. *Listy na Husovu obranu z let 1410–1412. Konec jedné legendy?* Prague, 1999.
Lambert, Malcolm. *Medieval Heresy. Popular Movements from the Gregorian Reform to the Reformation.* Oxford, 1977.
Lášek, Jan Blahoslav, ed. *Jan Hus. Mezi epochami, národy a konfesemi.* Prague, 1995.
Laynesmith, J. L. *The Last Medieval Queens. English Queenship 1445–1503.* Oxford, 2004.
Le Goff, Jacques. *The Birth of Europe.* Translated by Janet Lloyd. Oxford, 2005.
Lerner, Robert E. "Writing and Resistance among the Beguins of Languedoc and Catalonia." In *Heresy and Literacy*, edited by Biller and Hudson, 186–204.
Lewis, C. S. *The Allegory of Love. A Study in Medieval Tradition.* Oxford, 1936.
Lewis, Flora. "The Wound in Christ's Side and the Instruments of the Passion. Gendered Experience and Response." In *Women and the Book*, edited by Taylor and Smith, 204–29.

Loades, David. *Mary Tudor. A Life*. Cambridge, Mass., 1989.
Lochrie, Karma. *Covert Operations. The Medieval Uses of Secrecy*. Philadelphia, 1999.
Loserth, Josef. "Über die Beziehungen zwischen englischen und böhmischen Wiclifisten." *Mittheilungen des Instituts fur österreichische Geschichtsforschung* 12 (1891): 254–69.
Ludwig Jansen, Katherine. "Maria Magdalena. Apostolorum Apostola." In *Women Preachers and Prophets*, edited by Kienze and Walker, 57–96.
Machilek, Franz. "Privatfrömmigkeit und Staatsfrömmigkeit." In *Kaiser Karl IV*, edited by Seibt, 87–101.
Marotti, Arthur F. "Shakespeare and Catholicism." In *Theatre and Religion*, edited by Dutton et al., 218–41.
Marshall, Peter. *The Magic Circle of Rudolf II. Alchemy and Astrology in Renaissance Prague*. New York, 2006.
Mathew, Gervase. *The Court of Richard II*. New York, 1968.
McFarlane, K. B. *John Wyclif and the Beginnings of Nonconformity*. London, 1952.
McKisack, May. *The Fourteenth Century, 1307–1399*. Oxford, 1959.
McSheffrey, Shannon. *Gender and Heresy. Women and Men in Lollard Communities, 1420–1530*. Philadelphia, 1995.
Minnis, A. J. "De impedimento sexus. Women's Bodies and Medieval Impediments to Sexual Ordination." In *Medieval Theology and the Natural Body*, edited by Biller and Minnis, 109–39.
———. "'Respondet Waltherus Bryth . . . '. Walter Brut in Debate on Women Priests." In *Text and Controversy*, edited by Barr and Hutchinson, 229–49.
Mueller, Joan. *The Privilege of Poverty. Clare of Assisi, Agnes of Prague, and the Struggle for a Franciscan Rule for Women*. University Park, 2006.
Nechutová, Jana, "Ženy v Husově okolí. K protiženským satirám husitské doby." In *Jan Hus*, edited by Lášek, 68–73.
———. *Latinská literatura českého středověku do roku 1400*. Prague, 2000.
Nejedlý, Zdeněk., *Dějiny husitského zpěvu*. 2nd ed, 3 vols., Prague, 1955.
Nilson, Ben. *The Cathedral Shrines of Medieval England*. Woodbridge, 1998.
Odložilík, Otakar. "Cesty z Čech a Moravy do Velké Britanie v letech 1593–1620." *Časopis Českého Muzea* 59 (1935): 241–320.
Olson, Linda, and Kathryn Kerby-Fulton, eds. *Voices in Dialogue. Reading Women in the Middle Ages*. Notre Dame, 2005.
Oman, Carola. *The Winter Queen. Elizabeth of Bohemia*. London, 1938; rev. ed., 2000.
Omrod, W. M. "Richard II's Sense of English History." In *The Reign of Richard II*, edited by Dodd, 97–110.
Patterson, Lee. "Court Politics and the Invention of Literature. The Case of Sir John Clanvowe." In *Culture and History*, edited by Aers, 7–41.
Pearsall, Derek. *The Life of Geoffrey Chaucer*. Oxford, 1992.

———. *Gothic Europe, 1200–1450*. Harlow, 2001.
———. *Arthurian Romance. A Short Introduction*. Oxford, 2003.
Percival, Florence. *Chaucer's Legendary Good Women*. Cambridge, 1998.
Pleij, Herman. *Dreaming of Cockaigne. Medieval Fantasies of the Perfect Life*. Translated by Diane Webb. New York, 2001.
Polišenský, Josef V. *England and Czechoslovakia*. Prague, 1946.
———. *Anglie a Bílá Hora*. Prague, 1949.
———. *Britain and Czechoslovakia*. Prague, 1968.
———. *Komenský. Muž Labyrintů a Naděje*. Prague, 1996.
Prestwich, Michael. *Edward I*. New Haven, 1997.
Pujmanová, Olga. "Portraits of Kings depicted as Magi in Bohemian Painting." In *The Regal Image*, edited by Gordon et al., 27–32.
Richards, Jennifer, and James Knowles, eds. *Shakespeare's Late Plays*. Edinburgh, 1999.
Rosario, Iva. *Art and Propaganda. Charles IV of Bohemia, 1346–1378*. Woodbridge, 2000.
Ross, Charles. *The Wars of the Roses. A Concise History*. London, 1986.
———. *Edward IV*. New Haven, 1997.
Rubin, Miri. *Gentile Tales. The Narrative Assault on Late Medieval Jews*. New Haven, 1999.
Saul, Nigel. *Richard II*. New Haven, 1997.
———. "The Kingship of Richard II." In *Richard II. The Art of Kingship*, edited by Goodman and Gillespie, 37–57.
———. *The Three Richards. Richard I, Richard II and Richard III*. London, 2005.
Schleiner, Louise. *Tudor and Stuart Women Writers*. Bloomington, 1994.
Schmolke-Hasselmann, Beate. *The Evolution of Arthurian Romance. The Verse Tradition from Chrétien to Froissart*. Translated by Margaret and Roger Middleton. Cambridge, 1998.
Seibt, Ferdinand. *Hussitenstudien. Personen, Ereignisse, Ideen einer frühen Revolution*, Munich, 1987.
———, ed. *Kaiser Karl IV. Staatsmann und Mäzen*. Munich, 1988.
Sheingorn, Pamela. "'The Wise Mother.' The Image of St Anne Teaching the Virgin Mary." In *Gendering the Master Narrative*, edited by Erler and Kowaleski, 105–34.
Simpson, James. "The Other Book of Troy. Guido delle Colonne's *Historia destructionis Troiae* in Fourteenth- and Fifteenth-Century England." *Speculum* 73 (1998): 397–423.
Simpson, Richard. *Edmund Campion. A Biography*. London, 1896.
Šmahel, František. "Doctor Evangelicus super omnes evangelistas. Wyclif's Fortunes in Hussite Bohemia." *Bulletin of the Institute of Historical Research* 43 (1970): 16–34.
———. *Husitská revoluce*. 4 vols., Prague, 1993–95.

———, "Literacy and Heresy in Hussite Bohemia." In *Heresy and Literacy*, edited by Biller and Hudson, 237–54.
Somerset, Fiona. *Clerical Discourse and Lay Audience in Late Medieval England*. Cambridge, 1998.
Somerset, Fiona, Jill C. Havens, and Derrick G. Pitard, eds. *Lollards and Their Influence in Late Medieval England*. Woodbridge, 2003.
Spearing, A. C. *The Medieval Poet as Voyeur. Looking and Listening in Medieval Love-Narratives*. Cambridge, 1993.
Spinka, Matthew. *John Amos Comenius. That Incomparable Moravian*. Chicago, 1943.
———. *John Hus at the Council of Constance*. New York, 1965.
———. *John Hus' Concept of the Church*. Princeton, 1966.
———. *John Hus. A Biography*. Princeton, 1968.
Šroňková, Olga. *Die Mode der gotischen Frau*. Translated by J. Gaydečka. Prague, 1954.
Stewart, Alan. *Philip Sidney. A Double Life*. London, 2001.
Stříbrný Zdeněk. *Shakespeare and Eastern Europe*. Oxford, 2000.
Strohm, Paul. *Hochon's Arrow. The Social Imagination of Fourteenth-Century Texts*. Princeton, 1992.
———. *England's Empty Throne. Usurpation and the Language of Legitimation, 1399–1422*. New Haven, 1998.
Taylor, Andrew. "Anne of Bohemia and the Making of Chaucer." *Studies in the Age of Chaucer* 19 (1997): 95–119.
Taylor, Jane H. M., and Lesley Smith, eds. *Women and the Book. Assessing the Visual Evidence*. London, 1997.
Thomas, Alfred. "Czech-German Relations as Reflected in Old Czech Literature." In *Medieval Frontier Societies*, edited by Bartlett and Mackay, 199–215.
———. *The Labyrinth of the Word. Truth and Representation in Czech Literature*. Munich, 1995.
———. *Anne's Bohemia. Czech Literature and Society, 1310–1420*. Medieval Cultures at Minnesota, vol. 13. Minneapolis, 1998.
———. "King Arthur and His Round Table in the Culture of Medieval Bohemia." In *The Arthur of the Germans*, edited by Jackson and Ranawacke, 249–56.
———. "Women Readers and Writers in Medieval and Early Modern Bohemia." In *A History of Central European Women's Writing*, edited by Hawkesworth, 7–13.
Trevor-Roper, Hugh. *Princes and Artists. Patronage and Ideology at Four Habsburg Courts, 1517–1633*. London, 1991.
Tuck, Anthony. "Richard II and the House of Luxemburg." In *Richard II. The Art of Kingship*, edited by Goodman and Gillespie, 205–29.

Van Eerde, Katherine S. *Wenceslaus Hollar. Delineator of His Time.* Charlottesville, 1970.
Vauchez, André. *The Laity in the Middle Ages. Religious Beliefs and Devotional Practices.* Translated by Daniel E. Bornstein. Notre Dame, 1993.
Vidmanová, Anežka. *Laborintus. Latinská literatura středověkých Čech.* Prague, 1994.
Vilikovský, Jan. *Písemnictví českého středověku.* Prague, 1948.
Vincent, Nicholas. *The Holy Blood. King Henry III and the Westminster Blood Relic.* Cambridge, 2000.
Von Moos, Peter. *Consolatio. Studien zur mittellateinischer Trostliteratur über den Tod und zum Problem der christlichen Trauer.* 2 vols., Munich, 1971.
Wallace, David. "Anne of Bohemia. Queen of England and Chaucer's Emperice." *Litteraria Pragensia* 5/9 (1995): 1–16.
———. *Chaucerian Polity. Absolutist Lineages and Associational Forms in England and Italy.* Stanford, 1997.
———. ed. *The Cambridge History of Medieval English Literature.* Cambridge, 1999.
Watson, Nicholas. "Censorship and Cultural Change in Late Medieval England. Vernacular Theology, the Oxford Translation Debate, and Arundel's Constitutions of 1409." *Speculum* 70/4 (1995): 822–64.
———. "The Gawain-Poet as Vernacular Theologian." In *A Companion to the Gawain-Poet*, edited by Brewer and Gibson, 293–313.
Waugh, Evelyn. *Saint Edmund Campion. Priest and Martyr.* Manchester, N.H., 1996.
Webb, Diane. *Pilgrimage in Medieval England.* London, 2000.
Wilson, Richard. *Secret Shakespeare. Studies in Theatre, Religion and Resistance.* Manchester, 2004.
Wimsatt, James I. *The Margeurite Poetry of Guillaume de Machaut.* Chapel Hill, 1970.
Winston-Allen, Anne. *Convent Chronicles. Women Writing about Women and Reform in the Late Middle Ages.* University Park, 2004.
Wogan-Browne, Jocelyn. *Saints' Lives and Women's Literary Culture c. 1150–1300. Virginity and its Authorizations.* Oxford, 2001.
Woolley, Benjamin. *The Queen's Conjurer. The Science and Magic of Dr. John Dee, Adviser to Queen Elizabeth I.* New York, 2001.
Yates, Frances. *The Rosicrucian Enlightenment.* New York, 1972.
———. *Shakespeare's Last Plays.* London, 1975.

Index

Page numbers in italics refer to illustrations.

acculturation, 150–51, 165
Ackermann, Der. See Plowman, The
Adamites, 114
Agnes of Bohemia, Saint 35, 45, 87
Agnes of Lancencrona, 8, 19
Agnes of Štítné, 133, 138, 148
albas (dawn poems), 126, 142–43
Alexander III (pope), 134
Alexandreida, 158
Alfonso X, king of Castile, 12
allegories of love, 25–26
Ambrose, Saint, 175
Ambrosia (Campion), 175
Anderson, Benedict, 118
animal fables, 30
Anna of Frimburk, 133
Anna of Mochov, 133
Anne, Saint, 37–38, 54
Anne, wife of Charles IV, 58
Anne of Bohemia, wife of Richard II, 5, 201, 209–10; active/passive view of, 18–21, 64; betrothal and marriage of, 8, 26–31, 64; as cultural mediatrix, 9, 13–14, 21–22, 24–26, 27, 81; death and apotheosis of, 51–63; devices of, 40, 67–68, 95; flowers/pearls symbolism and, 27–28, 40–41, 43, 54–57; as intercessory figure, 18, 42, 64; languages/learning of, 9, 28, 37, 64, 98, 132–33; as patron of arts, 21–22, 24, 28, 31–34, 64; piety/chastity of, 9, 38, 46, 48, 64, 86, 98; tomb of, 54, *94*, 94–97; as validation of Richard's imperial ambitions, 12, 14, 65, 71, 78, 97
Annunciation, the, 36
apocalyptic imagery, 57, 59–60, 82–83, 85, 89, 111–12
Aquinas. *See* Thomas Aquinas, Saint
Arden, Robert, 175–76
Arian heresy, 175
Arnošt of Pardubice, 35, 91
Ars Poetica (Horace), 95
Arthurian legend, 11–12, 76–78, 80
Arthur, King, 11–12, 77–78, 79, 80
Arundel, Richard Fitzalan, 4th earl of, 66
Arundel, Thomas, archbishop of Canterbury, 14, 100

Arundel, Thomas Howard, 14th earl of, 196, 202–3
astrology, 93
Augustine, Saint, 43–44, 109, 204–5
Avellanedo, James, 174

Balbín, Bohuslav, 151
Baldhoven, Georg Martin von, 180
Barclay, Alexander, 154
Bartholomeus Claretus de Chlumec, 30
Bartlett, Anne Clark, 136
Bartoš, František, 6, 99, 103
Battle of the White Mountain, 4, 6, 192
Baxter, Margery, 137, 142
Beaufort, Henry, 153
Becket, Thomas, Saint, 155, 157–58, 199
"The Beguines," 120, 126, 137
Benedict, Samuel, 206
Bennett, Michael, 13, 66
Benoît de Sainte-Maure, 76
Benson, Larry D., 29
Bestul, Thomas, 136
Bethlehem Chapel, 117–18, 131, 133
Bible: Kralice, 171; as *sola scriptura*, 108; translation of, into vernacular language, 9, 14, 98, 118, 121, 132–33; of Wenceslas IV, 58, 81–82, 83, 89, 132, 144
Biceps, Nicholas, 99–100
bilingualism. *See* literacy and learning, female
Binski, Paul, 73, 83, 85, 89
Blanche, wife of John of Gaunt, 25, 52
Blanche, wife of Ludwig III of Bavaria, 56
Boccaccio, 24, 33–34, 81
Boehm, Barbara Drake, 35, 70
Boethius, 42, 54
Bohemian Brethren, 115, 117
Bohemian Lawes or Rights Defended against the Informer, The (Harrison), 185–86
Boke of Cupid (Clanvowe), 28
Bonne of Luxembourg, 22, 24, 25, 32, 52, 87
Book of the Duchess (Chaucer), 25, 52
Book of the Fraternity of the Assumption, 55
Book to a Mother, 136
Bowers, John, 54–55
Brant, Sebastian, 154

Breviary of Great Master Lev, 96
Bridget, Saint, 142
Broker, Nicholas, 94
Brtnický, Zdeněk. *See* Waldstein, Zdeněk Brtnický, baron of
Brut, Walter, 127
Buch der Ersetzung (Meyer), 131
Buch der Liebkosung, Das, 36, 49
"Bundle of Myrrh, A," 128
Burley, Sir Simon, 8, 18, 42
Burley, Walter, 40
Burns, E. Jane, 145

Caernarfon Castle (Wales), 12
Calixtus III (pope), 164
Cambridge University, 200, 206
Campion, Edmund, 16, 172, 174–76, 177, 194, 211
Canterbury Cathedral, 157–58, 198–99
Canterbury Tales (Chaucer), 47, 69
Carmina Burana, 143
Carruthers, Mary, 55
Catherine of Alexandria, Saint, 37–38, 46–47, 57–62, 64, 138–39
Catholics, English, 2, 168–70, 176, 210
Cecil, Sir Robert, 200
Cecilia, Saint, 47, 64
center / margin binary views, 3, 5, 7–8, 10–11
Chamberlain, Neville, 7
Chanson de Roland, 24
Chapman, George, 168
Charlemagne, 74, 75, 91–92
Charles I, king of England, 201–2
Charles IV, Holy Roman Emperor: ancestry of, 74, 85, 91–92; cult of the Three Kings and, 70; daughter's marriage and, 26–27; devices of, 81; governance model of, 71, 77–78, 91, 97; imperial views of, 71, 82–83; "mirror for princes" in autobiography of, 30; nobility, relationship with, of, 69, 80–81; as patron of arts, 19, 22, 33–37, 73–74; piety of, 45–46, 71, 81, 86–87; portraits of, 23, 97; progresses of, 13
Charles V, Holy Roman Emperor, 16
Charles V, king of France, 85, 86, 91, 93
Charles VI, king of France, 13
Charles IX, king of France, 175

Index   231

chastity. *See* virginity and chastity, female
Chaucer, Geoffrey: "Bohemia" for, 33, 209; English as language of writings of, 28, 37; "Europe" for, 5; *marguerite* tradition and, 40, 43, 55–56; *Book of the Duchess*, 25, 52; *Canterbury Tales*, 47, 69; *The Legend of Good Women*, 14, 21–22, 24, 28, 31–34, 38–40, 43, 60, 64, 134, 143; *Life of Saint Cecilia*, 47–48; *The Parliament of Fowls*, 28–31, 64; "Second Nun's Tale," 47; *Troilus and Criseyde*, 14, 21, 31, 50, 134; "Wife of Bath's Tale," 69
Chelčický, Peter, 15, 98, 107–16
Chrétien de Troyes, 25, 150
Church of St. Bartholomew (Kolín nad Labem), 96
church reform: Bible, vernacular language translation of, and, 9, 14, 118, 121, 132–33; corruption and, 15, 105–7, 109, 114–15; Eucharistic doctrines and, 107, 113–14, 140, 152; married clergy and, 139–40; priestly authority and, 107, 129–31, 139, 141; primitive/apostolic Church, identification with, and, 99, 104–5, 110; separation of church/state and, 15, 107, 109, 115; women's role in, 119–23, 133–35, 137, 145, 147–48
Císařová-Kolářová, Anna, 122
Clanvowe, Sir John, 28
Clare of Assisi, Saint, 35
Clementine Almanach (Thomas of Štítné), 96
Clement VI (pope), 91
Clement VII (antipope), 27
Clerk, John of Whalley, 76–77
clothing styles, 57–58, 81, 83, 145
Codex Heidelbergensis, 74
"Collyn Clout" (Skelton), 154, 175
Cologne Cathedral, 69, 71
Colonne, Guido delle, 76, 134
color symbolism, 59–60
Comenius, John Amos, 9, 17, 115, 172, 196, 203, 204–8
Commedia (Dante), 81
Compacts of Basel, 152
complaint literature, 126

Concordia facta inter regem Riccardum II et civitatem Londonie (Richard of Maidstone), 89, 91
Confessio Amantis (Gower), 14, 27–28
confession, sacrament of, 137–38
Consolation of Philosophy (Boethius), 42, 54
consolatio tradition, 53, 55
Constantine Donation, 92, 112
Constantine, Emperor, 92, 114
Constantinople, 69, 70, 150
Copeland, Rita, 137, 142
Council of Constance, 10, 107, 152
court culture, 65–97; Anne of Bohemia and, 22, 24–26; apocalyptic imagery and, 59, 82–83; architectural space and, 73–85; books/manuscripts and, 34–36, 87–93; fashion and, 57–58, 81, 83, 145; governance models and, 13, 69, 71, 73, 77–78, 80–81, 158; knot imagery and, 81, 95; relics of the Passion and, 85–87; satires of, 144–45; Trojan/Arthurian narratives and, 74–78, 80; Wilton Diptych in, 67–73
Cromwell, Oliver, 169
Crowne, William, 202
Curry, Anne, 97

Dalimil Chronicle, 20, 117, 158
Dante Alighieri, 26, 81
dawn poems. *See albas*
Dcerka (*The Daughter*) (Hus), 130–31
De Antichristo (Wyclif), 146
"Dear Radiant Day," 126
"Dear Student," 126
De Civili Dominio (Wyclif), 105–6, 108, 114–15, 120
De Civitate Dei (St. Augustine), 43–44, 204
De claris mulieribus (Boccaccio), 24, 33–34
Decree of Kutná Hora, 131–32
Dee, John, 172, 177, 205
De Ecclesia (Hus), 135
De eruditione praedicatorum (Humbert of Romans), 135
De Eucharistia (Wyclif), 100
De heretico comburendo (statute, 1401), 9, 100

Index

De Ideis (Wyclif), 100
"De inundatione Pragae" (Weston), 180–81
Dekker, Thomas, 168
De laudibus feminarum (Petrarch), 33
De libris hereticorum legendis (Hus), 102
"demon seed," 141–42
De sanguine Christi (Hus), 86
Descartes, René, 206
Destruction of Troy (Clerk), 76–77
De Triplici Vinculo Amoris (Wyclif), 14, 132
De vita et moribus philosophorum antiquorum (Burley), 40
Devotio Moderna movement, 145
Dialogus (Wyclif), 100, 111, 120
Dinshaw, Carolyn, 146
Divine Comedy (Dante), 26
Dominicans, 121–23, 131–33, 135, 145–48
Dragmaticon philosophiae (William of Conches), 93
dream vision genre, 52–53
Duke Ernest (*Herzog Ernst*), 49, 162
Duncan-Jones, Katherine, 178
Dymmok, Roger, 89, 91–92, 146
Dynter, Edmond de, 75

Edmund the Martyr, Saint, 67, 69, *frontispiece*
Edward I, king of England, 12, 73, 75, 169
Edward II, king of England, 69
Edward III, king of England, 73, 78, 80
Edward IV, king of England, 15, 159–61
Edward the Confessor, 69, 71, 73
Eleanor of Aquitaine, 24
Elizabeth I, queen of England, 2, 7–8, 169–71, 175–76, 184–85, 193–94, 198, 201
Elizabeth of Hungary, Saint, 183
Elizabeth of Pomerania, mother of Anne of Bohemia, 66
Elizabeth Přemyslovna, mother of Charles IV, 86–87
Elizabeth Stuart, wife of Frederick V, 169–70, 181–85, 191–92, 202
Elizabeth Woodville, wife of Edward IV, 55, 160–63

Elliott, Dyan, 139–40, 141, 147
emotion / reason debate, 53–54
English-man's Love to Bohemia . . . (Taylor), 187–88
Epiphany, cult of the, 69–70
Erastus, Daniel, 206
Erghum, Ralph, 165
Escanor (Girart of Amiens), 12
Esther, Biblical queen, 20–21, 47, 48
ethnic tensions, 99, 101–2, 117–18, 131–32
Eucharistic doctrines, 107, 113–14, 140, 152
Eugenius IV (pope), 154
European Union, 10, 211
Evans, R. J. W., 172, 205
Eve, as seductress, 126, 128, 140
exotic / familiar binary views, 3–4, 149–50, 165

Fall of Princes (Lydgate), 32
familiar / exotic binary views, 3–4, 149–50, 165
Faulfiš, Nicholas, 100
Ferdinand I, Holy Roman Emperor, 171, 174, 181
Ferdinand II, Holy Roman Emperor, 4, 196, 202
"Filia, si vox tua," 126
Flaška, Smil of Pardubice, 30, 92, 144, 158
flower symbolism: Anne of Bohemia and, 27–28, 40–41, 43, 54–55, 63; *marguerite* tradition and, 40, 55–56; Virgin Mary and, 40, 42, 55, 63
Fortescue, Sir John, 154
Foucault, Michel, 10
Four Articles of Prague, 106–7
Frauenlob, 48–49
Frederick III, Holy Roman Emperor, 15
Frederick V, Elector Palatine (later Frederick I, king of Bohemia), 169–70, 181–85, 192
Frederick, archbishop of Cologne, 66
Froissart, Jean, 40

Garden of Eden story, 126, 128
gardens, enclosed, 61
Gate of Things (Comenius), 206

Geoffrey of Monmouth, 11, 75, 77–78
geographical spaces, imagery of, 3–4, 60–63, 137–39, 149–50
George, duke of Clarence, 161, 165
George, Saint, 67, 152, 164
George of Kněhnice, 100
George of Poděbrady, king of Bohemia, 15, 151, 153, 154, 159
Gilles of Orleans, 145
Girart of Amiens, 12
Gloucester, Thomas of Woodstock, duke of, 66
Golden Bull, 89–90
Gordon, Dillian, 71
gossip, 137–38
governance models, 13, 69, 71, 73, 77–78, 80–81, 91, 97, 158, 185–86
Gower, John, 14, 27–28
Graña, César and Marigay, 1
Great Hospital (Norwich), 65–66
Greenblatt, Stephen, 159, 176, 194
Greene, Robert, 2, 11, 167–68, 192
Gregorius de Hungaricali Broda, 30
Gregory IX (pope), 35

hair styles, 57–58, 164
Harrison, John, 184–87
Hartlib, Samuel, 205–7
Harvard College, 207, 208
Harvey, Gabriel, 172
Hedwig of Silesia, Saint, 45
Heidelberg, 182, 204
Heng, Geraldine, 11, 149, 156
Henry II, king of England, 157
Henry III, king of England, 71, 73, 86
Henry IV, king of England, 9, 117
Henry V, king of England, 10, 117–18, 151–52, 164
Henry VI, king of England, 154, 159–60
Henry VIII, king of England, 97, 154, 157
Henry the Lion, duke of Saxony, 24
Hervorst, Hugh, 66
Herzog Ernst. See Duke Ernest
Higgins, Iain Macleod, 3, 62
Hildegard von Bingen, 35
Historia Destructionis Troiae (Colonne), 76, 134
Historia Regum Britanniae (Geoffrey of Monmouth), 11, 75, 77–78

Historia Trium Regum (John of Hildesheim), 70
Hoccleve, Thomas, 148
Höfler, Constantin, 5
Hollar, Wenceslas, 17, 196, 201–4
Horace, 95
Howard, Donald R., 150
Hübner, John, 101
Hudson, Anne, 104, 132, 136
Huizinga, Johan, 155
Humbert of Romans, 135
Humphrey, duke of Gloucester, 152
Hus, John: Arian heresy and, 175; church corruption and, 106–7; "England" for, 210; ethnic tensions and, 117–18; Eucharistic doctrines and, 113; priestly authority and, 129–31; sodomy, accusations of, and, 146; veneration of holy images and, 123; women, view of, by, 130, 134; Wyclif, influence of, on, 6, 98–107; *Dcerka* (*The Daughter*), 130–31; *De Ecclesia*, 135; *De libris hereticorum legendis*, 102; *De sanguine Christi*, 86; *On Simony*, 106; *On the Church*, 106
Hussites/Hussitism, 116–18; apocalyptic imagery and, 82; England as source of reforms for, 9, 105; ethnic tensions and, 99, 101–2, 117–18; friars and, 145–48; manifesto of, 106–7; pilgrimages and, 155; primitive/apostolic Church, identification with, and, 99, 104–5, 110; social class and, 148; veneration of holy images and, 123, 155; women's role in, 119, 121–23, 133–34

irenicism, 194–95
"I syng of a myden," 51
Itinerarius (Oderic of Pordenone), 156
Itinerary (Moryson), 189
Ivančice (Moravia), 171

Jakoubek of Stříbro, 107, 108–9, 113, 120
James I, king of England, 2, 183, 191
James of Compostela, Saint, 155
Jan of Chlum, wife of, 133
Jan of Kamenice the Younger, 133
Janua Linguarum Reserata (Comenius), 206, 208

234 Index

Janua Rerum (Comenius), 206
Jean de Meun, 25–26
Jena Codex, 112, 131
Jerome of Prague, 100
Jerusalem, celestial, 3, 59–61
jewels, symbolism of, 43, 55, 58–59, 95
Jews, 140–41, 169, 189–90
Jindřich of Rožmberk, 133
Joan, Pope, 134
John II ("the Good"), king of France, 32, 132
John XXIII (antipope), 102, 121, 146
John of Gaunt, 25, 106
John of Hildesheim, 70
John of Jenštejn, 140
John of Luxembourg, king of Bohemia, 22, 74, 76–77, 117
John of Nepomuk, 141
John of Středa, 33, 36, 80, 91
John the Baptist, Saint, 67, *frontispiece*
Jonson, Ben, 2, 167, 168, 185–86
Jugement du roy de Behaigne, Le (Machaut), 32, 74
Justice, Stephen, 116
Justina (Campion), 175
"just" war, the, 108–9
Juvenal des Ursins, Jean, 166

Karlstein Castle, 73–74, 81–83; Apocalypse cycle in, 57, 83, 89; Chapel of the Holy Cross, 37, 70, 74, 92; Lady Chapel, 49, 57, 83, 86; oratory of, 46, 59
Kelley, Edward, 177–78
Kempe, Margery, 38, 127, 133–34, 142
Kendall, Paul Murray, 3
Kerby-Fulton, Kathryn, 145
Klassen, John, 122
Knight of the Cart, The (Chrétien de Troyes), 25
Knížky (*Little Books*), 121
knot imagery, 81, 95
Kolda of Koldice, 35, 49, 87, 96, 136
Kralice Bible, 171
Kravař, Eliška, 133
Krumlov Madonna, 71–72
Kunigunde, Abbess, 24, 35–36, 45, 87, 96
Kutná Hora, 101, 131

Labyrinth of the World and the Paradise of the Heart, The (Comenius), 115, 204–5, 207
Laetus-Veselský, Jan, 205
"Lamenting to Heaven," 125–26, 131n21
languages. *See* literacy and learning, female
Languet, Hubert, 171
Laud Troy Book, 76
Lefl, Jindřich, wife of, 133
Legend of Good Women, The (Chaucer), 14, 21–22, 24, 28, 31–34, 38–40, 43, 60, 64, 134, 143
Legend of Saint Prokop, 115
Le Goff, Jacques, 211
Letter of Majesty, 186
Lewis, C. S., 25–26
Libellus Geomancie, 93
Liber contra duodecim errores . . . (Dymmok), 89, 91–92
Liber Regalis, 58, 87–89
Libri Sententiarum (Lombard), 127
Libuše, 122, 185
Life of Saint Catherine (Czech), 37, 46–47, 57–62, 85, 96, 134, 138–39
Life of Saint Cecilia (Chaucer), 47–48
Life of Saint Prokop, 139
Life of Saint Wenceslas, 45
Lis et Marguerite (Machaut), 60
literacy and learning, female, 9, 35–38, 54, 121–23, 132–37
Lochrie, Karma, 138
Lollard Knights, 92, 148
Lollards / Lollardism, 92, 116–18; *De heretico comburendo* and, 9, 100; English translation of the Bible and, 9, 14, 98, 118, 132–33; friars and, 146; primitive / apostolic Church, identification with, and, 99, 104–5; social class and, 148; support for Bohemian reform and, 102–4; women's role in, 119, 133–34
Lombard, Peter, 127
Loserth, Josef, 5–6, 99
Lote, Stephen, 94
Louis IX, king of France, 86
Louis VII, king of France, 157–58
Love, Nicholas, 136

Ludmila, Saint, 43–45, 71
Lupton, Julia Reinhard, 193
Luxembourg Genealogy, 74, 91
Lydgate, John, 32, 76–77, 134

Machaut, Guillaume de, 22, 24–25, 32, 40, 52, 60, 74
Mann, Thomas, 1
Margaret, Saint, 47, 64
margin/center binary views, 3, 5, 7–8, 10–11
marguerite tradition, 40, 43, 50, 55–56
Marie de Champagne, 24
Marie de France, 141
Mary, Blessed Virgin: active/passive gender models and, 20–21; cult of, 48–51, 95–96; flower symbolism and, 40, 42, 55, 63; hair of, 57; as intercessor, 20–21, 140; literacy/learning and, 36–38; as model of queenship, 20–21, 25–26, 48
Mary Magdalene, 47, 135
Mary Queen of Scots, 176, 193–94
Mary Tudor, queen of England, 8, 157
Masaryk, T. G., 122
Masque of Queens, The (Jonson), 168, 185–86
Massinger, Philip, 4, 192
Mather, Cotton, 207–8
Mathew, Gervase, 22, 95
Matilda of England, daughter of Henry II, 24
Matthew of Janov, 100
Matthias, Holy Roman Emperor, 190
Maximilian II, Holy Roman Emperor, 169, 170–71, 181, 190, 194–95
Meditationes Vitae Christi (pseudo-Bonaventure), 136
Meissen, Heinrich von (Frauenlob), 48–49
Meistermann, Ludolf, 101
Meyer, Johannes, 131
Mézières, Philippe de, 85–86
Milíč, Jan, of Kroměříž 120, 135
"mirror for princes" genre, 29–31
Mirror of the Blessed Jesus Christ (Love), 136
Monas Hieroglyphica (Dee), 172

More, Sir (Saint) Thomas, 180, 186
Morgan Diptych, 70
Morte Arthur, 77–78
Moryson, Fynes, 189
Mügeln, Heinrich von, 49

Narrenschiff, Das (Brant), 154
Na Slovanech Monastery, 49
Net of Faith, The (Chelčický), 112, 114
New Council, The (Smil Flaška), 30, 92, 144, 158
Nicholas of Kadaň, 93
Nicholas of Verdun, 69
Norfolk, Thomas Howard, 4th duke of, 176
Norfolk, Thomas Mowbray, 1st duke of, 176

Oderic of Pordenone, 156
Oldcastle, Sir John, 102–3, 105, 118, 148, 151
Old Fortunatus (Dekker), 168
Olympia (Boccaccio), 81
On Simony (Hus), 106
On Spiritual Warfare (Chelčický), 110
On the Church (Hus), 106
"On the Flood of Prague" (Weston), 180–81
On the Triple Division of Society (Chelčický), 110–12
Orbis Pictus (Comenius), 172
Ordo ad coronandum regem Boemorum, 87, 89
Orgel, Stephen, 167
Osmund, Saint, 164–65
Otakar II, king of Bohemia, 11–12
Other, the, 60–63, 140, 150, 165
Oxford, Robert de Vere, earl of, 8, 19
Oxford University, 9, 98, 100, 109

Palacký, František, 122
Pandosto. The Triumph of Time (Greene), 2, 11, 167–68
Pansophia, 172
Pansophiae Prodromus (Comenius), 206
"Parable of the Invincible Knight" (Kolda of Koldice), 49
paradise, location of, 3–4, 60–63

Parliament of Fowls, The (Chaucer), 28–31, 64
parodies, religious, 129
Parthenicon Elisabethae Joannaie Westoniae . . . (Weston), 180–81
Passio judaeorum secundum Johannes rusticus quadratus, 140–41
Passional (prose selection of saints' lives in Czech), 34, 37
Passional of Abbess Kunigunde (Kolda of Koldice), 35, 87, 96, 141n45
Passion of the Jews According to John the Stocky Peasant, The, 140–41
patrons/patronage, 24–25, 39–40
Paul II (pope), 153
Payne, Peter, 100, 154
Pearl, 3, 51–64, 81, 85
pearl symbolism, 27–28, 43, 54–58
Peasants' Revolt, 27
Pecock, Reginald, 153
Perchta of Rožmberk, 64
Percival, Florence, 38–39, 40
Perdita (*The Winter's Tale*), 2, 168, 186, 193, 194
Peregrinatio (Laetus-Veselský), 205
Peter of Zittau, 76–77
Petrarch, 22, 24, 33
Philip Augustus, king of France, 157
Phillips, Helen, 32
Physiologarius (Bartholomeus Claretus de Chlumec), 30
Picture, The (Massinger), 4, 192
Pierre de Lusignan, king of Cyprus, 86
piety and saintliness, female, 43–49, 87, 134–35
pilgrimages, 155, 199
Pius II, pope (Aeneas Sylvius) 153
Pius V (pope), 2, 169
Plowman, The (Der Ackermann), 39–41, 43, 50, 53, 95
Polišenský, Josef, 6
"Prayer of Kunigunde," 36, 128
Přemysl Otakar II, king of Bohemia, 11–12
Přemysl (Primislaus) the Plowman, 168, 186
Prest, Godfrey, 95
priests: authority of, 107, 129–31, 139, 141; celibacy of, 139–40

Primislaus. *See* Přemysl
Prise d'Alexandrie (Machaut), 25
private spaces, 137–39
Prokop, Saint, 115, 139
Prospero (*The Tempest*), 178
prostitution, 135, 137
pseudo-Augustine, 36, 136
pseudo-Bonaventure, 136
Pujmanová, Olga, 70
Putter, Ad, 81

Quadripartitus (Gregorius de Hungaricali Broda), 30

reason/emotion debate, 53–54
Rejčka, Elizabeth, 35
relics, 67, 85–87, 101, 152, 158, 164, 199
Remede de Fortune (Machaut), 25, 32, 52
"Remonstrance against Sir John Oldcastle" (Hoccleve), 148
Reply to Bishop Rokycana (Chelčický), 112–13
Richard, duke of Gloucester (later Richard III), 161, 163
Richard, earl of Cornwall, 12
Richard II, king of England, 209; ancestry of, 67, 69, 75, 85, 91; anticourtly criticism of, 144; astrology/astronomy and, 93; betrothal and marriage of, 8, 26–27, 29, 31; cult of the Three Kings and, 69–71; deposed, 24, 65, 97; devices of, 40, 65–67, 83, 95; governance model of, 71, 73, 77–78, 80; imperial ambitions of, 12–14, 65–67, 85, 91, 94, 97; "mirror for princes" genre and, 29–31; nobility, relationship with, of, 13, 66, 69, 80–81; as patron of arts, 24; piety/orthodoxy of, 9, 81, 86–87, 92; portraits of, 83–*84*, 97; tomb of, 54, *94*, 94–97; Troy narratives and, 75, 77; Wilton Diptych and, 3–4, 13, 40–42, 67–73, 86, *frontispiece*
Richard II (Shakespeare), 15–16, 174, 176
Richard of Maidstone, 89, 91
Ridolfi plot, 176
Rienzo, Cola di, 33
Roe, Sir Thomas, 184
Rokycana, Jan, 113
Rolandslied, 24

Roman de la Rose (Jean de Meun), 25
Roman de Troie (Benoît de Sainte-Maure), 76
Romano, Giulio, 195
rosemary, device of Anne of Bohemia, 67–68
Rožmberk, William of, 177
Rožmitál and Blatná, Leo, baron of, 15–16, 151, 154–55
Rudolf I, Holy Roman Emperor, 12
Rudolf II, Holy Roman Emperor, *173*; ecumenism of, 4, 93, 169, 181, 186, 190, 194–95; as patron of arts and sciences, 168–69, 172, 202; personality/learning of, 173–74, 178
Rupert, Prince, 184, 190
Rupert of Bavaria, 66

saintliness. *See* piety and saintliness, female
Salisbury, England, 164–65
Sandwich, England, 156–57
Šašek, Václav of Bířkov, 155–56, 158, 162–66, 210
Saul, Nigel, 19, 97
Second Cycle of Legends, 47–48
"Second Nun's Tale" (Chaucer), 47
separation of church and state, 15, 107, 109, 115
sexuality and heresy, 15, 141–42
Shakespeare, William: "Bohemia" for, 1–2, 10, 168, 194, 210; *Richard II*, 15–16, 174, 176; *The Tempest*, 169–70, 178; *The Winter's Tale*, 1–2, 11, 167–70, 172, 175–76, 181, 186, 193–95
Sheen (palace of Anne of Bohemia), 28, 201
Ship of Fools, The (Brant), 154
Short Relation of the Departure of the high and mightie Prince Frederick . . . (Harrison), 185
Sidney, Sir Philip, 7–8, 165–66, 170–74
Sigismund, king of Hungary (later Holy Roman Emperor), 10, 16, 67, 107, 152, 164
Simpson, James, 75–76
Šindel, Johannes, 93
Sir Gawain and the Green Knight, 41, 50, 77–81, 95

Six Books on General Christian Matters (Thomas of Štítné), 47
Skelton, John, 154, 175
Skirlaw, Walter, 103
Škopek, Jinřich of Dubá, wife of, 133
"Slovce M," 50
social class, 110–13, 133, 148, 155
sodomy, 146
Soliloquies (pseudo-Augustine), 36, 136
Solomon, king of Israel, 91
Somerset, Fiona, 91, 145
Song of Songs, The, 26, 50, 63, 128
Sophie, wife of Wenceslas IV, 34, 107, 121, 143–44, 148
spaces. *See* geographical spaces, imagery of
speculum principis genre, 29–31
Stanislav of Znojmo, 101
Stejna, John, 101
Strada, Jacopo de, 195
Strahov manuscript, 76
Strohm, Paul, 20–21
Sudbury, William, 86, 87

Taborites, 110, 113–14
Tanner, Tony, 167
Taylor, John, 16–17, 187–91, 211
Taylor his Travels (Taylor), 16–17, 188–91
Tempest, The (Shakespeare), 169–70, 178
Testament of Love, The (Usk), 25–26, 42–43, 64, 95
Tetzel, Gabriel, 155–59, 161–65
Theodoricus, Master, 37, 49, 57
Thirty Years' War, 4, 169
Thomas Aquinas, Saint, 199
Thomas of Štítné, 46–47, 96, 133
Three Kings, cult of, 69–71
Tkadleček. See Weaver, The
Tragedy of Alphonsus . . . , The (Chapman), 168
travelogues, 149–51, 156, 158, 165
Travels of Sir John Mandeville, 3, 37, 61–63, 149–50, 156
Třeboň altar paintings, 47
Trevor-Roper, Hugh, 194
Trialogus (Wyclif), 100, 120
Troilus and Criseyde (Chaucer), 14, 21, 31, 50, 134

Troy Book (Lydgate), 76–77, 134
Troy narratives, 74–78, 134
Tyler, Wat, 27

Unguentarius, 141, 141n45, 146
University of Prague, 98–99, 101, 131–32
Urban VI (pope), 27, 38
Usk, Thomas, 25–26, 42–43, 48, 55–56, 64, 95
Utraquists, 113–14, 153
utopia, perceptions of, 10, 16–17, 159, 169–70, 174–75, 181, 186–88, 210–11

veneration of holy images, 123, 155
Vévoda Arnošt, 162
Vilikovský, Jan, 120
virginity and chastity, female, 43, 45–47
virtues and vices, female, 38–39, 134
Visions of Saint Bridget, The (Thomas of Štítné), 46–47
Vitus Cathedral, Saint (Prague), 73, 85, 172, 183
Vladislav Hall (Prague Castle), 173, 183
Vlasta, 122, 186
"Vlka poznáš po srsti," 146–47
Voksa of Valdštejn, 103, 118
Vyšší Brod Altarpiece, 36

Wagner, Murray, 114
Wakefield, Henry, 137
Waldensian heresy, 127
Waldstein, Zdeněk Brtnický, baron of, 17, 169, 196–201
Wallace, David, 17, 21, 33, 56, 81
Wars of the Roses, 158–61
Warwick, Richard de Beauchamp, earl of, 152
Warwick, Richard Neville, earl of, 160–61, 163
Warwick, Thomas de Beauchamp, earl of, 66
Watson, Nicholas, 53
Weaver, The (Tkadleček), 39–41, 53, 143
Wenceslas, Saint, 45, 71, 73, 87
Wenceslas I, king of Bohemia, 45
Wenceslas II, king of Bohemia, 48
Wenceslas IV, king of Bohemia: ancestry of, 75; Anglo-Bohemian alliance and, 27; anticourtly criticism of, 144–45; astrology/astronomy and, 93; Bible of, 58, 81–82, 83, 89, 132, 144; deposed, 13, 65; devices of, 81–82, 83; governance model of, 97; Hussites/church reform and, 101–2, 106–7, 116, 121; imperial ambitions of, 65–67, 85; Jews and, 140n45; language/learning of, 37; "mirror for princes" genre and, 29–31; nobility, relationship with, of, 13, 30, 65, 69; as patron of arts, 34; portrait of, *90*; rival popes and, 101; Troy narratives and, 75
Westminster, 13, 54–55, 73, 83–*84*, 94–97, 193
Weston, Elizabeth Jane, 16, 177–81
"Wife of Bath's Tale" (Chaucer), 69
William of Conches, 93
Williams, John, 206–7
Wilton Diptych, 3–4, 13, 40–42, 67–73, 86, *frontispiece*
Wimsatt, James, 60
Winter's Tale, The (Shakespeare), 1–2, 11, 167–70, 172, 175–76, 181, 186, 193–95
Winthrop, John, 207–8
witches and witchcraft, 140–41
women: aberrant sexuality and, 15, 141–42; active/passive models of, 18, 20, 49, 64; gossip and, 137–38; heresy and, 120–22, 126–28, 137, 140, 142, 148; literacy/learning and, 35–38, 54, 121–23, 132–37; piety/saintliness and, 43–49, 45–49, 87, 134–35; private spaces and, 137–39; reason/emotion debate and, 54; religious activity by, associated with prostitution, 135, 137; virginity/chastity and, 43, 45–47; virtues/vices debate and, 38–39, 134
World in Pictures, The (Comenius), 172
Wotton, Sir Henry, 191
Wurmser, Nikolaus, 49
Wyche, Richard, 103–5, 118
Wyclif, John, 5–6; Arian heresy and, 175; Bible as sole source of authority and, 108; Chelčický and, 98, 107–16; church corruption and, 15, 105–7, 109, 114–15; civil dominion doctrine of, 105–6, 108–9, 115–16; dissemination of works of, 9–10, 100–101, 119–20; Eu-

charistic doctrines and, 107, 113, 140; Hus and, 98–107; influence of, 98–118; the "just" war and, 108–9; ordering of society and, 110–11; priestly authority and, 107, 130; relics of, 101; sodomy, accusations of, and, 146; ultrarealism of, 100–101; vernacular translation of the Bible and, 14, 132; *De Antichristo*, 146; *De Civili Dominio*, 105–6, 114–15, 120; *De Eucharistia*, 100; *De Ideis*, 100; *De Triplici Vinculo Amoris*, 132; *De vinculo amoris*, 14; *Dialogus*, 100, 111, 120; *Trialogus*, 100, 120
Wycliffite Mass, The, 129, 142
"Wycliffite Woman, The," 15, 119, 125–45; text of, 123–25, 213–15

Yates, Frances, 170
Yevele, Henry, 94
Yonec (Marie de France), 141
York Minster, 65–66, 71
"You will recognize the wolf by its coat," 146–47

Zbyněk of Hasenburk, 102
Žižka, John, 110, 117
Zmrzlík, Peter of Svojšín, 76, 133–34